Outdoor Instruction: Teaching and Learning Concepts for Outdoor Instructors

Maurice L. Phipps with Stephanie L. Phipps and Chelsea E. Phipps

DISCLAIMER

This book details the author's personal experiences with and opinions about outdoor instruction. The main author has a Ph.D. in Education from the University of Minnesota.

The authors and publisher are providing this book and its contents on an "as is" basis and make no representations or warranties of any kind with respect to this book or its contents. The authors and publisher disclaim all such representations and warranties, including for example warranties of merchantability and advice for a particular purpose. In addition, the author and publisher do not represent or warrant that the information accessible via this book is accurate, complete or current.

The statements made about products and services have not been evaluated by the U.S. government. Please consult with your own legal, accounting, medical, or other licensed professional regarding the suggestions and recommendations made in this book.

Except as specifically stated in this book, neither the author or publisher, nor any authors, contributors, or other representatives will be liable for damages arising out of or in connection with the use of this book. This is a comprehensive limitation of liability that applies to all damages of any kind, including (without limitation) compensatory; direct, indirect or consequential damages; loss of data, income or profit; loss of or damage to property and claims of third parties.

You understand that this book is not intended as a substitute for consultation with an education professional. Before you begin any change of your lifestyle in any way, you will consult a licensed professional to ensure that you are doing what's best for your situation.

This book provides content related to outdoor instruction. As such, use of this book implies your acceptance of this disclaimer.

Picture Credits

Preface

This book is intended for outdoor instructors and outdoor instructors in training. Many outdoor instructors start teaching with no prior education in pedagogy but eventually become interested in the 'science' of teaching. They may already have a flair for the 'art' of teaching but are intrigued by what else there is to know about educating in the outdoors. The outdoor environment often changes what you would normally do as a teacher and so traditional books on pedagogy for the classroom don't account for this very large difference.

This book then is to enable insights into teaching in the outdoors. As there are many teaching and learning theories, there actually is much to learn to become the most effective instructor you can be. This means delving deeply into both pedagogical and psychological theories. The legendary mountaineer and outdoor educator Paul Petzoldt used to say that outdoor instructors often needed to be psychologists in the way they analyzed situations. This book contains many psychological concepts that address Petzoldt's comment. The aim is not to become a psychologist but that psychological background knowledge will help to give many insights.

The theories and ideas are explained using examples from my past experience and thus, incorporate both theory and practice. Some sections have been published before, for example the Jung theoretical aspects and the Group Dynamics Teaching Model, both were published in journals and other books in the past but with modification have been included in this book because of their importance to the overall knowledge base for outdoor instructors.

Because of the strong influence of Paul Petzoldt, there are many references to Paul's ideas throughout this book. Each one will be referenced but may not be referenced specifically as to the exact place and date, as the information was gathered through working with Paul over many years. My association with Paul began with a Wilderness Education Association professionals' course in 1982, followed by a five-week apprenticeship on his last Teton Course the following year that he taught when he was seventy-six. Other expedition courses followed where Paul visited for shorter periods of time. We were both on the WEA Board of trustees for many years. Wherever possible specific references will be given - such as the *New Wilderness Handbook*, which although appearing as a second edition in 1984, is still a much quoted book to this day as his beginning chapters have concepts that are timeless.

The appendix includes some questionnaires to help instructors determine the group climate and to check the various aspects of instruction that are being covered. These instruments include: The Group Dynamics Questionnaire, The Instructor Effectiveness Check Sheet, the Instructor Effectiveness Questionnaire, and The Importance-Performance Instruction Questionnaires. The different questionnaires have been used in research by Phipps (1986, 1992), Phipps & McAvoy (1988), Phipps & Claxton (1997), Phipps, Hayashi, Lewandowski & Padgett (2005), Clarke & Phipps, (2010) and Richardson, Kalvaitis, & Delparte, (2014).

I would like to thank those who were helpful in the development of this book, Cindy, my wife who understood my "disappearances" while writing in my study for many hours at a time, and my daughters, Stephanie and Chelsea, who contributed the chapter on Male and Female Instruction. Of course I owe much to my own education at Sheffield Teachers' College, Leeds University and Carnegie College, Mankato State University, and the University of Minnesota. My early training through the British Canoe Union, especially courses at Plas Y Brenin were most helpful as was my introduction to the "American Way" through The Wilderness Education Association. Western Carolina University gave me a semester to work on the manuscript. Last but not least, I would like to thank my instructors, co-instructors and students who have made my progress through my career so enjoyable. These are too numerous to mention everyone but I would like to give special thanks to Joe Brown who inspired me at Whitehall Outdoor Center, Bob Dye and Jack

Elliott who encouraged me through scouting, Bewerley Park Outdoor Center, for my first outdoor position, the Australian Canoe Federation, the Mitta Mitta Canoe Club and my Australian friends as we developed their canoe coaching scheme, Paul Erickson for his support during my private outdoor company experiences and also his support to study in the US, Graham Clarke for his information on Importance –Performance, and Paul Petzoldt, Todd Murdock and Aya Hayashi with whom I taught many times.

References

Clarke, G., & Phipps, M. L. (2010). An investigation into the technical and soft skills instruction using an importance-performance analysis. *Unpublished study*. Cullowhee, NC: Western Carolina University.

Petzoldt, P. (1984). *The new wilderness handbook*. (2nd ed.). New York: Norton.

Phipps, M. L. (1986). *An assessment of a systematic approach to teaching outdoor leadership in expedition settings*. Doctoral Dissertation 268 pp. University of Minnesota, Dissertation Abstracts 8622633.

Phipps, M. L., & McAvoy, L. (1988). Teaching and evaluating the soft skills of outdoor leadership. *Outdoor Recreation Resource Journal*, Canada, volume 3.

Phipps, M. L. (1992). *The Group Dynamics Questionnaire.* The Proceedings of the 1992 WEANational Conferenc Pueblo CO: University of Southern Colorado.

Phipps, M. L., & Claxton, D. (1997). An investigation into instructor effectiveness using experiential education constructs. *Journal of Experiential Education*. 20 (1) 40-46.

Phipps, M. L., Hayashi, A., Lewandoski A., & Padgett, A. (2005). Teaching and evaluating instructor effectiveness using the Instructor Effectiveness Questionnaire and the Instructor Effectiveness Check Sheet combination. *Journal of Adventure Education and Outdoor learning.* Vol 5 (1) 69 – 84.

Richardson, R., Kalvaitis, D., & Delparte, D. (2013). Using systematic feedback and reflection to improve adventure education teaching skills. *Journal of Experiential Education, 37*(2) 187-206.

CONTENTS

FIGURES

TABLES

Introduction

"He who loves practice without theory is like the sailor who boards ship without a rudder and compass and never knows where he may cast."

- Leonardo Da Vinci

The skill of teaching is very different to the skill of an activity. Even though every outdoor instructor has had a variety of teachers in and out of school by the time they begin to instruct, there may still be much to learn on the subject of teaching. Instruction in the outdoors has many differences compared to classroom school teaching. Immersion into some relevant theory can help the outdoor instructor and correspondingly help their students.

This book is intended for current and prospective outdoor instructors who may or may not have had any formal education in teaching. The object of this book is to provide knowledge to help develop the characteristics of an effective instructor. Hefty tomes have been written on the subject of education, many of which may not be totally relevant to teaching in the outdoors, so an effort will be made here to include only useful information that will enable outdoor instructors to maximize the effectiveness of their teaching and their students' learning. How much should instructors know about educational principles and practices? The climbers, skiers, kayakers, and cavers etc., who rise in their fields because of their activity skill may not be natural instructors. Even if they are, could they improve? Certainly. Sometimes the expert performer didn't have to analyze their skill development because it came naturally. Is this a disadvantage when they then have to teach a learner that does not have that natural ability? Probably. What about interpersonal interactions in the group? How can that affect the learning? Should all outdoor instructors be proficient in these soft skills? Absolutely. What do outdoor instructors teach? The range is wide including, activity skills, expedition skills, navigation, geology, geomorphology, botany, hydrology, speleology, interpretation, teamwork, communication, and leadership.

An example of a teaching concept that may improve the teaching of kayak rolling could be mental imagery. The instructor might say "imagine putting your hand in a cookie jar" to enable a cocked wrist. The instructor may have been working on muscle memory by physically assisting with the stroke using what is called proprioceptive feedback and this may have not been enough.

A good example of the issue of the expert performer may be the ski instructors who learned to ski just after learning to walk and have no idea of how they, themselves learned. For some of us unfortunate 'Brits' in the sixties visiting the Alps, the instruction was reduced to watching incredibly good demonstrations and getting the following two instructions – "Bend zee knees", and "Lean forward". Needless to say, we often abandoned the lessons and went for it on our own to eventually realize that we truly needed some instruction to improve, as skiing is not a very intuitive sport to learn as an adult. This minimalist teaching has changed, but at times, even now, instruction given in the outdoors could be too minimal.

Much teaching is done in groups and the group experience can be good, bad, or something in-between. Group skills or interpersonal skills are most often an integral part of the learning experience. Understanding how a group works along with the practice of effective leadership is a critical aspect of teaching in the outdoors. Research has been conducted on groups by the National Space Agency (NASA) in extreme or remote environments such as mountaineering expeditions as analogs for planetary exploration and long duration space missions (Kanki, 1991). A researcher from the NASA Ames Research Center compared some Wilderness Education Association (WEA) outdoor leadership training to their research on crew coordination and communication (Irwin & Phipps, 1994). Observations included a lot of similarities and the point was made that the training must be credible, powerful and active, the trainee must regard it as being relevant, and the instructors are very important and so their training is critical. NASA refers to their research on interpersonal skills, group dynamics and leadership as Human Factors research and it is done for safety reasons. Outdoor instructors also need to include group and interpersonal skills in their teaching and training to enable both enjoyable and safe experiences.

Paul Petzoldt (1984) held that all outdoor leaders should be able to teach. Conversely, all instructors should be able to lead. Situations, conditions, and followers change all the time in the outdoors, so the leader cannot rely on one favored style. The leadership should be situational and adjust to fit varied factors related to participants and their readiness levels in the different situations and conditions that they will meet. Understanding how to do this can equip the instructor to enable highly motivated groups.

Effective teaching uses several purposefully chosen skills to maximize the students' learning. The students' level of activity skill, conceptual ability and group skills must be recognized to match the teaching for learning. Possessing great skill in a particular sport doesn't necessarily mean that one would have the skill to teach it.

Understanding some educational foundations, concepts, strategies and techniques can improve the teaching and learning situations that outdoor instructors will encounter. The breadth of possible teaching experiences in the outdoor field is quite large as the outdoor instructor may instruct physical skills such as climbing or paddling, leadership and group skills (how to behave in groups), confidence building, environmental education, self-realization, and self-actualization. The environment will also vary, as it could be a classroom, a pavilion, a crag, a river, a mountain, a snow slope, a cave or other outdoor setting. With judicious selection of the educational components found in this book outdoor instructors may improve the effectiveness of their diverse instruction in different environments.

Besides leading, what are the characteristics of a good instructor? Schumann, Paisley, Sibthorpe, and Gookin (2009) studied some National Outdoor Leadership School groups and found being patient, knowledgeable, empathetic, inspiring, fun, and entertaining contributed to student learning. These qualities, along with good teaching skills and role modeling, help to create a supportive learning environment. What do effective outdoor instructors look like? What are their characteristics?

Characteristics of Effective Instructors

The following list gives an idea of important characteristics an instructor can strive for and careful study of this book will aid the instructor in achieving their full potential.

Good judgment. The ability to size up the situation and make a good decision is paramount in the outdoors as environmental and group conditions change and interact. Rigid rules and procedures alone just don't cut it, though some may help the less experienced. A focus on avoiding survival situations rather than becoming an expert in survival is a better approach for most instructors/instructional situations.

Other directedness. The instructor and leader should direct their attention to individual clients or the group to highlight their strengths and abilities, rather than direct attention to themselves for egotistical reasons. Doing a stern squirt on the river or a couple of 360's down the snow slope while taking down some beginners may liven things up for the instructor but at the same time may create anxiety for the student who is not ready for that yet. Try and get in your students' "shoes" as much as you can. They are often struggling with skills that may be easy for you so a lot of patience is needed - shown through what you say, how you say it, and by matching your non-verbal behavior.

Outcomes orientation toward students. Establishing the intended outcomes for the teaching is probably easier for skills based courses, but harder for process oriented courses dealing with character, team building, personal growth, etc. Pushing the students to do their best is the goal, method(s) enable them to achieve it, and outcomes assessment is the check that learning happened.

Leadership ability. Understanding effective leadership theories coupled with the ability to apply them in ways best suited to the individual or group is necessary. One must be able to project legitimate power so as not to lose the leadership of the group, and yet also share power within the group. Sometimes owning unpopular decisions is necessary as you can delegate some decision-making but not responsibility. Have a willingness and ability to address conflict. Be a good role model, consistently leading by example, as students will follow what you do even if it contradicts what you say. This extends to hygiene on expeditions and clothing, to name a few. You don't need the best gear when your students have the cheap stuff. Carefully check who and what you are advertising on your cap or t-shirt. Is that shirt cotton, when you gave a list saying "no cotton"? Should you be wearing sunglasses? Firmness but sensitivity in delivery of instruction to encourage expected standards will help to motivate students.

Motivating abilities. Is your leadership based on motivation? How do you motivate? Do you intrinsically motivate by inspiring others, or extrinsically motivate with grades, fear, or punishments? Do you give out frequent praise, or do you try and catch students doing something wrong? This is called the Seagull Leader. "Seagull managers fly in, make a lot of noise, dump on everyone, then fly out" (Blanchard, 1985). Do you have some on-the-spot activities you can use to lift the group's spirits during down times (such as "Have you ever", "Evolution", or "Look up and Die")? Are you enthusiastic most of the time? Do you have a sense of humor? Is your sense of humor appropriate? The experiential learning model recognizes that mistakes have to be made. Do you accept mistakes? Those mistakes mustn't harm the students. Carefully choose the most appropriate outdoor environment for the group. Another motivating characteristic for students is an instructor who is fair and kind. Disputes must be resolved, and students do seem to have sensitive antennas to fairness.

Planning ability. Effective instructors are optimistic pessimists - their outlook and personality is sunny, but they are prepared for the worst related to weather, expedition behavior, possible accidents, etc. How many students will forget necessary personal items or equipment? Do you have a plan for that, like an extra spray skirt or helmet? Is your personal planning and preparation comprehensive so you don't forget anything? If you are one stove short on an expedition, you will have lot of inconvenience, if you are short on cooking fuel, the expedition may have to be terminated. Your memory must be excellent and guided by lists and charts! Proper planning is not limited to logistics; one must plan how leadership will be introduced, taught, and practiced on the course. Leadership is best taught systematically by introducing students to favored styles through an inventory, then practicing non-favored styles on the course along with education on group dynamics. Teach about conflict and conflict resolution before it happens so students can deal with it more effectively. Learning about interaction between leadership and group dynamics is complex. Are you planning your instruction well? What methods will you choose? Do they match your students' abilities? Are you using a checklist for effective instruction? Did you develop a lesson plan? With all the complexities for instruction, logistics and group issues combined with a somewhat unpredictable outdoor environment, being flexible is also essential to planning.

Excellent communication. Excellent communication is concise, clear, and consistent. Understand and know how, and when to use verbal and non-verbal communication well. Know when to say nothing.

Have some quotes, phrases and stories to emphasize your important points. Show that you have a sense of humor but be careful that it is appropriate. Know when to be brief.

Psychological understanding. Paul Petzoldt used to say that an outdoor leader should also to be a psychologist. When interviewed about their teaching, some of the Nantahala Outdoor Center instructors said that they would like to crawl inside the students' heads so they could understand how to best present something, or make sense of some seemingly strange behavior. Can you recognize diversionary tactics? For example, a student might start talking up a storm just before they are supposed to try a kayak roll to gain some time before their attempt. Can you recognize defense mechanisms going in the group dynamics? Understanding them is a good first step, but what is the best way to deal with these problems? Sensitively deactivating them comes through knowledge and careful practice.

Being sensitive to the group's mood could mean a change in plans. Perhaps there have been too many early starts and long days, and the group really needs a rest day. Is the teaching session going on too long? Do you need to take a break and do some fun activity? Paying attention to the mood of the group can keep motivation high. Huntford (1985) emphasized Earnest Shackleton as the psychological leader in his book *The Last Place on Earth.* Shackleton's ill-fated but well-known expedition, where he survived an epic journey, must have included reacting to the mood of his group while saving them all in extreme circumstances.

Skill in the activity. The instructor needs to have more skill than the level being taught. If the teaching instructor can't handle the multi-pitch rock climbing, or can only just barely manage it, disastrous results could ensue. Being knowledgeable about the activity is great, but being confident and well-practiced is a necessity. If you as the ski instructor mess up the demonstration turn over the mogul, then Bandura (1977) would suggest that your students' perception of what they can do, their self-efficacy, will probably decrease. What if there is an accident? Another set of skills would be expected of an instructor – first-aid and/or first-response evacuation techniques. What if a student gets into a dicey situation? Do you have the skills to get to them to help? Are you willing to put yourself in harm's way to help them? Consider this quote, used by Petzoldt, from Robert Service's (2009) poem, *The Creation of Sam McGee,* "A promise made is a debt unpaid." If you take students out in a hazardous environment, even though you were banking on "perceived risk", something unexpected could result in real risk, so the unwritten promise that you made as an instructor is to do everything possible to help them.

You will have plenty of experience with the activity you are teaching, or 'expeditioning' in general, but remember that the students will be comparatively green with little understanding of consequences, so be anticipatory. Anticipate possible reckless behavior, like a student wanting to jump into a mountain pool. Anticipate students forgetting things or losing things. Anticipate that students may not pay attention to navigation in class and when on the trail. What is your plan if they get lost and you are not with them? Having a lot of experience can help develop better judgment if one recognizes past mistakes. Over time tacit knowledge is developed such that you don't have to constantly work through that decision tree all the time.

A Love of Teaching. If you are enthusiastic and love to teach, it shows. You probably know your subject matter well. How well are you versed in the art and science of teaching? Knowing a variety of teaching concepts can enable you to adapt your methods. It can give you insights into what and how to plan your lessons and educational structure. Cooperative learning, which includes many structures, can enhance group work and prevent group dynamic disasters. Individual learners have different learning styles and so being able to adapt to those styles can help. Being a gymnastic thinker can enable you to switch analogies that you may be making or different techniques. Is your questioning pitched at the right level or did you start out with a higher-level thinking question and end up with silence from the students? These are just a few concepts to illustrate how studying pedagogy can help. It can give you the foundations, concepts, and strategies to help develop your teaching. Read on for further information through the following chapters. Don't forget that the skill of teaching, as well as the skills in the outdoor pursuits that you intend to teach, needs enlightenment and practice.

Powerful Learning Situations

There is a greater sense of power in many adventure situations. For example, just being in Teton Canyon had a powerful effect on my students visiting from North Carolina. Adding in the adventure activity and the experiences that we provide can be very powerful. Tapping into the powerful learning situations that we have needs controlled teaching for most effective learning. Hattie (2009) addresses this in a meta-analysis related to achievements in learning. He quoted Clinton (1987) who stated that for improving self-concept, "the most successful programs were Outward Bound or Adventure Programs" (p.24). Hattie (2009) suggested that there were four major features:

1. Quality of the experience
2. Setting difficult but specific goals (challenge) but with adequate preparation and social support
3. An increase in quality feedback which the students usually want
4. Understanding of when to reassess and how to redirect student's coping strategies.

Coping strategies Hattie (2009) explains "… can be cognitive (learning strategies), personal (building of self-efficacy, perseverance in the face of challenge), and social (help seeking, cooperative learning). These four major features are the keys of successful teaching and learning" (p. 25).

Figures 1, 2, 3, and 4 illustrate the foundations, concepts, strategies and techniques suggested in this book.

Figure 1. Foundations

Figures 1-4. From "Effective Teaching in the Outdoors" by M. L. Phipps, (2002). *The Proceedings of the National Conference for Outdoor Leaders*. Paul Brawdy and Ping Luo (Eds). Copyright 2002 by The Wilderness Education Association. Reprinted with permission.

Figure 2. Concepts

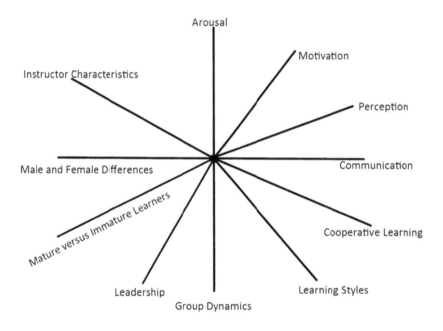

Figure 3. Strategies

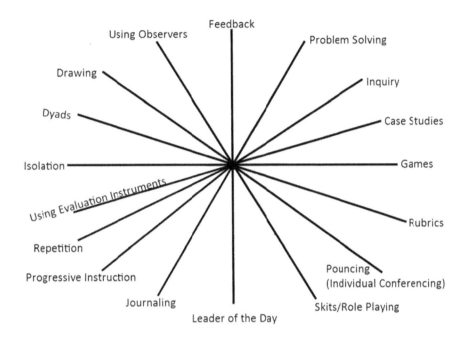

Figure 4. Techniques

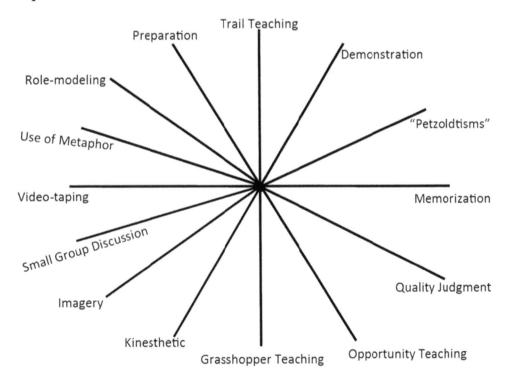

Chapters one and two will explain the Foundations. Concepts, Strategies, and Techniques will then be interwoven into the following chapters: Arousal, Motivation, Perception, Communication, Group Dynamics, Leadership, Male-Female Instruction, and Outcomes Assessment. Pedagogical theory is fairly dense so dive in slowly.

References

Bandura, A. (1977). Self-efficacy: Toward a unifying theory of behavior change. *Psychologist,* 37, 122-147.

Clinton, J. (1987). *A meta-analysis of the effectiveness of programs to enhance self-concept.* Unpublished M.Ed., University of Western Australia, Perth, Western Australia.

Hattie, J. A. C. (2009). *Visible Learning: A synthesis of over 800 meta-analyses relating to achievement.* London and New York: Routledge, Taylor & Francis Group.

Huntford, R. (1985). *The last place on earth.* New York: Atheneum.

Irwin, C., & Phipps, M. L. (1994). In L. McAvoy (Ed.), The great outdoors and beyond; common threads in leadership training on land in the air, and in space. *Research Proceedings of the Research Symposium for the Coalition of Education in the Outdoors* (pp. 43- 52). Minneapolis MN: University of Minnesota.

Kanki, B. (1991). *Performance factors and leadership: Problem-solving, crew coordination and communication.* Paper presented at the National Conference for Outdoor leaders: Public, Commercial, and Non-profit Partnerships in Outdoor Recreation. Crested Butte, CO.

Phipps, M. L. (2002) Effective teaching in the outdoors. In P. Brawdy and P. Luo (Eds.), *The Proceedings of the 2002 National Conference for Outdoor Leaders.* Indiana University: The Wilderness Education Association.

Petzoldt, P. (1984). *The new wilderness handbook.* (2nd ed.). New York: Norton.

Service, R. W. (2009). *Songs of sourdough.* Charleston, SC: BiblioLife.

Schuman, S. A., Paisley, K., Sibthorpe, J., & Gookin, J. (2009). Instructor influences on student learning at NOLS. *Journal of Outdoor Recreation, Education and Leadership.* 1(1), 15-37.

Chapter 1

Experiential Education and Experiential Learning

"If they say they have climbed the Matterhorn – take an extra rope."

- Glen Exum

Probably the most important theories to begin with are Experiential Education and Experiential Learning as these concepts lie at the heart of what the outdoor Instructor does. The majority of outdoor instruction is experiential in nature. Johnson and Johnson (1982) suggested that experiential learning affects the learner in three ways:

1. The learners' cognitive structures are modified
2. The learners' attitude are modified; and
3. The learners' repertoire of skills is expanded.

Experiential learning suggests a lot of independent learning, but some guidance (in the form of feedback) is often necessary; few people learn from experience alone. This is demonstrated frequently in the outdoors as people continually venture out with improper gear. Exum's quote above, taken from *The New Wilderness Handbook* (Petzoldt, 1984, p. 55) illustrates where someone may have been taken on an activity such as climbing with someone else, and they now think they know it all and as such are a liability. Also, some experience might be too much for the learner. In the case of adventure activities, they might be too fearful. Some research on effective instruction with a Wilderness Education Association (WEA) Expedition course found that three of ten students perceived their fear levels to be too high half way through the course, though this decreased to two by the end of the course. This was caused by the rock climbing on the course (Phipps, Hayashi, Lewandowski, & Padgett, 2005). The fear levels needed to be toned down some. In Dewey's (1963) *Experience and Education*, regarded as the precursor of the modern experiential education movement, the point is made that "Any experience is miseducative that has the effect of arresting growth or distorting the growth of further experience" (p.25). Outdoor educators must make active efforts to ensure that the students' experiences are not 'miseducative'. If, for example, first-time caving students are led through "Hydrophobia Passage" – a 'nice bit of cave' that is in reality a tight scary squeeze where you can barely get your mouth above the water in a small stream passage while crawling for about 45 minutes – the experience might put those students off caving.

We can also aspire to make the experience as educational as possible. It is possible to experience a trip to a museum, a zoo, or the mountains and be bored, anxious or unaware of the salient points of the experience. To prevent this and maximize the experiential learning, two models will be discussed in detail. Kolb (1976) and Joplin (1981) have both been very influential in the Experiential Education field. "Kolb, looked at the process of experiential learning and drew on the legacy of the perspectives provided by Lewin, Dewey and Piaget" (Beard & Wilson 2006, p. 32).

Joplin's approach is from the instructor's point of view. The learning cycles developed can be seen in Figures 5, 6, and 7.

Figure 5. Dewey's Learning Cycle

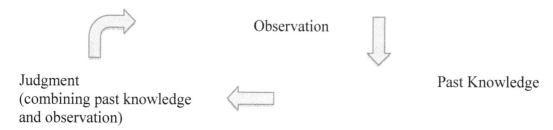

Observation

Judgment
(combining past knowledge
and observation)

Past Knowledge

Arsoy A. & Özad (2002) noted "Dewey's ideas are revised by Kurt Lewin (1946) who schematized Dewey's ideas in a diagram and named it as the Lewinian Learning Cycle" (p.48).

Figure 6. Kolb's Interpretation (in parentheses) of Lewin's Experiential Learning Cycle

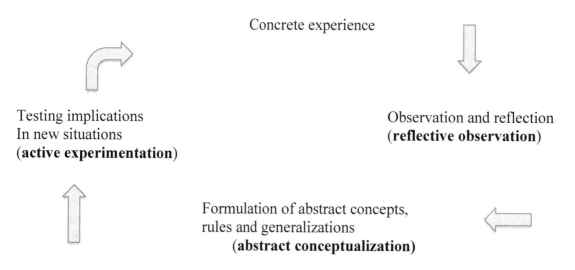

Concrete experience

Testing implications
In new situations
(active experimentation)

Observation and reflection
(reflective observation)

Formulation of abstract concepts,
rules and generalizations
(abstract conceptualization)

The use of learning cycles however, has been questioned by Seaman (2008). Referencing Kraft (1990) and Wichmann (1980) he states "For nearly three decades, however, researchers and practitioners have recognized a gap between the powerful learning often witnessed during experiential programs, and the ability of the most common conceptual models and research to explain the most common conceptual models and research to explain how this learning occurs" (p. 4). Baldwin, Persing, and Magnuson (2004) refer to this as the "black box" which contains our ability to think beyond traditional concepts, such as learning-cycles. On these limitations, Beard and Wilson (2006) state, "It may result in false conclusions, may not help us understand and explain change and new experiences, and it may cause mental laziness and dogmatic thinking" (p. 41). They quote others, (Holman, Pavlica, & Thorpe, 1997; Reynolds, 1997; Taylor, 1991) suggesting more complex models in addition to contend with the obvious complexity of learning. Learning cycles shouldn't be regarded as the "be all and end all" of experiential education – there are many other available theories. However, there is a logic to them that makes them useful thus they are recommended here and will be discussed in more detail. Joplin's (1981) five-stage model of experiential education also needs full discussion as where the experiential learning cycles concentrate on the learner, Joplin concentrates on enabling the teacher to maximize the learning by adding focusing, feedback, support, and debriefing to the action. The outdoor instructor should use the different models in conjunction with each other.

Kolb's Experiential Learning Model

Kolb's (1984) idea is that there are two goals to learning. One concerns the subject matter. The other is to learn about one's own strengths and weaknesses as a learner (learning how to learn from an experience). He recommends that opposing perspectives like action/reflection, and concrete involvement/analytical detachment, are all necessary for optimal learning. Care should be taken to not let one perspective dominate in the learning process.

.... Since the learning process is directed by individual needs and goals, learning styles become highly individual in both direction and process. For example, a mathematician may come to place great emphasis on abstract concepts, whereas a poet may value concrete experience more highly. A manager may be primarily concerned with active application of concepts whereas a naturalist may develop observational skills highly. Each of us in a more personal way develops a learning style that has some weak points and strong points. (Kolb, 1984, p. 32)

Kolb (1976) suggested that people have favored learning styles that relate to the experiential learning cycle. He identified four styles that can be seen added into the learning cycle in Figure 7. The four styles are *accommodator*, *diverger*, *assimilator* and *converger*.

Figure 7. Kolb's Learning Styles in Relation to the Experiential Learning Cycle

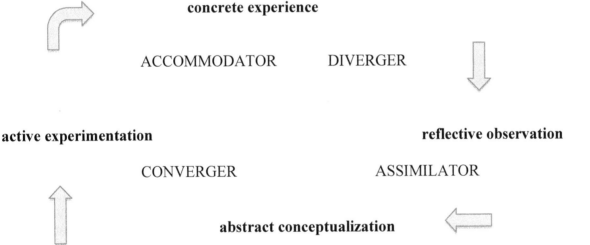

1. The converger's dominant learning abilities are abstract conceptualization and active experimentation. He or she can focus in on specifics.

2. The diverger is best at concrete experience and reflective observation. He or she excels in brainstorming.

3. The assimilator's dominant learning abilities are abstract conceptualization and reflective observation; His or her strength is in the ability to create theoretical models.

4. The accommodator is best at concrete experience and active experimentation. Doing things and involving themselves in new experiences are their strengths.

Let us take the example of teenage students in a class learning how to use a compass. How would students with different styles prefer to learn?

1. The convergers might immediately jump into holding it, turning it around, twisting the dial, holding it next to metal objects wanting to get it onto a map and perhaps work out a bearing. They would focus on the technical task and problems and would not be too concerned about others in the session.

2. The divergers might prefer to see a demonstration of how to use the compass from different perspectives like a good PowerPoint and a large model compass or a compass projected from an 'Elmo' projector (if in a classroom). They would prefer the lesson in small groups where they could interact with others talking about the various aspects – trying to gain a 'gestalt' or a feeling for the big picture.

3. The assimilators would like to create a theoretical model and so would like some information about the compass but would like to 'put some things together' themselves. They would require little interaction with other people. They would like abstract ideas, so verbal and pictorial explanations would be well received. They would like the precise nature of compass bearings. If they were on compass course and the facts looked wrong, they would probably reexamine the facts and systematically address a problem.

4. The accommodators would want to have a concrete experience and be allowed to experiment with the compass. They would like a work sheet to let them just get on working with the compass, then to just go out and do it without worrying about the risks of getting it wrong. If the worksheet or perhaps a follow-up compass course appeared wrong, they might discard the plan or theory. They would probably be using intuition, trial and error. They would be at ease with other people but may come off as 'pushy'.

Imagine your next compass class. You now know that the faces looking at you have all kinds of different expectations and needs - so what do you do? It would be impractical for every class that you teach to give them all a learning styles inventory then split them up into learning style groups and teach each group differently. Instead, compromise in the lesson and try to cater to all the styles. Knowing their different needs means that you can address them appropriately when they need extra help or clarification. Teaching to all the different learning styles also helps the students develop their weaker styles. It does help to know why some students seem to 'get it' easier than others when you have tapped into their style – so you can change your teaching methods to tap into the other students' styles that may still be struggling.

Kolb (1984), suggests that the integration of scholarly and practical learning styles increases educational capacity, and he recommends experiential education to enable this. As instructors, we need to vary our teaching methods to cater to different learning styles, but also include both scholarly and practical learning where we can. We also need to encourage students to use their least favored styles.

As with Kolb's learning styles, other learning styles such as visual, auditory, and kinesthetic, pose similar considerations. A class of ten students may have all of these different preferred learning styles. An effective modality can be chosen for a lesson and then changed if one or more students are not "getting it".

For example, when teaching river techniques, you could draw a river diagram on a beach with rocks, twigs, and lines in the sand to represent eddy lines. Using a visual modality for instruction, with a small model boat you could show exact angles of entry into and out of eddies and ferries. Afterwards, on the river this could be fine-tuned with an actual demonstration. By this point some students will "get it," but some may need some verbal explanation; especially, for example, with the reasons why you are using a specific angle. So, the instructional modality changes. If you are watching the students' non-verbal communication as well as their performance, you can ascertain their needs. This means, of course, that you really have to pay attention to each student's confidence level or nervousness and adjust your teaching to what you think they need. They may tell you, but only if you have set a positive communication climate. One option is to try and find out to what extent the students understand the concepts. You might ask them to repeat and describe what you have asked them to do. If their arousal levels are too high, they may have missed everything you said. One-on-one conversation can have the added effect that you are really showing interest in each student, which is usually something they appreciate. If instructors are too wrapped up in themselves, it can be very distancing. An instructor frequently talking about their successes in climbing could well detract from an effective teaching relationship with students on the crag.

If students are anxious, their learning style may change and your communication, however you are trying to transmit it, may not be being received. If you are teaching a one-on-one lesson, searching for your student's preferred learning style would be essential. This would involve using different teaching modalities and looking for how they are received. For example, if you have been physically guiding a student's paddle standing next to them while teaching kayak rolling (kinesthetic learning) and the student is not successful, then switch to some other type of instructional modality. In this case, you might try a verbal approach and say something like "Try to scrape your paddle across the top of the billboard, rather than paint a stripe down the middle" to give them a different mental image to effect a sweep. See how this works for them by looking at the level of success in the skill, by looking at their non-verbal signals, and by listening to their comments. As the instructor, you must also play the role of a detective, feeling out what works best for them. Use some 'gymnastic thinking' to generate different, creative ways of teaching to suit their learning style at that specific time and place.

There has been some controversy on learning styles in education circles. Pashler, McDaniel, Roher, and Bjork (2008) were commissioned to review research on learning styles related to the growing industry in selling learning style surveys and inventories. Seaman (2012) referenced these authors in a paddling education article saying that diagnosing a learning style objectively is tricky business and "It isn't just a matter of asking questions about what kind of information people prefer - visual vs. verbal vs. kinesthetic – since people don't necessarily even know what's best for them" (p. 2). However, both asking a student and then assessing their reactions to a modality in regard to anxiety, confidence and success could be the key here – truly focusing on the student to find out what is working for them at that moment in time. This could be much more effective than an overbearing, repetitive method regarded in the past as the "best" way.

Seaman (2008) admitted that he had difficulty matching his co-instructor in recognizing learning styles. He underscores this difficulty by referencing another researcher, Willingham (2005) who "concluded that a teacher's job is not to search (in vain, he says) for a student's best learning style, but rather determine (a) what modality is central to the information or skill to be learned and (b) how modalities can reinforce each other to deepen understanding or expand skills" (p. 4). Interestingly, Seaman's co-instructor was female. He describes her teaching: "She seems to be able to diagnose learning styles on the spot and adapt her instructional methods accordingly – a little more talking here, a slightly longer drill there and some visualization exercises for others" (p.1). She could truly connect with the student. Perhaps she was looking for all those cues in different ways and perhaps females find this more natural, but, more on male and female differences in chapter 9. We could all endeavor to search for the cues to diagnose our students favored learning styles where possible while also taking into account advantageous modalities.

Joplin's Five-Stage Model of Experiential Education

Joplin (1981) devised her five-stage model to include, (1) focus, then (2) action, then (3) debrief while all the time giving (4) feedback and (5) support. The model can be seen in Figure 8.

Figure 8. The Experiential Education Model

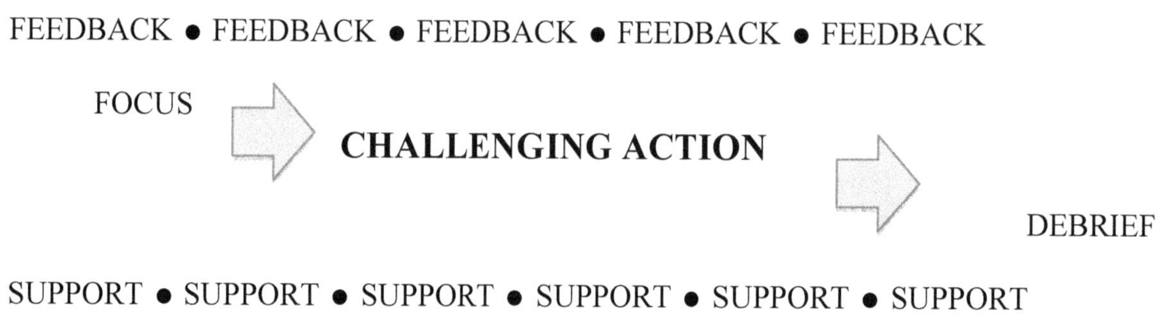

FEEDBACK ● FEEDBACK ● FEEDBACK ● FEEDBACK ● FEEDBACK

FOCUS

CHALLENGING ACTION

DEBRIEF

SUPPORT ● SUPPORT ● SUPPORT ● SUPPORT ● SUPPORT ● SUPPORT

Adapted from "On Defining Experiential Education," by L. Joplin, 1981, *The Journal of Experiential Education, 4(1)*, pp. 17-20. Copyright 1981, by The Association for Experiential Education. Reprinted and adapted with permission.

Joplin's (1981) model enables the instructor to maximize the experiential learning of the students by making sure that they have learning objectives (during focusing) and ensuring that they reflect (during debriefing) while giving feedback to correct skills or concepts during each phase. At the same time, support is necessary as it is an expectation that in experiential learning, students will fail as they try new things.

Focusing

Focusing includes presenting the task and isolating the attention of the learner for concentration. It defines the subject of study and prepares the student for encountering the challenging action to follow. A good focusing stage is specific enough to orient the student but not so specific that it rules out unplanned learning (Joplin, 1981). When teaching something that may be fearful like a river crossing or a Tyrolean traverse, instructors should limit the introduction to the amount of information needed for the bare basics and safety. The students' arousal levels (in this case anxiety driven) will already be high, probably too high to allow any kind of detailed listening. An introductory canoe or kayak session would have a similar effect on arousal levels (in this case - interest in getting in the boats), so the students might be better off trying to paddle without instruction for a few minutes until their arousal levels have diminished to a level at which they are more willing to listen. Initially, their anticipation of kayaking usually means that a tirade of instructions would probably go unheard. However, an activity that doesn't have such levels of fear or excitement could use more detailed focusing. A nature trail or pond exploration would require more detailed focusing to enable the students to know what to look for.

Focusing requires presenting at the students' level. We can build on their experiences as there is no point in re-inventing the wheel for every concept. Focusing fulfills the purpose of the experience. Dewey (1963) explained purpose as involving foresight and uses his learning cycle:

1. Observation of surrounding conditions.
2. Knowledge of what has happened in similar situations.
3. Judgment that puts together what is observed and what is recalled to see what they signify.

Dewey (1963) states, "The teachers' business is to see that the occasion is taken advantage of" (p.71). Focusing with purpose clarifies the learning experience, removes unwanted stimuli, and builds on experience. It is where the goals and objectives of the class can be expressed and clarified.

Action or Experience

One of the most critical aspects of Experiential Education is the selection of the most appropriate environment to ensure a quality, educational experience. The experiences could be as diverse as mountaineering, reading a book, or viewing a video. If this is the case, are all the conditions suitable to enable students to concentrate on the learning? Will communication be maximized or is there too much "noise" interfering with the message such as a cold temperature, a blizzard, a poor-quality video, a book that is too advanced, or the wrong atmosphere. In the outdoors, some distractions will become habitual and remain unnoticed if the experience is right and the focusing effective. Try and control conditions to make the focusing most effective by choosing a sheltered spot away from the noise of the river, for example. Safety however is the most important aspect to consider. A nature walk with young students requires more careful safety consideration than a literary exercise in the classroom.

Safety in the environment is a key issue for adventure activities. Joplin (1981) suggests that the action phase in experiential education gives the learner responsibility but that the student must be given the freedom to fail. The rock climber protected by a rope can experience this reasonably safely during a fall, and the whitewater paddler's boat can capsize without the experience being "miseducative", if the students are working at the correct level for the environment. Should you choose a cliff that is 500 feet or 30 feet? Should you introduce students to a rapid that is grade II or III? Ropes course experiences often include an early element, after some orientation, where the students are likely to fail so they can learn how to communicate better. However, continued failure on subsequent elements could be demoralizing, so instructors in this case need to be able to divert to easier elements. This should be included in instructor training, as there may often be a set pattern of activities considered "the norm", but judgment should be used to modify the selection of elements to suit the group. This could also be the case for rock climbing, caving, skiing or boating.

What if we complicate the situation and place the students under the leadership of a student teacher? The environment then becomes very critical because we must allow the students and st udent teachers to make mistakes in order for them to learn how to teach and make good decisions. Those mistakes should not be miseducative or too dangerous. There will always be some element of risk in adventure activities. Otherwise it would not be adventure. However, risk should be kept to a minimum as mishaps could be serious but for the judgment of the teacher trainer in selecting an appropriate site, being prepared to step in and take over from student leaders or teachers to modify what they are doing, and being prepared to abort an activity.

Add to the above risks the fluid environment of the outdoors. The river may be grade II normally, but today it has swelled with rainfall and is now a grade IV. The snow slope last year is not the same this year having just had a dump of fresh snow, now creating a possible avalanche danger. Is the sea running high today with an offshore wind compared to last time when it was relatively calm? Judgment about the site must include present conditions, as they most likely will have changed from prior visits. Another fluid dynamic is the group. Last year's group on a trip had excellent group skills, this year's group, on the same trip, may have poor skills and negative group dynamics with passive aggressive behavior, or with youth at risk there may even be violent behavior. Does the trip need modification, a different route, or abandonment of the planned peak? It could be a wise decision to not go. Is it hard to change the plan on a group? Yes, it can be very hard. I remember having to tell American students from the mid-west visiting England, who had never seen the ocean before - that we had to be tourists and ride in the van instead of kayaking down the coast to Robin Hood's Bay in Yorkshire on the North Sea. Their position was that this might be their last opportunity to do the trip. Mine was similar in that it could be their last trip because they may not have made it to Robin Hood's Bay!

There may be great pressure for instructors to go against their better judgment. There have been rafting incidents when guides went ahead on rivers in flood stage and clients have been killed because the river was too high. In cases like this, students or clients don't know what they don't know. As Petzoldt used to often say "Know what you know and know what you don't know." The instructor must be able to say "no" and educate the students about what they don't know about the situation. Figure 9 illustrates the fluid environments in which we work.

Figure 9. Fluid Environments

Changing Physical Environment	Changing Human Environment
Rivers	Personalities
Snow	Group skills
Ice	Conflict
Oceans	Group Dynamics
Lakes	Individual needs
Caves	Attitudes
Weather	High-low motivation
Trail conditions	
Rocks/cliffs	
Deserts/forests/mountains	

When you look at the combination of changing conditions in both physical and interpersonal environments, it's clear that the instructor has many things to consider when choosing the location for the activity. A change in weather, like a storm, can affect interpersonal behavior. An interpersonal conflict could make a climb too 'dodgy' because it requires the group to communicate cooperatively in a difficult situation.

Giving students the opportunity to practice real decision-making is necessary even if they suffer, to some extent, the consequences of a bad decision. This is especially true when teaching outdoor leadership. Otherwise, they will feel that the experience is unrealistic, not relevant, and not worthwhile. However, open communication based on trust between the teacher and the student will encourage Joplin's suggested feedback and support in the activity. The teacher trainer oversees the activity and should monitor the students or student leaders. There should be no hesitation in turning back or not going if the situation looks too hazardous. The designated trip leader can delegate decision-making, but cannot delegate responsibility. This means that the designated leader may have to make an unpopular decision, which may also have to be what Petzoldt used to call a "Maasai Chief Decision" (one that will not be questioned). Such decisions are often pressured because of the lengthy preparations for an expedition style course or because of a "we won't get another chance" attitude. That attitude could prove fatally true. Remember, decision-making in the outdoors is fluid. The weather, environment, terrain, or group members can all change, and often do. It is always good policy to ask yourself, "Within what safety margins are we working, in the conditions that we have right now?"

Stressing safety responsibilities and awareness during activities is a good feature to include during focusing. Sometimes students stop thinking for themselves, believing that instructors will be omnipresent in maintaining their safety. They place complete faith in them and their ability to ensure complete safety. In an adventure environment, this mentality is to be discouraged because one of the educational goals should be to enable the students to go on common adventures with their peers or for student leaders to lead others in the future. The elements of self-responsibility and responsibility for others that they should show in a common adventure should be shown in the education exercise. An example would be that everyone in a kayak group should be encouraged to look out for each other's release straps on their spray skirts, or that their personal flotation devices are cinched. This kind of awareness should be present at all times and not just left to the instructor to be constantly checking. One way to initiate participants' safety awareness is to do a safety briefing that requires everyone to brainstorm possible hazards.

Over the years, I have used the Petzoldt technique, "Nick the Greek". Paul used to be an accomplished gambler and often said that mountaineers should look at the Las Vegas odds in regard to safety so that they could live to be old mountaineers. So, he used the character Nick the Greek[1] in his safety briefings. "Where would Nick the Greek bet we could have accidents in this activity?" Nick the Greek always looked at the odds. Similarly, we should always consider the odds before embarking on (or stepping back from) an activity. The advantage of using this approach is that everyone started to think like Nick the Greek in relation the 'odds', but also asked questions like, "Should we be doing this?" or, "What would Nick the Greek say right now?" I remember a student holding out a cup and requesting hot water, for some hot chocolate to which I suggested, "Nick the Greek would say that the mug would be better on the ground so if I slip I won't pour boiling water on your hand!" My co-instructors and I also encouraged students to call a "Nick the Greek" any time they felt that there was a 'dodgy' situation. Involving students in the safety process is empowering and also gives them a sense of belonging, which brings us to Joplin's (1981) inclusion of feedback and support during her five-stage experiential model.

Feedback and Support

Building a supportive climate is essential if we are going to allow students to fail at times in experiential education. This includes setting a positive communication climate with each individual and the entire group. So, be as positive as you can, give plenty of praise where it is due, and make time to engage with everyone during one-on-one-sessions. Informal support can be given on expedition courses by visiting cook groups, where food is an easy conversation starter.

Perceived supportiveness can be lost by insensitive feedback but accurate feedback has to be given. Insensitive feedback where the student would feel embarrassed or fearful of speaking up in the group again should be avoided where possible. There may be times when an instruction has to be barked out like, "Paddle hard now!" for someone to make an eddy on the river, or "Leave it!" if someone's pack has started to roll down a steep hill. If you have time to think before giving feedback, remember, how you say something is as important as what you say.

How much feedback should you give? People vary in their expectations and comfort levels on receiving feedback. Some students prefer lots of feedback when learning a skill like skiing. Others prefer

---

[1] "King of Gamblers" was the editorial tribute Nick the Greek received as he lay dying in a hospital bed in 1966 from his admiring friend Hank Greenspun, founder of the Las Vegas Sun Newspaper. Retrieved 2/2/09 from http://www.pokerplayernewspaper.com/viewarticle.php?id=1400

some, and then like to be left to practice for a time. You as the instructor can ask the students how much they prefer to enable you to adjust how much feedback to give.

When giving feedback on a physical skill like kayak rolling, sometimes you need to focus on one part. For example, making sure that the bent arm stays bent, acting as a pivot. Isolating that part of the skill for the student can prevent all manner of subsequent mistakes. Slipping the other arm into a short-padded drainage pipe that will not bend could isolate keeping this other arm straight for a sweep roll. Isolating a part of many complex skills can be the secret to curing poor technique.

Giving feedback on group skills can sometimes be enhanced if half of the group is asked to observe - while the other half participates in an initiative. After the activity, the observers can give their feedback, which often brings many different points of view. This can improve feedback skills, but can also be used if you have a large group so that the activity is more manageable.

When your group's objectives are leadership teaching or instruction, then the group sometimes gives feedback to the trainee instructor or leader, often referred to as the "Leader of the Day" . This requires guidelines on how to give feedback and how to monitor by the facilitator to make sure that these guidelines are upheld (details on how to do this are given in the communication chapter.) Group feedback sessions can and should include feedback on expedition behavior. This is easier to do if group norm setting has been done prior to or at the very beginning of an expedition style course. How to do this is also detailed in the chapter on group dynamics.

Research conducted by Schuman and Millard (2012) on feedback in adventure based education supported feedback research in traditional education in that it is valued when it is "…timely, specific and contains positive and constructive components" (p. 122). A careful balance needs to be achieved when giving feedback.

We enable students to learn judgment by allowing experimentation while providing both feedback and support. Sometimes the judgment may be about various skills, but proper judgment also means knowing if you should pursue this type of activity alone after the course, or with more accomplished people. Teaching the value of understanding personal limitations is extremely important, especially with student instructors and leaders. Again, Petzoldt's saying, "Know what you know and know what you don't know" applies here. Students should sometimes be exposed to environments to show them the hidden dangers and that there is much more to learn in taking groups mountaineering than in taking them low-level backpacking. Added complications such as rope work, snow and ice techniques, and understanding of moats etc., must be considered for mountaineering. The students' exposure to all this can be to show them what they need to learn and so this must be stressed in feedback sessions unless they are truly advanced and well on track to be mountaineers.

It should be remembered that the students have to experience decision-making, as they will eventually replace you as the teacher or leader in the learning cycle and experiential education model. But remember to affect this judgment in relation to the external (physical) and internal (group) environment. Feedback is often a part of the processing or de-briefing of the activity so let us look more closely at this aspect of Joplin's model.

De-briefing

An experience must be interpreted, analyzed, and internalized if it is to be useful (Vanderwilt, 1982-1983). This stage of the experiential education model is to enable the synthesis of the experiential learning cycle. It is often necessary to assist the students in reflecting, forming abstract concepts, and developing new personal theories. This will then assist them in extracting meaning from current and/or future experiences.

Feedback and support are often given in the form of skill or safety corrections during the action phase. During the debriefing, however, the processing doesn't need to be as leader or teacher centered. Much valuable insight can and should come from the students. Their insights should be presented sensitively though and detail on how to do this is covered under *giving and receiving feedback* in the groups dynamics chapter. The de-briefing session could immediately follow an exercise or could be a 'round-up' of the day. Reviewing the day is particularly useful for tying up loose ends. Students may have had questions earlier but it may have been an inconvenient time to ask because of the activity (like in the middle of a steep ski run) or you may have been in the middle of a storm. Particularly when a situation is hazardous, dealing with what decisions and techniques were used to explain the "whys" of the chosen decisions is essential. Applications to other situations can be made, whether it be directly related to the activity or indirectly related, such as group process and maintenance. No two situations are exactly alike, and an awareness of this is essential.

If the group is not very vocal, a technique to overcome this and ensure individual analysis is to provide a processing sheet with a few questions related to the activity. If the students have ten or fifteen minutes to organize their thoughts and to write them down, they will have more to offer in the discussion. Instead of writing, the students could be asked to draw how they felt, or how the activity progressed. This may be a way to open up younger children. Another very effective technique is to use a daily journal. Structuring the journal can make it more effective. Figure 10 shows two examples for a kayak and canoe course and a kayak/canoe trainee instructor course.

Figure 10. Example Journal Formats for Kayaking and Canoeing Beginner Student Journal

Kayak Journal
Describe what was important in your learning today for 4 different techniques, safety or environmental issues. Refer to judgment factors.
1.
2.
3.
4.
Elaborate on the following concepts that we covered today addressing the "whys"
Paddling in a straight line
Paddling backwards
Turning and spinning
Moving sideways
Rafting up
Support strokes
Edging
Switching edges
Self-rescue
Deep-water rescue

Trainee Instructor Journal Format

Reactions and insight are required from each teaching session. You will be teaching each other as part of the course. Write your comments under the following headings:

How did it feel to be the learner? What observations and reactions did you have?
How did it feel to be the teacher? What observations and reactions did you have?
What insights did you get from the videos and readings?
Overall what new things did you learn from this session?

What elements of the IEC/IEQ² did we cover? Explain them an discuss their effectiveness for this session

Reprinted from "Teaching and Evaluating Instructor Effectiveness using the Instructor Effectiveness Questionnaire and the Instructor Effectiveness Check Sheet Combination", Phipps, M. L., Hayashi, A, Lewandowski, A. Padgett, A. H., 2005, *Journal of Adventure Education and Outdoor Learning*. 5 (1) 2005, p. 53. Copyright 2005, by Routledge, Taylor & Francis Group. Reprinted with permission.

The two journal format examples are designed to help the students think more deeply about their experiences related to the skill of kayaking, and to the skill of teaching and learning. The Instructor Effectiveness Check Sheet (IEC) (Phipps & Claxton, 1997) is for instructors to look at as they progress through a course to make sure they are covering educational concepts suggested in this book – structure, communication, perception, motivation, arousal levels, feedback, group processing, action/practice, leadership and safety. The Instructor Effectiveness Questionnaire (IEQ) uses the same content to ask the student whether the concepts in their minds are being covered (Phipps, Hayashi, Lewandoski, & Padgett, 2005). The instruments can be used together – the IEC for instructors to keep them 'on track' and the IEQ to check the students' perceptions. Both the IEC and the IEQ can be found in the appendix. A case example of an entry used and published in the Journal of Adventure Education (Phipps, et al., 2005) follows.

Case Example Journal

Reactions and insight are required from each teaching session. You will be teaching each other as part of the course. Write your comments under the following headings:

How did it feel to be the learner? What observations and reactions did you have?

Learning in the C2. I have canoed for several years now and even led many basic canoe classes, but it wasn't until last week that I really learned some new things about canoeing. This included winding up and twisting my torso for a more powerful stroke, popping quick prys in the stern and doing cross-bow rudders and bow rudders. It felt good to practice some of this today in the C2. I felt very much like a ripening learner, as there were many concepts and visualizations I had in my mind. The short time in the C2 wasn't adequate enough to practice and feel comfortable though (i.e., my leans when doing the bow rudder when hitting the eddy).

How did it feel to be the teacher? What observations and reactions did you have?

I am really glad the instructor gave me the chance to be the trip leader (though I am working through this). It felt good to be asked to trip lead as it helps me feel more confident about my boating. It was frustrating in that I wanted to do it well and safely and it feels peculiar to be a trip leader under another leader because there can be conflicting (not bad, just different) ideas of expectations and methods of doing things. I felt that the debriefing went well. It wasn't rushed or too unnatural, and it helped the group to see what was important for others today.

What insights did you get from the videos and readings?

From the video on my forward stroke - dig the paddle deep and use a good torso rotation.

Overall what new things did you learn this session?

The importance of the safety briefing and review of river hazards. I learned good group movement on the river – going down and waiting in eddies; also, the value of repeated eddy-catching practice. Trip leading entails a complex range of things. I think one thing I can do well as a leader is to

___

[2] The Instructor Effectiveness Check Sheet (IEC) and Instructor Effectiveness Questionnaire (IEQ) are instruments that were developed by Phipps and Claxton (1997) during research for the Nantahala Outdoor Center. They can be found in the appendix.

attend to personal and group needs but adding the kayaking, the physical demands, and skills, as well as the instructional techniques makes the task even more complicated and difficult. I am learning that I need to work on my own skills before I reach an autonomous instructor level. Also, I think I am realizing how important it is to take safety precautions in my recreational boating (z drag kit, ropes, knife, etc.).

What elements of the IEC/IEQ did we cover? Explain them and discuss their effectiveness for this session. Use the numbers of the IEC/IEQ in your answers

Structure

1.* Learning at appropriate levels of difficulty: I think being the trip leader with a group of people who know how to paddle, with an instructor who is very versed, capable and confident, in conjunction with a class teaching me how to teach, provided me the right amount of difficulty. I still had the opportunity to make decisions, to consult with my instructor, and to practice some leadership skills.

2.* A clear focus on goals was evident: I tried having people set personal goals for themselves and I think it puts the task in the forefront of peoples' minds and makes them conscious of practicing and perfecting skills. I thought that asking our group to pick a goal and then talk about how they met their goal at the end of the session proved to be beneficial to evaluating the outcomes of the day.

Communication

13.* Appropriate amounts of new information: The C2 instruction demonstrated this best. The beginning of the class called for a brief introduction to "C2ing", (some of the strokes and principles). Then, when we practiced "C2ing" the instructor gave new information, introducing new versions of the strokes like the cross bow rudder to help us catch river left eddies.

14.* Information given in understandable ways: I feel that sometimes my words are scrambled and my messages get misunderstood. Some of this takes place because I didn't make the effort to get the group together, turned facing me, and I didn't speak loudly enough for it to carry over the sound of the water.

Perception

21.* Developing judgment: This was enabled by my role as the trip leader and picking my way down the river. This meant choosing which eddies to catch, which places to ferry, where to turn around and look, consulting with the instructor on safety and programming decisions, and being empowered to lead helped me think about the well-being of our group.

Motivation

23.* Physiological needs: My needs were met. I kept an eye and ear open to see that everyone was warm, especially Eric after he swam. I brought extra tops to share.

24.* Meeting individual needs: The instructor made efforts to meet my needs by responding to my desire to take more initiative and letting me lead today as well as Brad's wish to teach more.

---

*Numbers refer to the IEQ and IEC question numbers

Verbalizing is an effective tool, but according to Greenaway (1983, 2009) sometimes relying on words can be unhelpful for both the articulate and inarticulate. For such cases, Greenaway suggested active reviewing to set up new languages, conventions or norms, and turn theory into action. Examples are given below.

1. Setting up new languages. Conflict styles as described in the Group Dynamics chapter where the terms suggested by Johnson (1981), shark, owl, teddy bear, turtle, and fox are used, become a way to address a sensitive issue and this new vocabulary can in essence be a new language that is needed for group processing.

2. Setting up conventions or norms such as active appraisal. An example may be a 'morale graph' where individuals can show their state of morale by the height if their hand above the ground. Human sculptures could reflect group dynamics.

3. Turning theory into action. Theories could be portrayed by events being re-enacted. Re-enactments of things that actually happened can bring out different points of view and resurrect emotions.

Imagination used in active reviewing can create interesting and effective processing sessions where reflecting, usually thought of as a mental activity only, becomes an experiential activity. The use of symbolism can get directly to the point and is often more accurate. Greenaway adds that one is more likely to use language accurately, responsibly, and sensitively. When communication and action are no longer safely separated, the quality of one's language can only improve (Greenaway, 1983).

As mentioned earlier, using a journal can produce talking points at group sessions but it can also be used for individual briefings; for example, the instructor can discuss decision-making with a student by reviewing their record of important decisions that have been made each day. Phipps (2009), and Grube, Phipps & Grube (2002) describe a structured journal which enables individual conferencing. The instructor may ask to see the previous day's journal entries to try and get inside the head of the student(s) in regard to their thinking about leadership and decision-making. This can lead to discussions about the theories being taught and learned. It also encourages the student to think as a leader at all times and not just when they are 'Leader of the Day'. An example of a journal entry is shown in Figure 11.

Figure 11. Leader and Decision-Making Journal Example

Date *May 18*
Decision Number *4*

 a. Describe the situation
 A cooking lesson. The group has set up camp and needs to know how to cook with basic food ingredients

 b. What did you do as the leader? (or what would you have done as the leader?)
 I would have had the group sit in a circle so everyone could see. I would have all the ingredients to make fry-bread ready. First I would wash my hands, sterilize utensils, then demonstrate making the dough and then frying it while explaining the important points like amounts and safety.

 c. Why did you do this? (or why would you have done this?)
 I would have done this so the group had the basics for cooking a lot of different meals besides fry-bread like, cheesy bread, pizza, calzones etc. I role modeled the hygiene and safety factors so that the students would be more likely to follow those guidelines.

 d. How did you implement this decision? (or how would you have implemented this decision?) <u>Underline</u> your choice

 Select the readiness level according to Situational Leadership theory[3]
 Select the readiness level: Select the corresponding style:
 R4   R3   R2   ***R1***   S4   S3   S2   ***S1***

---

[3] For detail on Situational Leadership, see the leadership chapter

Highlight the name of the **style** used:

Delegating/Participating/Selling/***Telling***

e. Was this decision related to task or relationship or both? Underline your choice.

    T   R   Both

It was mostly task – teaching the cooking and everyone was a beginner at this new task

Follow-up papers, projects, and presentations are all ways to affect synthesis. Presentations really demand careful organization and offer an alternative for someone who might not have a flair for writing. Hopefully the students will be inspired by experience to initiate their own research. If the teachers offer students the opportunity to choose their research topic, they may be more intrinsically motivated to research areas that have relevance to them without external coercion. If students feel that they are jumping through hoops, their creativity will likely suffer. Developing creativity is now being regarded as more important to counter the stagnating effect of the overpowering testing being administered in education today. Their interest should also be sufficiently engaged to produce and explore with peers. After all, as students progress from elementary to higher education, and then on to the workplace, they will nearly always be working with colleagues. In the case of student teachers, assisting with other groups will also add to their growing armory of educational experiences.

Processing encourages reflective observation and abstract conceptualization in the learning cycle, and it is also a convenient way to discourage elitism, negative competitiveness, and hero complexes. However, judgment should be used in deciding whether to leave the processing for another time. It may be too late in the day to process events, the students may be too tired. It may be an inopportune time for group dynamic reasons. Maybe it would be better to wait until the following morning, or another day. Do remember though that if the processing involves conflict resolution, the longer the conflict remains buried, the bigger it could become when it is unearthed by you or when it unearths itself. There may be times when a de-briefing could even spoil the moment. According to James (1980) a course director named Rustie Baillie coined the phrase, "Let the mountains speak for themselves." If the students have just had an exceptional experience watching a glorious sunset on summit, it may be best to let 'the mountains to speak for themselves'. This point has been made by some Outward Bound Instructors, who have recognized that processing may sometimes detract from an experience.

Although a staunch advocate of reviewing, Greenaway (1996) also maintains that sometimes reviewing can be omitted or replaced by 'reviewing-while-doing' but notes that learning would be limited. He also suggested that you could rely on unconscious forces, such as archetypal experiences in Outward Bound type courses (archetypes are discussed further in the motivation chapter). These experiences are isomorphic; they have a similar structure or storyline. Greenaway (1996a) quotes Stephen Bacon (1983) from his book, *The Conscious Use of Metaphor in Outward Bound*, "Instructors can afford to be less concerned with the discussion and more focused on providing appropriate course experiences. It puts the emphasis back into … the sphere of action, adventure and experience" (p. 10).

Reviewing can take different forms: sometimes quick, sometimes long, sometimes during an experience, shortly after it, later in the day, or even the next day. The instructor needs to assess the timing and consider weather, group dynamics, group needs, and any other variables that may come into play. Instructors from different schools may review differently. The 'team's course' review may involve front loading, framing, and metaphoric transfer. The Outward Bound Instructor may choose some, or all, of these techniques when reviewing a challenge. NOLS or WEA[4] instructors may direct their reviewing toward an aspect like judgment by asking questions like, "What judgment factors did we see while climbing today?" The instructor may well take Greenaway's active reviewing to heart to inject more action and interest. A paddling instructor from the NOC[5] might address technical questions related to a particular stroke when doing an eddy turn.

The important thing about these differences is what Greenaway (1996 a) refers to as 'fit'. He suggests that there needs to be a good fit between the reviewing style and the experience. "When the reviewing style 'fits', learners sense its value, and it is then the whole process – of activity and review – that becomes the adventure" (p. 4). Greenaway (1996 b) suggests a four-stage reviewing sequence:

1. *Experience* or re-live what happened which can produce different perceptions.
2. *Express* in terms of feelings about what the experience was like.
3. *Examine* what you think about the experience by stepping outside of it - a critical analysis.
4. *Explore*, perhaps something that has been brought up in the other stages – what next? What can you take from what you have learned to the next activity?

This is somewhat similar to Borton's (1970) commonly used questions for reviewing, "What? So what? Now what?" (p. 89). This where, again, you begin with being descriptive before progressing to higher levels of thinking as suggested by the cognitive hierarchy of Bloom's (1956) Taxonomy (see chapter 2).

1. What?
- Describe what you did.

2. So what?
- Address the "whys" of what you did (the judgment factors) in relation to:
    - Activity skills
    - Concepts
    - Personal growth
    - Group skills
    - Teaching skills
    - Leadership skills

Select from the above based on the activity goals. Don't try to address all these at one session.

3. Now what?
- How can you use what you learned in #2?
    - Where do you go from here? For example, practice with friends, go on a more advance course, or do some reading, find a mentor, etc.

---

[4] NOLS – The National Outdoor Leadership School
WEA – The Wilderness Education Association
[5] NOC – The Nantahala Outdoor Center

Constructivism

Experiential education, linking experiential learning cycles and Joplin's (1981) Experiential Education Model uses the philosophy of learning that we construct our own understanding by reflecting on our experiences where learning is the process of adjusting our mental models for new experiences. This kind of epistemology (theory of knowledge) is known as constructivism.

Constructivism relates strongly to experiential education, contemporary education and outdoor education. This theory was advocated by John Dewey, (1963) who was an early proponent of experiential education. The central theme is "building on students' prior knowledge and experience to help them construct new learning" (Gilbertson, Bates, McLaughlin & Ewert, 2006, p. 29). Compared to behaviorist models, constructivism places the learning far more on the students' shoulders. It is active learning. DeLay (1996) gives a good example:

> The teens talked about why they did not make the top of the peak. "It looked like it was going to storm," said one. That's the reason, others agreed. "No way," said Ryan. "We knew weather might blow in and still we got up late." After further discussion the rest of the group agreed and suggested other contributing factors. The discussion then turned to taking responsibility and not blaming outside things. Janene said that was like when she blames her mother for when she gets grounded.

> The participants in this example are engaging in reflection upon their experience. In the process, they are making new connections between their present and prior experiences, generalizing and applying principles from one context to other contexts. The participants are constructing knowledge. (p. 76)

DeLay (1996) also makes the point that besides emphasizing the importance of reflection after an experience to see relevance and to form connections between the experience and their 'outside' world, students should be alerted beforehand to what they could learn. This would be done in Joplin's *focusing* – before the activity (front loading) the instructor can 'frame' whatever issue needs to be emphasized. In the above example, it appeared that there was no front loading and it is less commonly used for adventure activities other than ropes courses. It can be used in many situations and is used quite often however, for a safety briefing before a new activity, or a technique demonstration for kayaking or skiing, or a strategy demonstration on the beach of a river with a model kayak and hazards drawn in the sand. The following are guiding principles of constructivism according to Funderstanding (2009):

- Learning is a search for meaning and begins with concepts that students are investigating to find meaning.

- Parts need to be understood in relation to wholes and in that way, concepts are more important than isolated facts.

- Students perceive the world in their own way with their corresponding assumptions so instructors need to understand these perceptions.
- Rather than just memorizing answers learning is the construction of meaning and so assessment needs to be be part of the learning process.

The constructivist teacher guides students and encourages active, rather than passive, learning. They use problem solving and inquiry-based learning in which the students formulate and test ideas in a collaborative learning environment (Funderstanding, 2009). Student collaboration is perhaps best framed as cooperative learning - which is another kind of epistemology.

Cooperative Learning

Three methods of instruction have often been experienced by students, individual, competitive, and cooperative. In the outdoors, the 'umbrella' should be cooperative learning. Cooperative learning is far more than just group work. The premise is that students need group skills and the ability to process how they are working together to enable a high functioning group. Besides these two skill sets, there must be interdependence, individual accountability, and face-to-face promotive interaction. Cooperative learning can be used by instructors and places emphasis on the students doing a lot of the talking and discussing rather than the instructor assuming a 'sage on the stage' role. When students talk about a subject, they are engaging in cognitive rehearsal. This imprints the information more effectively than just listening, and allows for perception checks from other students or the instructor who can also verify or question perceptions. It does, however require considerable preparation and monitoring. Working together and ensuring that everyone masters the material trumps the competitive system, where each student competes to gain the best grade. The concept of cooperation is well illustrated by Johnson, Johnson, and Smith (1998):

> On July 12, 1982 Don Bennett, a Seattle businessman, was the first amputee ever to climb Mount Rainier (Kouzes & Posner, 1987). He climbed 14,410 feet on one leg and two crutches. It took him five days. When asked to state the most important lesson he learned from doing so, without hesitation he said, "You can't do it alone" (p. 1: 20).

David and Roger Johnson, directors of the Cooperative Learning Center at the University of Minnesota, have completed much research on cooperative learning. They emphasize that structuring cooperation is critical. This entails using five basic elements:

1. *Positive interdependence.* The perception must be that one cannot succeed unless everyone else succeeds. Each person's efforts benefit all.

2. *Individual accountability* and personal responsibility. Each member must be accountable for contributing a fair share of the work and learning.

3. *Face-to-face promotive interaction.* Through interpersonal interactions, cognitive learning and communication skills are increased. Such interaction includes discussions, testing each other, cooperative note taking, shared work sheets, jigsaw-type exercises and so on.

4. *Interpersonal and small group skills.* Members practice effective group skills, including leadership, decision-making, trust-building, communication, and conflict management.

5. *Group processing.* Members discuss how the group is working. How effective are relationships? Are goals being met, and is the task being accomplished? How well? How can the group improve?
   (Johnson, Johnson, & Smith, 1998, p. 1:38)

In an environmental class, for example, the students are given the task of learning about Leave No Trace (LNT) principles using an LNT Pamphlet. The instructor sets up the five elements in the following ways.

Positive Interdependence

To integrate the above five principles, the instructor strives for positive interdependence by using goals, roles, resources and rewards. The students must agree on both the strategy and answers. They must perceive that they sink or swim together. Johnson, Johnson, and Johnson-Holubec (1992) suggested using the following example roles to produce positive role interdependence:

1. The *reader* reads the issues aloud to the group.
2. The *checker* makes sure that all members can explain how to solve each problem or issue correctly.
3. The *encourager* encourages all members of the group to participate.

Only one copy of the LNT information is given to each group so they have to share this and subsequent thoughts. For a test, interdependence can be encouraged by the instructor by giving extra points - if each individual in the group achieves a certain score.

Individual Accountability

Each individual is assessed (and in this case), it could be a written quiz. If it is a joint project, like a poster, a skit, or a paper, it is important to avoid any student piggy backing or hitch hiking. For large projects, this can be a big issue and sometimes breaking down the task into smaller job descriptions can help. Quizzes taken for fun and personal feedback bring different emotions to quizzes done for grade. Shared grades can affect emotions even more. For an LNT class, a simple quiz, taken individually, or in the form of a game would be appropriate. For individual accountability however, any grade should be an individual grade.

Face-to-Face Promotive Interaction

In face-to-face promotive interaction, the students discuss concepts and strategies to promote everyone's learning. At the beginning of a cooperative task the instructor should emphasize and encourage face-to-face seating as sometimes the students may just sit in a line, which doesn't promote interaction as well. As a group size increases, communication usually becomes more difficult and therefore face-to-face interaction is best enabled by dyads, triads (knee to knee, head to head), or a circle formation. To more effectively enable cognitive learning, small groups of two or three are best. To illicit brainstorming or to initiate group interaction problems, then larger groups would be better. In this LNT lesson, the students would be sent off in small groups of three to sit or lie facing each other (head-to-head or knee-to-knee). The task and the method (cooperation) would be explained clearly, along with time and material restraints. It may be to construct a visual on different parts of the LNT process.

If you have been doing a lot of cooperative learning and then switch to some individual or competitive learning, it is very important to be very clear about which method is expected. For example, you might say, "The task today is individual, so you will be working on your own without collaboration." This is sometimes forgotten by instructors who, when the students naturally get together may think that they are cheating whereas it was probably poor instructions given by the instructor that didn't clarify the task. Be very clear with your instructions as to whether there should be interaction or not.

Interpersonal and Small Group Skills

Have you taught any interpersonal skills yet? Have you set any group norms yet? Both have to be done deliberately as many students have never worked cooperatively in groups before. If they have no group skills, working in a group can be very difficult. In fact, it is quite unfair to expect students to work in groups without teaching these skills. Detail of how to do this is given in the group dynamics chapter. In this LNT lesson, the students will be encouraged to discuss civilly and to listen to others' points of view. If no one is listening, then cooperation isn't happening. Real listening is a critical ingredient to cooperation. The instructor will be circulating the groups and helping with the interpersonal communication as well as the LNT principles. Some aspect like giving compliments could be targeted and the instructor can note each time a compliment is heard. This often invokes a lot of tongue in cheek compliments, but it is all practice as that is a good group norm to encourage. If the students have been taught positive group roles, and they are able to initiate them, then they can practice distributed leadership. Anyone moving the group forward in the task or relationship is using distributed leadership. The students, by now, probably know that you will ask about how the interactions went at the end of the session. If so, this will likely encourage them to interact appropriately, which brings us to group processing.

Group Processing

At the end of their session, group members could ask each other, "What is something that each member did that was helpful? And what is something we could improve on?" This allows each student to focus on the social skills that are and are not working and get feedback on their participation. Remember to give time for this and remind students to be sensitive when giving feedback (detail on this is given in the group dynamics chapter).

Omitting any of the five elements can result in the lesson deteriorating. The two elements most often omitted in regular schooling are the group skills ones (interpersonal communication and processing). In the outdoors, group skills are a major part of what we do. They are especially important on expedition courses where if taught haphazardly, disastrous group dynamics can evolve, so structured and systematic teaching of group skills is highly recommended. The leadership and group dynamics chapter focuses on how to teach these in systematic way.

Cooperative learning can be informal or formal. Informal cooperative learning is where the students are resolving a problem in one lesson or listening to a presentation that is broken up with small group discussion pairs that focus on different parts of a presentation. At the end of a presentation pairs can check each other's notes. Students can have small study groups. The lesson can use a worksheet that is cooperatively completed or involve a 'jigsaw' where the initial group breaks up and studies with others to then return to teach those concepts to the initial partner. A lesson where students teach each other is a very effect way of learning but be careful about having a student teach the whole class, rather than each other in small groups. The students do need to see you teach and perhaps a substantial amount depending on what the course is about.

Formal cooperative learning is more for regular schools but it could be used in camps and outdoor science schools. This is for long-term projects, where the students work on something for several weeks or at a camp that may be several days. It sometimes involves shared grades, so the hitch-hiking problem can be common. To avoid that, set group norms, and insist on regular group processing. Setting detailed job descriptions is a good use of time and can be used for reference during group processing. Successfully working with groups to effect cooperation then requires a lot structure.

Expeditionary Learning

Expeditionary Learning is a branch of Outward Bound that builds on Kurt Hahn's original concepts with some enrichment from some contemporary educationalists. The Expeditionary Learning Schools (ELS) Model is being implemented in more than 150 schools including 45,000 students and 4,300 teachers. Support is given to students from their 'crews' who have a school-based adult at the 'helm'. This idea is similar to base groups as suggested by the Johnsons from the Cooperative Learning Center at the University of Minnesota. The idea is that the students get academic and emotional support through their school career from a small 'base' group.

ELS build service into the learning expeditions and "Unique to ELS, learning expeditions are long term, "real world" investigations, by teachers and students, of compelling subjects, which culminate in public presentations" (Expeditionary Learning Schools Outward Bound, 2009). There are ten principles:
1. The primacy of self-discovery
2. The "having of wonderful ideas"
3. The responsibility for learning
4. Empathy and caring
5. Success and failure
6. Collaboration and competition
7. Diversity and inclusion
8. The natural world
9. Solitude and reflection
10. Service and compassion.

The intent is to foster a culture within the schools embedded with practices and rituals that foster team work and character building.

References

Arsoy A. & Özad B. E. (2002). The experiential learning cycle in visual design. *The Turkish Online Journal of Educational Technology* 3 (2). 48-55.

Bacon, S. (1983). *The conscious use of metaphor in Outward Bound*. Denver, CO: Colorado Outward Bound School.

Baldwin, C., Persing J., Magnusen D. (2004). The role of theory, research, and evaluation in adventure education. *Journal of Experiential Education*, 26 (3) 167- 183.

Beard, C., & Wilson, J., P. (2006). *Experiential learning* (2nd Ed.). Philadelphia, PA: Kogan Page.

Bloom, B. S. (Ed.) (1956). *Taxonomy of Educational Objectives, the classification of educational goals – Handbook I: Cognitive Domain.* New York: McKay.

Borton, T. (1970). *Reach, touch and teach.* New York, NY: McGraw-Hill.

DeLay, R. B. (1996). Forming knowledge – constructivist learning and experiential education. *Journal of Experiential Education*, 19(2), 76-81.

Dewey, J. (1963). *Experience and Education.* NY: Collier Books.

Expeditionary Learning Schools Outward Bound. (2009). *Overview and history: Expeditionary learning schools Outward Bound.* Retrieved from http://www.elschools.org/aboutus/elhistory.html

Funderstanding. (2009*). Constructivism*. Retrieved from http://www.funderstanding.com/content/constructivism

Gilbertson, K., Bates, T., McLaughlin, T., & Ewert, A. (2006). *Outdoor education: Methods and strategies.* Champaign, IL: Human Kinetics.

Greenaway, R. (1983). *Active reviewing.* Paper presented at the National Conference on Education and Development in Organization. University of Lancaster, UK.

Greenaway, R. (1996a). *Reviewing adventures: Why and how?* Sheffield, UK: NAOE Publications.

Greenaway, R. (1996b). *Active reviewing.* Retrieved 2009, from http://reviewing.co.uk/actrev.htm

Greenaway, R. (2009) Why active and creative reviewing? Unpublished manuscript. http://reviewing.co.uk/articles/why-active-and-creative-reviewing.pdf

Grube D., Phipps M. L., & Grube, A. J. (2002). Practicing leader decision-making through a systematic journal technique: A single case design. *The Journal of Experiential Education*, 25(10), 220-230.

Holman, D., Pavlica, K. and Thorpe, R (1997). Rethinking Kolb's theory of experiential learning in management education, Management Learning, Sage, London.

James T. (1980). *Can the mountains speak for themselves?* Unpublished manuscript, Colorado Outward Bound School.

Johnson, D. W. (1981). *Reaching Out: Interpersonal effectiveness and self-actualization.* Englewood Cliffs, NJ: Prentice Hall.

Johnson, D. W., Johnson, R. T., & Johnson-Holubec, E. (1992). *Advanced Cooperative Learning.* Edina, MN: Interaction Book Company.

Johnson, D. W., Johnson, R., & Smith, A. (1998). *Active learning, cooperation in the college classroom.* Edina, MN: Interaction Book Company.

Johnson, D. W., & Johnson F. P. (1982). *Joining together.* Englewood Cliffs, NJ: Prentice Hall.

Joplin, L. (1981). On defining experiential education. *The Journal of Experiential Education*, 4(1), 17-20.

Kolb, D. A. (1976). Learning and problem solving: On management and the learning process. *California management review*, 18(3), 21-31.

Kolb, D. A. Irwin, M., R., & McIntyre, J., M. (1984). *Organizational Psychology: An Experiential Approach to Organizational Behavior* (4th Ed.). Englewood Cliffs, New Jersey: Prentice-Hall, Inc.

Kraft, R. (1990). Experiential learning. In J. C. Miles & S. Priest (Eds.), *Adventure Education* (pp.175-183). State College, PA: Venture.

Lewin, K. (1946) A Research & Minority Problems. *Journal of Social Issues* 2 p. 34-46.

Pashler, H., McDaniel, M., Rohrer, D., & Bjork, R. (2008). Learning styles: Concepts and evidence. *Psychological science in the public interest*, 9(3), 105-119.

Petzoldt, P. K. (1984). *The new wilderness handbook*. New York: W.W. Norton and Co.

Phipps, M. L. (2009). Using situational leadership theory in decision-making. In R.Stremba & C. Bisson (Eds.). *Teaching adventure education theory: Best Practices* (pp. 195-205). Champaign, IL: Human Kinetics.

Phipps, M. L., Hayashi, A., Lewandoski, A., & Padgett, A. (2005). Teaching and evaluating instructor effectiveness using the Instructor Effectiveness Questionnaire and the Instructor Effectiveness Check Sheet combination. *Journal of Adventure Education and Outdoor learning*, 5(1), 69 – 84. www.tandfonline.com

Phipps, M. L., & Claxton, D. B. (1997). An investigation into instructor effectiveness. *The Journal of Experiential Education*, 20(1), 40-46.

Reynolds, M. (1997). Learning styles: a critique, *Management Learning*, 28 (2) pp. 115-33, London: Sage.

Schumann, S., & Millard, N. M. (2012). The nature of feedback in adventure-based education. *Journal of Outdoor Recreation, Education, and Leadership*, 4(2), 120-123.

Seaman, J. (2008). Experience, reflect, critique: The end of the "learning cycles" era. *Journal of Experiential Education*, 31(1), 4-18.

Seaman, J. (2012). Learning styles as a basis for paddlesports instruction: A review of the literature and some alternatives to add to the conversation. *Journal of Paddlesport Education*. December.

Taylor, H (1991). The systematic training model: corn circles in search of a spaceship? *Journal of the Association for Management Education and Development*, 22 (4), pp 258-78.

Vanderwilt, R. (1982-1983). Mankato State University Bulletin, Mankato, MN.

Wichmann, T. F. (1980). Babies and bath water: Two experiential heresies. *Journal of Experiential Education*, 3(1), 6-12.

Willingham, D. T. (2005). The content's modality is key. American Educator. Retrieved from http://www.aft.org/newspubs/periodicals/ae/summer2005/willinghamsb2.cfm2009.

Chapter 2

Some Useful Theories of Teaching and Learning

"Learning and teaching should not stand on opposite banks and just watch the river flow by; instead, they should embark together on a journey down the water. Through an active, reciprocal exchange, teaching can strengthen learning how to learn."

- Loris Malaguzzi

The theory of knowledge is known as epistemology and can cover methods, validity and scope. Nicol (2003) supports a four-point epistemology suggested by Heron (1996) and Reason (1998) for outdoor learning that includes *experiential knowing*, *presentational knowing*, *propositional knowing*, and *practical knowing*.

Experiential Knowing

Experiential knowing is a direct result of an 'active learning' experience or activity. Experiential education, or 'learning by doing', and is perhaps the most commonly associated method of learning for outdoor instructors. However, "Experience and education cannot be directly equated to each other" (Dewey, 1963, p. 25). Because some experiences are not as educative as others the instructor needs to plan the experience in a way that it will be educative. If an experience 'puts off' a student, then Dewey would refer to this as a miseducative experience. Because of the physical nature of outdoor activities that may take place in a harsh environment, with the added component of fear, an experience could easily become miseducative, especially if one of the course goals is challenge. As outdoor instructors, we have to monitor the quality of the experience.

Presentational Knowing

Nicol (2003) explains presentational knowing: "This form of knowledge allows learners to reflect on their experiences. In this way, the experience becomes a unification of the mind and world as the individual endeavors to internalize the experience and then bring it forth as talk, text or image" (p.19). Reason (1998) suggested that this could include drawing, sculpture, movement, dance, poetry and stories. This is where the instructor assists the students to understand the experience in relation to the activity, interpersonal or intrapersonal facets, environmental or even wider concepts to be taken away from a course. This adds to reflection in that the students turn their abstract ideas into communication in a structured way. The quality experience is made more meaningful when the students express themselves in different ways.

Propositional Knowing

Experience alone cannot teach students about abstract concepts and symbols. Moving beyond experiential and presentational knowing, where the student learns about concepts through theories is propositional learning (Nicol, 2003). It allows students "...to explore the world beyond their experiential and presentational knowing." "It provides the student with another form of knowing not accessible by direct experience alone (Nicol, 2003, p.20). This is where the outdoor instructor directly teaches or enables students to explore different theories, individually or cooperatively.

Practical Knowing

Reason (1998) states that practical knowing involves "How to do something and is expressed as a skill, knack or competence" (p. 44). Although this may seem a natural fit for outdoor pursuits and physical skills, it refers also to self-realization, informed attitudes along with informed decisions, and courses of action, which may be social, personal or environmental. As outdoor instructors, we should ask ourselves "What are our students taking away from our courses – what are they going to do with the skills, theories and concepts that we have imparted? Have we given them the useful skills to enable them to go further with their own learning?

Besides the above four-point epistemology, learning can be categorized in other ways, as there are many theories of learning. Priest and Gass (1997) suggested the categories of cognitive, behavioral, and experiential for outdoor learning.

Cognitive Theory

Cognitive theories stress the absorption and retention of knowledge (Priest and Gass, 1997). Students learn facts for short-term memorization and if they connect this within a larger context, the long-term memory is activated. In the outdoors, it is more common for instructors to *only* teach what students really need to know and then use it in context. There is less emphasis on students studying just for just a test. Some memorization of the new terms or jargon involved with the activity however, is necessary. Beginners in rock climbing would have to learn and remember the names of knots, hardware, such as carabiners, belay devices, rappel devices etc. They would have to learn a set of climbing calls and safety procedures, like what to do if there is rock fall and where to stand and clip in to be safe at belay points. The advantage for the outdoor instructor is that the student is often already motivated to learn. They know that this new information is going to get them active in some rock climbing so they already have an incentive.

Koriat (2003) suggested that the active delivery of contents and concepts aid episodic memory systems; something is recalled for particular events and this relates to remembering. Tulving (1983) supported the idea that there are two memory systems, *remembering* and *knowing*. Remembering relates to recalled experiences and events, whereas knowing relates to the person's conceptual knowledge about the activity or field of study. Knowing such facts without episodic cues is called semantic memory but episodic cues can be embedded in semantic memory (Tulving, 1983). Park Service interpreters often use this by creating a "hook' in their presentations, such as old artifacts that can be handled in a history program. Actually feeding a red-tailed hawk flying from student to student produced a significant episodic event for my students at an interpretive workshop. Events are more likely to be remembered as an episodic memory and can be woven into more contextual information (knowing). Later the episodic memory can help cue the *knowing* memory system.

If information is presented in relation to how the new facts fit into what the students are about to do, then it is being connected to a larger schema where the information is more likely to be retained. Repetition can then help with retaining that knowledge. Semb and Ellis (1994) found that repeated exposure to concepts in different contexts can increase the episodic recall which will strengthen the actual knowledge. This can be used in most outdoor pursuits; an example would be setting up belay systems in different situations or practicing a parallel turn when skiing on different gradient slopes and terrain such as piste, moguls or deep snow.

Behavioral Theory

Behavioral theories ignore conscious thought and personal experience in favor of external conditioning and personal control (Priest & Gass, 1997). Students subjected to this theory are conditioned by external forces (rewards, or punishments), which are given out by authority figures. Rather than intrinsic motivation, behaviorists suggest external motivation. We have all experienced this in positive and less positive ways. In elementary school, we received stickers and stars. Later we may have received supportive comments on papers or, if we didn't do so well, constructive comments and lower grades. Most school systems use grades as an external motivator – how they are applied makes them more or less effective. This brings in other issues like fairness, accurate goal setting by the teacher, and good rubrics to assist with expectations. Some outdoor instructors do give grades as both punishment and reward; some don't and use other methods of motivation to effect learning.

Problem Solving

Beames, Higgins, and Nicol (2012) noted Dewey's belief that for effective learning to take place, students need to be given "forks in the road" rather than just be led "down the road". In other words, classes should be structured to allow students to problem solve. Students need the opportunity to choose from many variables to achieve a goal. Instructors must structure the learning environment to allow for safe, effective, problem solving.

Experiential Learning

Experiential learning reverses the traditional learning process of information assimilation through cognitive learning with symbols, words, or numbers, followed by assimilation and organization of the knowledge. "This sequence progresses from structure to substance" (Priest & Gass, 1997, p. 15). In experiential learning, the learner acts first, observes, and then starts to understand the concepts and processes. Beginning with an experience effects more intrinsic motivation and often aids the cognitive process in that it is often easier to think about an experience than an abstraction. The teaching and learning processes often require structure to increase effectiveness.

Structure

Psychological foundations. Experiential education is more effective when linked with the psychological foundations of teaching and learning: arousal, motivation, communication, perception, and competitive and individual learning within cooperative learning. Detailed chapters follow on each of the psychological foundations. Structuring the teaching and learning to aid in effectiveness may differ with the teacher, the group, and the environment. Developing the students' potential is important, but it may be best brought out through cooperative learning rather than individual learning. When should the structured learning be individual, competitive, or cooperative? Expedition style courses offer many opportunities for cooperative learning: Menu planning, route planning, group dynamics, and so on. Individual learning and competitive learning can be placed under the umbrella of cooperation. Remember that the positive development of the group dynamics enhances the experience.

Lesson plans. A traditional way to structure lessons is to complete a lesson plan. Careful planning is often the hallmark of a good lesson. An example is shown in Figure 12.

Figure 12. Lesson Plan

1. Lesson Title
2. Purpose and objectives
3. The audience – individual or group and size of group
4. Location
5. Time Control Plan - how long will each part of the lesson take?
6. Content – the information being given
7. Method – how is the lesson being taught?
8. Risk management considerations
9. Bad weather alternative
10. Equipment needed
11. Where can the student go from here for more information or more training?
12. Where did the information given come from (references)?

Progressive instruction.

Structuring is important to allow progress at a sensible rate carefully judged by the instructor who has gauged the students' level of psychological maturity and readiness level for the task or skill. Teaching in stages is often necessary. This is sometimes referred to as scaffolding; the instructor provides scaffolds or supports to assist the learner's development. The scaffolds facilitate a student's ability to build on prior knowledge and internalize new information. The activities provided in scaffolding instruction enables the learner to progress just beyond the level of what the learner can do alone (Olson & Pratt, 2000).

Imagine a student looking at someone doing a kayak roll, then getting in a kayak and doing it. It has been done but is extremely unlikely. Even a complex description of what to do would not be sufficient. A scaffolding approach to teaching kayak rolling would be to break down the skill into smaller parts, then practice each skill, building on the last one. The smaller parts in learning a sweep roll would consist of the student being:

1. Comfortable upside down in an oxygen free environment.
2. Confident in making an exit if needed.
3. Able to successfully do a 'hip-flick'.
4. Able to keep their head down as they roll the boat up.
5. Able to hold the paddle in a set up position.
6. Able to sweep the paddle out to the side from an upside-down position without pulling down.
7. Able to keep the paddle blade flat or slightly angled upward during the sweep.
8. Able to coordinate the hip flick with the start of the paddle sweep.
9. Able to keep their head down as the boat is 'kicked up' with the knee (hip-flicked) up by looking at the paddle blade.
10. Able to rotate the body while making the sweep.
11. Able to finish upright looking down the shaft of the paddle --which has finished its sweep just past the cockpit.

This should result in the student rolling unaided. The accompanying scaffolding would be as follows for each step as the student progresses and becomes, comfortable, confident, and able in the 11 steps or skills. The instructor should not try and skip a step unless the student is comfortable, confident and able in each preceding skill. The instructor would be standing in the water next to the learner through the whole process.

1. Comfortable upside down in an oxygen free environment:
    The instructor could start with games getting the learner to be comfortable 'hanging out' underwater. This could be an instructor standing at the side, rolling them over and up again, the student could practice getting in from upside down, they could do that and try and put the spray-skirt on while upside down (that takes a lot of hanging out!).

2. Confident in making an exit if needed:
    This would be followed by a 'wet exit' where the student practices exiting the kayak while upside down.

3. Able to successfully do a 'hip-flick':
    The instructor would stand next to the kayak and hold the hands of the learner who is seated in the boat. The learner would tip over towards the instructor and then right the boat by driving up the near side knee (the hip-flick).

4. Able to keep their head down as they roll the boat up:
    The hip-flick is then done with the same support making sure that the learner keeps their head down so as the knee drives up, the head drives down toward their hands.

5. Able to hold the paddle in a set up position:
    The learner holds the paddle and places it on the side of the boat, parallel to the boat on the deck and holds it tight to the deck.

6. Able to sweep the paddle out to the side from an upside-down position without pulling down:

    The instructor stands next to the boat and the learner, who capsizes over to be supported by the instructor who holds them just high enough that their mouth is out of the water. The student then practices first pushing the paddle up to the surface (still parallel to the kayak) and then making the sweeping action with the paddle.

7. Able to keep the paddle blade flat during the sweep:

    The instructor or another person makes sure the action is correct – sweeping out and wide with the paddle blade flat or with some wrist "wind up" to lift the forward edge of the blade.

8. Able to coordinate the hip flick with the start of the paddle sweep:

    While still being supported, the learner practices kicking up with the knee at the same time the paddle sweep is initiated.

9. Able to keep their head down as the boat is 'kicked' with the knee (hip-flicked) upwards:

   The learner capsizes completely towards the instructor then pushes the paddle to the surface as high as possible, keeping it as level as possible. The instructor pulls the paddle around making a wide sweep that the learner can feel. As soon as the learner feels the paddle move, the right knee drives upwards and the head is kept down by looking at the sweeping paddle blade.

10. Able to rotate the body while making the sweep:

    Assistance is given with the sweep (paddle being pulled around by the instructor) while the learner feels the wide sweep and body rotation.

11. Able to finish upright looking down the shaft of the paddle - which has finished its sweep just past the cockpit:

    The learner looks at the paddle blade throughout the sweep, which enables the body rotation and the finish (looking down the shaft of the paddle).

12. The learner tries the roll unaided.

It's easy to see that teaching the kayak roll requires the use of scaffolding. Much feedback and support has to be given, perhaps with mental imagery techniques to complement the proprioceptive techniques where the instructor guides the paddle action allowing the feel of the action. In this particular skill, each scaffolding stage has to achieve an acceptable level of performance. If the hip-flick is not strong enough, the next step should not be made. If the learner is panicking while underwater, then more confidence exercises are necessary until they can 'hang-out' upside down comfortably.

In a complex skill, like kayak rolling, the difficulty level needs to increase gradually to avoid learner frustration. Learning in a swimming pool is the best starting place, then moving up to a lake, then a river, then a rapid on the river, then executing moves like a stern squirt to move on to a combat roll, where the roll is 'unexpected' and hasn't been set-up for. Similarly, all activities should be carefully graduated. The learner should progress onto a class II river after a lake session rather than jump straight onto a class III. The learner would most likely experience frustration learning to do eddy turns and ferries if the water is too pushy. Similarly, the beginner skier needs to learn on green runs until their skill level has progressed sufficiently to move up to blue runs, or the climber needs to start on easier climbs.

Bloom's Taxonomy

Bloom's (1956) Taxonomy of Educational Objectives was first published in his Handbook I. It has since been expanded by both Bloom and others, such as Anderson and Krathwohl (2001), and Marzano, (2001). It was developed as a response to the education of the day focusing on fact-transfer and information re-call, which is the lowest level of learning. The taxonomy is shown in Figure 13 below.

Figure 13. Bloom's Taxonomy

---

1. Knowledge (recall data or imitate)
2. Comprehension (understand and follow instructions)
3. Application (apply, use the information and develop precision)
4. Analysis (analyze aspects and integrate skills)
5. Synthesis (synthesize by putting aspects together)
6. Evaluation (assess and judge ideas and skills)

(Bloom, 1956 p. 201)

In levels 5 and 6, the cognitive domain levels of synthesis and evaluation were inverted by Anderson and Krathwohl (2001). The psychomotor domain (which involves physical movement) was added by Dave (1970). There is a hierarchy, and Bloom's (1956) Taxonomy suggested that the levels should be mastered in order. An example of considering what level to choose may be to begin a de-briefing session at the first level by asking a memory question like, "What did we do first in the lesson today?" That would be far better than starting with, "How did you feel about that?" That higher-level question relates to higher-level thinking that would probably inhibit an immediate reply. After the session is 'warmed up' with some simple memory questions, then some progression can be made into higher-level questions. For outdoor instructors, besides pitching at the correct level during processing, understanding the levels of Bloom's taxonomy can be useful in the following ways.

Knowledge. This is where the expectation is learning new information like a bedding plane or a rift in a cave or a figure of eight knot or prussic loop for climbing. When being introduced to new activities, there are some new terms to be learned through basic memorization. The expectation is that the information can be recalled.

Comprehension. The student at this stage is expected to be able to interpret a concept or activity with an understanding of certain principles. What causes an eddy on a river, which way is the current flowing in the eddy and why is it flowing back upstream? What un-weights the back of your skis? Why is pushing against the front of the ski boots with your shins more effective than just leaning forward? Why is leaning back when going over the edge of a rappel important? If students are taught these things, then they are developing an understanding enabling more success and they will also start to develop judgment.

Application. The understanding gained in 'comprehension' is now applied, the knowledge is put into action in real circumstances. This may be where the kayaker actually tries an eddy turn after having practiced basic strokes and edging, or the skier practices making the turn while pushing forward with the shins. The caver or climber actually gets to be talked into leaning back over the edge of the drop.

Analysis. The student now organizes principles on how much to edge the boat on an eddy turn, when to lean, how much angle to use when hitting the eddy etc. The skier begins to work out when to pole plant, bend their knees, when to un-weight, when to straighten the legs in their parallel turns. The caver/climber begins to understand how their toes will slip down resulting in a face plant if they do not lean back and how they will get more friction on the soles of their boots by leaning back.

Synthesis. The student has become proficient enough that adaptations can be made in the skill to meet different situations. The kayaker would run a river with different rapids with small and large eddies and could adjust the angles of approach, leans and paddle strokes to meet the new situations. The skier can negotiate different slopes adjusting for the steepness and bumps etc. The climber/caver can negotiate different 'take-offs' when rappelling, perhaps including a free rappel.

Evaluation. The student has reached a point where good judgment can be made to assess the effectiveness and safety of what they are doing. They have the capability of doing the activity -- which could be running the Tuckasegee river, skiing down from the top lift or completing a through trip from the Ice Cave to the Wind Cave in Wyoming or Dowber Gill Passage in Yorkshire. This includes assessing whether the activity is doable with their current skill sets. It involves the decision whether to run a certain river, snow slope or attempt a certain cave.

From the above examples, it's clear that the instructor can aid the teaching and learning by assessing at what level the instruction should be pitched and aiming to get to synthesis and evaluation wherever possible.

Evaluation of instructor and program effectiveness are more complex type of evaluations. Research on whether student needs are being met or whether pre-planned objectives are being met can be achieved using outcomes assessment techniques (details can be found in the outcomes assessment chapter).

Judgment

Paul Petzoldt used to say, "Rules are for fools," to explain that situations are often unique in the outdoors and so the instructor needs to adapt to changes rather than rely on set rules. Situations may be different because of many factors such as different locations, changing weather, varied and sometimes unpredictable, terrain, group dynamics, and leadership. Petzoldt pushed the application of judgment as he started the National Outdoor Leadership School (NOLS) and documented his ideas on judgment in *The Wilderness Handbook* (1974) and *The New Wilderness Handbook* (1984). He tape-recorded his ideas on his "Teaching in the Wild Outdoors" chapter on the 1983 National Standard Wilderness Education Association (WEA) course to add into the New Wilderness handbook and discussed his favored teaching style "the quality judgment" method. Wherever possible he maintained that we should teach the "whys". Wagstaff (2001) elaborates from Petzoldt's field notes:

- Why are we teaching the subject?
- Why are we teaching it now?
- Why is our decision working?
- Why does it apply to our purpose?
- Why is it being done the way it is being done?
- Why, Why, Why?

If the student has the reasoning related to the specific thing being taught – the student is storing information and experience related to reasoning and purpose. This kind of learning is far superior in making future decisions in related circumstances than just memorized storage without the whys. (p 5). Cain and McAvoy (1991), defined quality judgment as:

… the measure of the leader's mental and physical ability to, and process by which he/she anticipates and recognizes needs or opportunities for some degree of action in relation to the groups' collective goals and in relation to the priorities of his/her responsibilities. These needs or opportunities are characterized by the situational interactions of what they perceive, observe, and know about themselves, the group, and the circumstances of any specific situation. (p. 17)

The instructor can develop judgment by addressing the "whys" throughout a course; perhaps during instruction, review sessions, evaluation sessions, or through journaling. Petzoldt continued this theme through the WEA. John Jackson also stressed the importance of judgment at Plas y Brenin, the National Mountain Leadership Centre in North Wales. His idea was documented in his unpublished manuscript, Notes on Party Leadership (no date).

> There is plenty of room for an individual approach, and each good leader will solve problems in his or her own way, but the decisions made and the solutions to problems will obey certain basic rules and will be determined by the individual's ability to make sound judgments based on knowledge and experience. (Jackson, quoted in Cain, 1991. p. 19)

Judgment is regarded as the "glue" holding together outdoor leadership competencies (Cain, 1991). Miles (1987) suggested the following attributes that contribute to judgment:

> *Knowledge* (related to the situation)
> *Skill* (in the activity or process)
> *Self-confidence* (believing the eventual decision to be correct)
> *Selflessness* (the decision is made with the group and leader in mind)
> *Commitment* (to the decision and its consequences especially related to safety)
> *Expedition* (Promptness and deliberate speed without vacillation)
> *Experience* (What was done in the past? What have others done? And what have been the consequences?) (p. 505)

How does the instructor use judgment in decision-making? Cain and McAvoy (1991) suggested the use of the Normative Model as outlined by Reitz (1977) with some modification based on Cain's Delphi Study on judgment (1988). The process is as follows:

1. The observation and recognition of a need or opportunity to act on behalf of maximizing the group's collective goals and objectives;
2. The collection of all available information that describes the conditions of the need or opportunity;
3. The identification and analysis of potential options of action that can be executed to satisfy the need or opportunity based upon the observations and collection of information;
4. The identification of potential consequences that may be incurred by execution of each individual option or combination thereof;
5. The selection of one or any combination of the most appropriate options;
6. The execution of that decision; and
7. The evaluation and action if necessary.
   (Cain & McAvoy 1991 p. 22).

Guthrie (1995) however, brings up the concept of tacit knowledge - which shows that all is not as simple as the above model. Tacit knowledge is primarily acquired through experience working with qualified professionals and can function pre-consciously. He gives the following example:

> You are cross-country skiing on a snow-covered trail with a bunch of beginner leaders. As you follow the trail, you look for the subtle signs indicating the trail. You look for old blazes, for unnaturally straight breaks in the trees, or logs or branches, which have been sawed off, for depressions in the snow.

You find that you are following the trail, with difficulty perhaps, but nevertheless you know you are on the trail. Yet your students are confused. They do not see the signs which you see, and they are skeptical you know what you are doing. As you were following the trail, you may or may not have been consciously looking for the various signs. However, if you were not, once your students start questioning you, you will become more conscious of what you are looking for. You could then point out the signs to students....

The knowledge you have of following the trails is tacit knowledge. It has been acquired through experience, possibly with a mentor showing you the signs. This knowledge is not acquired easily, not through books alone, and can be only acquired through considerable practice. (p.107)

Tacit knowledge includes "how to" knowledge, perception knowledge (not obvious to the untrained) and a conceptual or theoretical underpinning. Guthrie's (1995) criticism of the Cain (1991) model above is that it doesn't explain how the instructor or leader knows the most appropriate option or best decision. He likewise critiques the Priest and Dixon (1990) model of judgment and decision-making likened to a computer process (since elaborated as cycle - specific experiences, inductive reflection, general concepts, deductive reflection, specific predictions, right or wrong, and finally evaluative reflection, Priest & Gass, 1997). This also requires that before judgments can be deduced, prior judgments have to be made based on knowledge and more importantly, tacit knowledge. In the outdoors, hundreds of seemingly small decisions can compile to lead to good decisions or can lead to an accident. Errors may be unconscious and made due to poor or absent judgment. Guthrie (1995) defines sound judgment: "Good judgment, then, is based on an innumerable number of conscious and pre-conscious decisions which are made on an on-going basis" (p. 110).

Guthrie (1995) suggests that because of the large number of decisions that have to be made on an ongoing basis, habits, routine practices, or what may be referred to as Standard Operating Procedures (SOPs) help. For example, I don't consciously decide each time we cook on an expedition course whether or not to boil a pot of water first as it is standard practice to do this and then sterilize all our eating utensils, followed by making a drink. This is now more tacit knowledge, which aids in preventing sickness and dehydration and is done pre-consciously. He also suggests that in emergencies, we don't go through the 'list' – but act immediately. Guthrie's (1995) comprehensive description of a leader with good judgment is:

A person who, as a consequence of experience, knowledge, and practice, has developed sound habits leading to proper preparation and prevention of problems, has developed the ability to recognize and forestall potentially dangerous situations, and has acquired the ability to make decisions and react quickly and appropriately enough in situations imposing immediate danger. (p. 114)

Besides tacit knowledge, there are other aspects to the psychology of judgment that outdoor leaders should know. Clement (1996) states that judgment can plummet with ambiguity and when uncertainty combines with factors like desire or ego needs. He uses research by Plous (1993) to show why this is so. Plous suggested evolutionary and social theories. These suggest that if we face problems that our predecessors did not, then we are likely to reason poorly. Clement (1996), suggested that in the outdoors we can be at a disadvantage, for example, when a lead climber has to compute the physics of falling, the condition of the rock, and one's own mental condition (not to mention the reliability of the one holding the rope) as he/she places a piece of protection. He suggests help through *self-checks* on selective perception, context effects, heuristics (with their biases), and groups, as well as considering common traps in decision-making. These self-checks are explained below.

Selective Perception

Memory is reconstructive which means that we don't necessarily remember exactly what happens in an incident. A group of people would probably all perceive an incident differently. Personal biases, memories, attitudes, etc., can affect what we see. Our knowledge base may then be compromised. Plous' (1993) self-check would be:

1. Am I motivated to see things a certain way?
2. What expectations did I bring into this situation?
3. Would I see things differently without these motivations?
4. Have I consulted others who do not share my expectations and motives? (p.21)

Context Effects

Judgment will be affected by the context of a situation. If you have some professionals on your local course who have previously climbed in the Himalayas, your perception may be biased as to their actual real capabilities. If a river has to be crossed again and the group has just successfully shown their skills in swift water, will that color your judgment in deciding whether to cross again or search for an alternative? The self-check would be to step back and observe from a distance, consider the details of the big picture (keep an eye on the 'Himalayan' climber or his axe that may whistle past your ear), and again ask others. Taking input from everyone could reveal more than what you as the instructor can see. Be open to opinions but be prepared to make an unpopular decision if necessary.

Heuristics

Heuristics or 'general rules' simplify decision-making but can be treated as rules, so a distinction has to be made regarding what you are doing in relation to a change in the ever-fluid environment of the outdoors or a new location. The self-check would be to keep asking the question, "Why do we do this?" The general rule of not standing under a tree in a thunderstorm is good advice for the Florida golfer, but won't apply on the banks of the Chattooga River. Organizations can check actual accidents and near misses regarding procedures and places they use to eliminate these kinds of mistakes in their judgment.

Groups

Clement (1996) makes the point that groups are subject to the same biases as individuals. The more diverse the group is, the less likely this would be. Imagine a group of people from the same organization on an outing, meeting 'hippie' people on the trail. Their group's view of this person may be fairly similar and may be even reduced to "group-think" which could affect communication. A diverse group may include someone with a hippie type nature. In this case, if interaction between the groups was necessary, then it could be more successful. The more differing points of view in a group, the more possible solutions there are, and more misperceptions may be dispelled. This produces conflict – conflict of ideas – but if the group has 'group skills' which includes the use of conflict styles and conflict resolution techniques, then better decision-making is possible. The self-check would be to encourage dissenting opinions, let the group members speak first and encourage someone to be the Devil's Advocate.

Decision-Making Traps

The final section of Clement's (1996) Psychology of Judgment for Outdoor Leaders is about decision-making traps (overconfidence, self-fulfilling prophecies, and behavioral traps). Self-check overconfidence by assuming that you are probably 70-75% correct, even if you think you are 90% correct (Plous, 1993), and consider why alternate answers may be correct (Clement, 1996).

Choosing something that affirms your original belief would be a self-fulfilling prophecy. Self-check your suggestions by seeking out disconfirming observations. A simple question like "What am I missing here?", when going over a plan with a group, assuming that there is an open communication climate, could bring up alternate observations.

Cross and Guyer (1980) created five traps: *time delay, ignorance, investment, deterioration and collective*:

1. Time delay trap - if you leave something and think about dealing with it later. Conflict is a good example of this. If a small conflict is confronted and dealt with immediately, it can be done with but if left, it usually becomes bigger and is much more difficult to handle.

2. Ignorance trap – just not knowing what the consequences or hazards may be. Several groups have fallen into the moat (under the snow waterfall) in the couloir on Symmetry Spire in the Tetons because they didn't know about such hazards. People have been trapped in low head dam 'hydraulics' as they just didn't know how dangerous they are. The usefulness of attending a wilderness travel course rather than just learning on your own helps to avoid this problem and teaches you to "Know what you know and know what you don't know" as Petzoldt would often say.

3. Investment trap – when you have taken weeks of preparation and invested lots of money, you are more likely to, say, push and do the Peak rather than give up on it when the weather may be 'iffy'. The 1996 Everest disaster had quite a lot to do with the investment trap. Be prepared to turn back whatever the financial costs – safety is always a better investment.

4. Deterioration trap – over time people need more risk to feed satisfaction levels and are therefore more willing to take bigger risks. As instructors, are you seeking more difficult runs when skiing or kayaking, or more difficult climbs or caves for the right reasons?

5. Collective trap – an individual may push for doing something not in the best interest of the group, which results in bad consequences for the group. Part of Petzoldt's 'New Ethic" in the *New Wilderness Handbook* (1984) addresses this suggesting that the leader should be honest to self and others in choosing where to go – somewhere that suits the group and that is within the capabilities of the leader.

Clement's (1996) above research on Plous (1993), and Cross and Guyer's (1980) psychology of judgment, helps to illustrate its complexity and how we are often biased when trying to make judgments. What comes through very strongly is the need for instructors to be open to others in the group suggesting alternatives and that we are willing to follow the alternative course of action if needed. We do have to remember that while we can delegate decision-making to group members, we cannot as instructors delegate responsibility, which means that as designated leaders, we still own any consequences of a poor decision.

Guthrie's (1995) research on tacit knowledge illustrates the need for developing our judgment through courses, and mentorship. We also should instill judgment in all our courses through methods like reviewing, and constantly addressing the whys in our teaching and journal prompting. Shooter and Furman (2011) concluded that it is now recognized that there is variability and a contextual nature to the decision-making process in relation to the environment, the type of decision, and the experience of the decision maker.

Hunt (1984) wrote an opinion piece on the dangers of substituting rules for instructor judgment because of the fear of lawsuits. He wasn't arguing for an absence of rules, but for the ability of an instructor to make a decision in new situations that may develop in the future. "Intelligent interpretations of rules is what links their past efficacy to the novel future. The instructor on the spot must make these interpretations" (Hunt, 1984, p 21). He noted that the assumption would be that the instructor would have to have good judgment.

Psychological Aspects of Teaching

Whiting (1975) suggested sub-grouping the psychological concepts of arousal, motivation, perception, and communication when addressing any skill development including teaching as a skill. The following chapters will illustrate these concepts.

References

Anderson, L. W., & Krathwohl, D. R. (Eds.) (2001). *A taxonomy for learning, teaching, and assessing: A revision of Bloom's taxonomy of educational objectives.* New York: Longman.

Beames, S., Higgins, P., & Nicol, R. (2012). *Learning outside the classroom: Theory and guidelines for practice.* New York and London: Routledge.

Bloom, B. S. (Ed.) (1956). *Taxonomy of Educational Objectives, the classification of educational goals – Handbook I: Cognitive Domain.* New York: McKay.

Cain, K. D. (1988). *A delphi study of the development, evaluation, and documentation of judgment and decision-making ability in outdoor leaders of adventure education programs.* (Unpublished doctoral dissertation). University of Minnesota, USA.

Cain, K. D. (1991). Judgment and decision making ability. In D. Cockrell (Ed.). *The Wilderness Educator* (pp.13-34). Merillville, Indiana: ICS Books.

Cain, K. D., & McAvoy, L. (1991). Experienced based judgment. In J. Miles & S. Priest (Eds.), *Adventure Education* (pp. 241-250). State College, PA: Venture Publishing.

Clement, K. (1996). The psychology of judgment for outdoor leaders. In S. Guthrie, J. Macke, & R. Watters (Eds.), *Back to Basics: Proceedings of the International Conference on Outdoor Recreation and Education* (pp. 45-51). Boulder, CO: Association of Outdoor Recreation and Education. ED 417042.

Cross, J. G., & Guyer, M. J. (1980). *Social traps.* Ann Arbor: University of Michigan Press.

Dave, R. H. (1970). Psychomotor levels. In R. J. Armstrong (Ed.), *Developing and Writing Behavioral Objectives* (pp. 33-34). Tucson AZ: Educational Innovators Press.

Dewey, J. (1963). *Experience and Education.* New York: Collier Books.

Greenaway, R. (1996b). *Active reviewing* Retrieved 2017, from http://reviewing.co.uk/actrev.htm

Guthrie, S. (1995). The role of tacit knowledge in judgment and decision making. In R. Koesler, & R. Watters (Eds.), *Proceedings of the 1995 International Conference on Outdoor Recreation and Education* (pp.105-114). Boulder, CO: Association of Outdoor Recreation and Education. ED404083, 1996.

Heron, J. (1996). *Co-operative inquiry: Research into the human condition.* London: Sage.

Hunt, J. S. (1984). The dangers of substituting rules for instructor judgment in adventure programs. *Journal of Experiential Education,* 7(3), 20-21.

Koriat, A. (2003). Memory organization of action events and its relationship to memory performance. *Journal of Experimental Psychology,* 132(3), 435-454.

Marzano, R. J. (2001). *Designing a new taxonomy of educational objectives.* Thousand Oaks, CA: Corwin Press.

Miles, J. C. (1987). The problem of judgment in the outdoor leadership. In J. Meier, T. Morash, and G. Welton (Eds.), *High Adventure Outdoor Pursuits: Organization and Leadership* (pp. 502-509). Columbus, OH: Publishing Horizons, Inc.

Nicol, R. (2003). Outdoor education: Research topic or universal value? *Journal of Adventure Education and Outdoor Learning,* 2(1). 29-41.

Olson, J., & Pratt, J. (2000). The instructional cycle. In *Teaching Children and Adolescents with Special Needs* (pp. 170-197). Upper Saddle River, NJ: Prentice-Hall, Inc.

Petzoldt, P. K. (1974). *The wilderness handbook.* New York: W.W. Norton and Co.

Petzoldt, P. K. (1984). *The new wilderness handbook.* New York: W.W. Norton and Co.

Plous, S. (1993). *The psychology of judgment and decision-making.* New York: McGraw-Hill, Inc.

Priest, S., & Dixon, T. (1990). *Safety practices in adventure programming.* Boulder, CO: Association for Experiential Education.

Priest, S., & Gass, M. (1997). *Effective leadership in adventure programming.* Champaign, IL: Human Kinetics.

Reason, P. (1998). A participatory world. *Resurgence,* 168, 42-44.

Reitz, H. J, (1977). *Behavior in organizations*. Homewood, IL: Richard D. Irwin, Inc.

Rogers, R. J. (1979). *Leading to share – sharing to lead*. Monograph. Ontario, Canada: Council of Outdoor Educators of Ontario. (ERIC ED178 234)

Semb, G. B., & Ellis, J. A. (1994). Knowledge taught in school: What is remembered? *Review of Educational Research*, 64(2), 253-286.

Shooter, W., & Furman, N. (2011). Contextualizing recent judgment and decision-making concepts for outdoor leadership research. *Journal of Outdoor Recreation Education, and Leadership, 3(3), 189-203.*

Tulving, E. (1983). *Elements of episodic memory*. New York: Oxford University Press.

Wagstaff, M. (2001). Remembering our roots : Why ask why? *The WEA Legend: Newsletter of the Wilderness Education Association*. Spring.

Whiting, H. T. A. (1975). *Lecturing as a skill*. Unpublished paper. Leeds, England: University of Leeds.

Chapter 3

Communication

"Words mean nothing."

- Paul Petzoldt

Most teaching for an outdoor instructor will probably be done as an open skill, that is, subject to feedback rather than as straight lecturing, which means that communication is paramount. The teacher then needs to develop an open communication climate with the group and with each individual. Special attention needs to be given to interpersonal communication skills in the outdoor situation as groups are closely confined within each other's personal space for long periods of time. Any kind of defensive postures can divert energy into hidden agendas and antagonistic endeavors. Berne (1964) described three 'life' positions: "I'm OK – you're OK," "I'm OK – you're not OK," and "You're OK, - I'm not OK". A way to achieve open communication is to give positive unconditional regard to the students demonstrating an "I'm OK – you're OK" position. Having both instructors and students in the OK position can make the communication climate more positive.

Develop supportive communication by being empathic, egalitarian, and spontaneous. This will create personalization, openness, non-role behaviors and creativity (Gibb, 1961). Reduce defensiveness as this can cause depersonalization, façade building, role taking, hostility, circumvention, aggression, and dependence. Being rigid, inflexible, superior directed or just neutral can create this kind of defensiveness (Gibb, 1961). Emotional warmth is important for teachers but fundamental for outdoor instructors. Neill (1997) stated, "Outdoor education places participants in unfamiliar situations without many of the usual anchors for emotional security" (p.97).

Communication skills are involved whenever there is direct interaction with students and transmission of information. In a new learning situation, redundant (already known) but relevant information helps the assimilation of novel information. Novel information needs to be presented against the backcloth of redundant information so that we can see or hear things in context. The good teacher strikes an appropriate balance between the presentation of redundant and novel information (Whiting, 1975).

The Communication Channel

The channel is the means of conveying the message. The communicator is the sender, and the student the receiver (see Figure 14). Noise is any element that interferes with communication. Sender noise refers to such things as attitudes, prejudices, frame of reference of the sender, and the appropriateness of the language or other expression of the message. Receiver noise refers to such things as attitudes, background, and experiences that affect the coding process. According to Johnson (1981), "in the channel" noise refers to, environmental sounds, speech problems, and annoying or distracting mannerisms.

Figure 14. The Communication Channel

Originator and Sender ------------------------------ **Receiver of Message**
Encodes message   ***Channel* Noise**   Must have access to the same
Defines terms   code as the originator
***Sender* Noise**   ***Receiver* Noise**

In outdoor situations, communication channel noises literally interfere if, for example, teaching sites are close to a roaring torrent or if the wind is whistling through the trees. Voice projection becomes very important. Perhaps request that students use a "20 foot" voice (speak loud enough that you can be heard 20 feet away). Feedback from students can assist in determining if 'noise' in the communication channel is too great to allow learning to take place.

Overloading the students with too much information, especially new information, usually encourages him/her to switch off or select only some of the input. False information might get into the communication system. The teacher should always look for feedback. Even if giving a lecture, the instructor should look for non-verbal signs indicating the degree of attentiveness and effective communication and encourage verbal feedback from students as well.

Timing can be an issue in outdoor pursuits as there may by moments that instructions cannot be given. On the Chattooga River, on the last rapid above Sandy Ford, the river splits at an island and there is an enormous amount of wood at the confluence. In lower water levels, there isn't enough water to run the left side of the river and get all the way down without having to get out and drag your boat. The right side is very narrow with possible snags – depending on how much work the raft guides have done that year to clear it. As there is a longish rapid approaching the island with no convenient eddy just above the confluence, the best place to discuss this is further upriver in an eddy before the lead-in rapid. Explaining this at the very beginning of the trip at Earl's Ford wouldn't be a good idea because it may raise anxiety levels too much throughout the trip.

"Words mean nothing". I can see Petzoldt shaking his head at a debriefing after students had pitched their tents under a huge widow-maker (dead tree), after we had just explained the old three W's for selecting a camp site – wood, water, and widow-makers. In later years, this phrase came up especially on Teton trips. Students from North Carolina had not experienced camping on snow and so had 'noise' in their minds as receivers in the communication channel. We knew that this would be the case, so we had had pre-trip meetings to show clothing that would be good to take. We explained the 'man-on-the-move' phenomena (see the Perception Chapter) where a student who 'ditched' his booties just before we drove out to Teton Canyon, never stood still in the evenings when we were on the snow as his feet were still in his cold boots, so he had to keep moving to stay warm. This gets old on an extended trip and we explained that sitting on an insulating pad in a snow kitchen wearing your booties is the ultimate in 'toastiness' and comfort. The last few springs in the Tetons haven't been cold enough for just booties so now you also need lightweight over boots, so the booties stay dry. How many students didn't bring their booties and over boots on a subsequent trip? Three men 'on the move'. So, they had several nights to ponder what kind of 'noise' affected the communication. I have to say that they didn't complain too much and were creative with some plastic bags inside their camp shoes. They got some together time warming their feet on each other's bellies as well, but I am sure that they won't eliminate booties from their kit for future snow trips. It's a bit like expecting all snake-loving students to follow the instruction, "Don't pick up any snakes". Sometimes experience ends up being the most effective teacher. However, a trip would have to be modified if there was any danger of frostbite or serious trench foot or a snakebite. Ignoring instructions can affect the whole trip for everyone if you have to return to a shop to get vital clothing or the hospital in the case of a serious medical concern.

Noise in the communication channel when climbing can be a safety issue, hence the development of climbing calls so climbing partners know what words to listen for when they may be over a hundred feet apart and perhaps in noisy, windy conditions. There are different sets of climbing calls throughout the world so if climbing with someone from another country it would be wise to settle on a common set. Figure 15 illustrates a British set and a North American set developed by Petzoldt. Petzoldt's calls were invented with syllables in mind, for example "up-rope" has two, whereas "slack" has one – the idea being that individuals would be less likely to mistake the words if they were reduced to grunts in the wind. His system also always included a response – often "Thank you", which makes for very polite climbing!

Figure 15. Comparison of Two Different Sets of Climbing Calls

Petzoldt's Climbing Calls		A Set of British Climbing Calls	
Belayer	**Climber**	**Belayer**	**Climber**
"On belay"	" Climbing"	"Safe"	"Take in"
"Climb	"Up-rope"	"Taking in"	"That's me"
"Thank you"		"Climb when ready"	"Climbing"
	"Rock"	"Climb on"	"OK"
"Twenty-five" *(feet)*			
" Fifteen"			"Tight rope"
"Zero"	"Thank you"		"Take in"
	"Falling"		"Slack"
	"Slack"		"Below"
"Thank you"	"Belay off"		"Tension"
"Thank you"			"Safe"

Active Listening

This is a way of listening that is designed to improve mutual understanding. It includes listening attentively. Sometimes someone may be thinking of what they want to say rather than focusing on what the speaker is saying. Active listening has structure as the listener should paraphrase what the speaker said to test for accuracy and further explanation can be given if necessary. You might start by saying, "This is what I am hearing you say" and, "Am I missing anything?" It can be used for communication clarification in instruction or for conflict resolution where feelings can also be included. It is important that full attention is given to the speaker. Value judgments should be suspended while listening. Reading body language can help interpret feelings. Cooperative intentions can also aid the discussion concerning feelings. Using this technique can really help a group to reach a consensus if this is needed in decision-making.

Role Modeling

An interesting role modeling incident happened to me at the beginning of a WEA professionals course in North Carolina one July. As we were preparing and outfitting the group, I offered everyone a cagoule (long rain jacket). The members of the group were not familiar with cagoules and were balking at the idea of taking them as they don't look fashionable. They were however very waterproof, not being made of 'Leaktex'. One guy asked, "What are you taking?" What a great lead in. I said, "A cagoule of course - as it can rain every day in this part of the country". Sure enough, we had nine days of rain out of the ten-day course, but that bit of role modeling improved the experience for everyone. We didn't have the same success with the Outbound shelters which are like Megamids, bottomless pyramid shaped shelters which are very light and roomy with good ventilation for North Carolina summers. One professional got very upset after we found a rattlesnake near our campsite. He shouted, "You didn't tell me these weren't tents! Someone said – "Yes, he said these are *not* tents!" Again, another "words mean nothing" situation. He hadn't heard the words. He was a little anxious about rattlers joining him in his shelter, but he did stay dry in his cagoule and Outbound.

Role modeling becomes an important part of communication as students will copy you – even if you have said not to do so. If you are camping and you want your drink topped off with hot water, then you had better put the cup on the ground, so they will imitate you. The same goes for being on time to meetings, taking care of hygiene, having a tidy kitchen at your campsite, camping away from the trail or the stream, etc. Role modeling group norms that have been set is essential. One very useful norm in particular is being 'other-directed'. Petzoldt (1995) noticed that some of his first guides at his American School of Mountaineering were more interested in their own goals:

> Training and selecting guides was difficult. I soon found that some of the people who were the most agile and experienced climbers were not suitable guides. While taking people up the mountain, they were thinking mostly of themselves, what they wanted to climb, and the different chimneys and snow slopes they wanted to try. It turned into a climb that pleased them, and the clients were just along for the ride. In my opinion, they should have been doing the type of climb that was best for the client. (p. 206)

Being 'other-directed' as the instructor, looking after the concerns of students, creates a group culture where everyone is more likely to help each other. Instructors can model this on expedition courses by letting the students pick their tent sites first. Rushing ahead of the students to pick the best one would send the wrong message. Throughout the course, checking in with all the students, maybe by visiting them when they are cooking, is another great way to make sure their needs are being met. They can be asked at de-briefing sessions at the end of the day but that isn't the same and they are less likely to confess their anxieties to the rest of the group. I nearly always do ask the group each day or evening if there are any anxieties or problems that need discussing but have found that more is revealed in informal one-on-one 'check-ins'.

Soliciting Hidden Information

When students are in the group as a whole, I have found that an exercise to illicit communication is necessary unless they have a totally open communication climate. For example, facilitate students writing an anonymous note about their anxieties, and put them into a hat. Mix up the notes and then ask everyone to take one and read it out loud. This will likely bring out issues that can be dealt with. Sometimes the issues are about group dynamics and sometimes they are misperceptions that just needed clearing up. Good facilitation skills are sometimes needed in these situations as participants may use inappropriate communication tactics that Thorenson (1972) called defense mechanisms. (Detail on this can be found in the group dynamics chapter.) An example that I experienced is when someone failed to help out when we pitched camp in a storm – he got his tent up and dived into it straight away. A group norm was to help each other in adverse conditions and he obviously ignored that. He was confronted in a group meeting the following morning and someone who had also been ignoring group norms on occasion jumped right in to defend him. This is called "red-crossing," encouraging mutual aid, so I had to say, "Let George speak for himself," so that he wasn't let off the 'hook'.

Confronting behavior issues requires good feedback skills (this is also addressed in the group dynamics chapter). Using the note in the hat exercise can be a way to check on group norms (that are pre-set) and communicate what needs to be addressed. A good way to re-visit group norms is to suggest that everyone write down one thing that they perceive the group to be doing well and one thing that needs improvement. Again, put the notes in a hat and then re-distribute them for everyone to read one out. Clarification is often necessary as you discuss everything. If this is done on a regular basis, it communicates to the group that you are revisiting the group norms and haven't forgotten about them - which tends to improve behavior. It is very important to give praise for meeting the group norms, so this should never become just a negative session.

Non-Verbal Communication

Non-verbal communication plays a very important role. Contradictory verbal and non-verbal communication should be discussed as this often hides conflict. Buried conflict usually emerges later having grown out of proportion to what it was originally. Display openness in your non-verbal communication as you are trying to establish an open communication climate.

As an instructor, it is helpful to understand some detail of non-verbal communication; it is generally regarded as contributing far more to communication than words. *The Backcountry Classroom* (2005) states that body language accounts for 55% of the message, tonality (how the words are said), 38%, and actual words only 7% (Drury, Bonney, Berman, & Wagstaff, 2005). Research using video instead of tape-recorded words found that non-verbal cues had 4.3 times the effect of verbal cues (Argyle, Salter, Nicholson, Williams, & Burgess, 1970). Study results may vary with different situations, but it does seem that non-verbal cues are extremely important. Non-verbal cues include:

() Kinesics (facial expressions and body movements)

() Posture

() Gesture

() Vocalics (Tone, pitch and accent)

() Haptics (touching)

() Eyes

() Clothing and bodily characteristics

() Proxemics (how physical space is perceived and used)

() Chronemics (time).

() Kinesics (facial expressions and body movements). A nod, a smile, a grimace, a cold hard stare, a frown, a raised eyebrow, a sneer, a jutted chin, an open mouth, gritted teeth, a wrinkled brow, a curled lip, a yawn, all tell us something. They are often unintentional, but can be intentional, and the timing of these kinesics communicates something as well. Ekman & Friesen (2003) explained that someone trying to convey an emotion has a faster onset and offset than someone showing a spontaneous emotion. That being said, the ability to interpret others' expressions is key. Being aware of your own expressions can be helpful but trying to mask your emotions is difficult as ingenuous expressions can be picked up very easily. Some changes in expression can be so fleeting they are referred to as micro-momentary movements, "facial expressions that are so short lived that they seem to be quicker than the eye", and can slip in, in a number of ways (Haggard and Isaacs, 1966, p. 154). When referring to control Cook (1997) says, "It can slip from those parts of the body least under voluntary control, through nervous gestures of hands or through a trembling of the stiff upper lip when the person thinks no one is watching" (p. 56).

People can read each other fairly accurately in regard to genuineness. Be aware of that in your expressions as an instructor and look for that in students who may be verbalizing one thing but saying something different through their expressions. This could happen, for example, with a student entering a cave or rappelling for the first time. In classes, nods, smiles, and quizzical looks are common and keep the conversation going, helping in the communication process.

() Posture. Body orientation and posture can also communicate things, like attentiveness. Leaning in or forward, facing into the circle of students can reflect fondness, whereas a disengaged student might face sideways and/or lean backwards. Be aware of indicators like direction of lean, arm position, body openness, and body orientation. Posture matching can enhance rapport between/among the group and instructors; non-congruent postures can illustrate differences of opinion or relationship distance.

() Gesture. Gestures can include obvious things like pointing, giving a thumbs-up, making a T shape with the hands to signal a time out, or less obvious things, like a knitted brow, clenched fist, or behaviors mentioned above, like leaning forward or backward. Other common, purposeful gestures include waving, eye rolling, and winking. To avoid looking incompetent or anxious, avoid hair twirling, putting a hand in front of your mouth and wringing your hands. Gestures can be used to emphasize things like the sweep of a hand across the 'valley', or pointing directly at a mountain when teaching navigation. They can also reflect nervousness or boredom. Common positive gestures in one country may have very different negative meanings in other countries. For example, the 'thumbs up' sign is positive in the U.S. and the UK but negative in Asia.

() Vocalics (tone, pitch, and accent). When leading groups, instructions can be given in positive or negative ways, so thinking about how to deliver your message is very important. How you say something can be more important than what you say. Are you suggesting that something be done, insisting, or telling in a civil way, or do you sound demeaning? Do you sound authentic? Try to always be civil and as natural as possible. Monotone pitch could make your presentation sound dry. Liven it up with variations of rhythm, speed, inflection, timbre, loudness and pitch. Intonation also affects your delivery. The same words said with a different intonation can mean the exact opposite as with the use of sarcasm – like, "Well thanks".

Accents can both help and hinder. Some accents are pleasant to people and some are grating. In America, an English accent is often liked whereas in Australia it is nothing out of the ordinary (speaking from personal experience). I remember advising a student in North Carolina who let me talk in my fairly mixed accent including Derbyshire, Yorkshire, Australian, and southern US. Though the student said, "I love your accent," it was soon followed by, "What did you say?" The actual message was totally lost. Words for sure meant nothing at that time! Accents can unfortunately result in prejudice. Prejudice should not be a part of any instructor's repertoire. Accents and dialects are part of each and every one of us. They reflect where we are from, whether we are proud of that or not, and they do have an effect on other people.

() **Haptics** (touching). There should be a 'red alert' on this. While touching can give encouragement and support, it can also create embarrassment, or worse, if misinterpreted. It could be interpreted as sexual harassment. People react very differently to touching whether or not it is a cultural norm. Pats on the back or a touch on the arm could be relatively safe. Shaking hands is usually safe, as are high fives, or fist bumps but hugs can vary. I am British, and not a hugger, but many Americans have to hug - a lot! For folks who have never met, hugging would be inappropriate. Use good judgment in this.

Also use good judgment when you have to touch students. There are many occasions for this in the outdoors. It could be when supporting students on a ropes course or spotting students rock climbing. You are actually holding students during one of the stages of teaching kayak rolling; do it in a way that doesn't affect the students' comfort zones. Male-female touching is especially tricky. Organizations may even have strict rules on this. Backrubs may be nice but be careful with this as that may lead to special friendships or miss-communicated intentions of special friendships. I have seen this on expeditions and the resulting problems once biological attraction kicks in can be very hard to deal with.

() **Eyes.** Ralph Waldo Emerson said, "When the eyes say one thing, and the tongue another, a practiced man relies on the language of the first." Charles Darwin, one of the original researchers of non-verbal behavior said:

> From the continued use of the eyes, these organs are especially liable to be acted
> on through association under various states of mind, although there is manifestly nothing to be seen.
> A man…who vehemently rejects a proposition, will almost certainly shut his eyes or turn away his
> face; but if he accepts the proposition will nod his head in affirmation and open his eyes widely.
> (1998, p. 33)

Do they mirror the soul? There are many sayings associated with eyes: "mirroring the soul", "shifty eyes", "come-hither look", "evil eye." They could be the most dominant features of the face; much is 'said' by the eyes. The study of eye contact is called *oculesics*. In western cultures using eye contact is expected when communicating. In other cultures, this may not be the case such as in Asia or Islamic countries. Where eye contact is acceptable, duration affects a person's comfort level; too long a gaze becomes a stare, too short becomes 'shifty eyed'.

In Western cultures as eye contact is expected, it is often used by a teacher as a cue for a student to speak. A blank stare from a student may mean that they don't understand something, or they are mentally processing. Phelps, Doherty-Sneddon, and Warnock (2006) suggest that students look away from the teacher while thinking about the answer to a question as that mental demand shouldn't be compromised by the extra demands of reading the teacher's expressions. When presenting as a teacher, not looking at the audience will give the perception of nervousness or a formal reading. Students looking around generally, looking at watches, and/or exhibiting restless behavior signals a lack of attentiveness.

Eye contact is used for other social communication like aggression or flirting. Both of these compromise teaching in the human dimension. When in bear country it is recommended not to have eye contact with bears as this can reflect a challenge and trigger an attack.

◐ **Clothing and bodily characteristics.** Gender, weight, height, color, body odor, and clothing are all non-verbal cues. They may instill an immediate effect, which can be lasting, but overall the students are looking at teacher traits such as fairness, liveliness, and knowledge. Some characteristics, like height and gender cannot be changed, but hygiene and clothing can. Height, according to Melamed and Bozionelos (1992), does create an initially more favorable impression. Body type and weight can produce the stereotypic generalizations associated with skinny, muscular, and overweight people. These generalizations are usually dispelled. I have seen very slightly built students show enormous strength, and muscular people need the help of others in carrying large packs.

Good hygiene practices should always be used, especially on expedition courses, as role modeling greatly affects student behavior in that regard. Clothing should also be role-modeled by the instructor for example, by wearing a hat for sun protection as well as long sleeves and long pants - the same for serious bush pushing for protection from brambles. The opinion that clothing or gear should be considered high fashion is alive and well in the outdoor industry. Is your clothing, helmet, or tent very different from that provided to the students? They will notice if it is and wonder why they aren't getting what they may perceive as the best.

 Could whatever you are wearing be some kind of barrier? What kind of sunglasses do you have – are they mirrored? Do you wear them only when you have to, or all the time? The eyes of the instructor are important as described above, so sometimes during instruction they should not be worn. At times they have to be worn, for example, on snow for sun protection, but it does affect communication.

Are you wearing any insignia that sends a message? North Face, or Patagonia brands communicate "I have good (but expensive) gear". Patches from the organization you work for communicate that you have an allegiance. What does your favorite T-shirt say? Is it conveying what you really want to say?

◐ **Proxemics** (how physical space is perceived and used). In the outdoors, lighting, noise, and temperature can affect the communication. Proxemics looks at the space between sender and receiver. In the outdoor classroom, we often have some wonderful teaching spots. Think about the environment you choose in relation to how quiet it is, aesthetics, or distractions, like a river or view. Have you been meeting in the same place time after time and need a change of scenery? Does the space allow for students looking down on you, or up at you? Does it allow for a circle, horseshoe shape, or more of an auditorium formation? This can have an effect on communication with different students who may choose their seating or standing position based on how they are most comfortable or for more or less interaction with the instructor. More outgoing or extroverted students might choose places with the best line of sight to the instructor. Anxious or introverted students might seek positions less available for eye contact (furthest away in auditorium settings and closer to in a circle or horseshoe).

People have different comfort zones regarding actual distance between each other when communicating. Initial study on this was done by Edward Hall (1966) who devised four zones; intimate, personal, social, and public. However, according to Griffin (2009), modern researchers view proxemics as part of other communication cues like gender, topic of conversation, perceived status, and surrounding noise. How close two people get depends then on more than intimacy levels. Instructors should be aware that students may be uncomfortable with very close proximity, especially at the beginning of a course. Different cultures have different norms in this regard. Normally classes in social and public domains are four feet or more apart, but when conversing one on one, care should be taken to not to go beyond the personal zone (18 inches to four feet) into the intimate zone (0 to 18 inches) as this would likely be perceived as an intrusion. People are affected by whether they are looking up or down. Discussing a journal would be best done sitting side by side. Giving a 'commanding' lecture may be better received if the instructor stands while the students are sitting down. If you are trying to achieve a sense of egalitarianism, then communicate at the same level.

() **Chronemics** (time). On an outdoor leadership course in the 1980s, I remember being told that group dynamics were incredibly important – but we spent virtually no time on the topic. I, as the student, might have thought that perhaps it wasn't all that important, except we were on a 23-day expedition with lots of meaty group dynamics happening, often provoked by time.

Time is always an issue with newly formed groups. Some people believe in "Island Time", "Irish" time, "Mormon Standard" time and other labels for the student who wish to arrive "whenever". This often creates the first conflict in the group as many students do believe in arriving on time and the instructor usually believes in punctuality as well. A group norm set very early in the course is helpful, as is synchronizing everyone's watches. If someone is constantly late, what are they saying to you or everyone in the group?

The pause. After asking a question, there may be an uncomfortable pause if no one immediately jumps to an answer. You want students to think before speaking, so the pause is good. Rather than you give the answer, wait awhile. Don't try and save the pause by calling on someone. If the pause is getting unproductively long, ask the students to verbally discuss the question with their neighbor. This nearly always elicits a response. Perhaps the question was not worded well and needed clarification. If the same students continue jumping to answer, then change tactics and call on others. People have different response times. Waiting with a longer pause can enable students with longer response times to participate in answering a question thrown out to the group.

How fast or slow do you talk? Do you change the pace to emphasize something? How long are people willing to listen? I have seen introductory climbing session talks detail rope breaking strains and other unnecessary information while the campers were looking at the climbing wall, probably fantasizing about being up there. For sure, they had shut down on the communication because of the length of time the instructor driveled on without paying attention to the students' cues (sighing, fidgeting, yawning etc.). Saying more than is needed often spills information as the 'cup' is filled to overflowing.

Verbal and Non-Verbal Communication Interactions

There is interaction between verbal and non-verbal communication. Knapp and Hall (2007) give six ways: repeating, conflicting, complementing, substituting, regulating, and accenting/moderating. Remember that the communication is a two-way street where the instructor should always be looking for non-verbal as well as verbal cues indicating whether the student understands the message being given. The outdoor instructor can use these interactions in the following ways:

■ **Repeating.** A ski instructor may lean forward herself when giving a verbal message to lean forward. A kayak instructor may point or throw a rock into an eddy when discussing that eddy. A climbing or caving instructor may demonstrate leaning back while explaining the body position required for a rappel. A verbal message is strengthened by some kind of gesture or body movement.

■ **Conflicting.** Verbal and non-verbal messages that do not match send a conflicting message. An eye roll will pretty effectively negate any verbal instructions. If the students ask you how far the hike is going to be and you say, "Not so far", but your body shows signs of anxiety, like fidgeting, the students will probably read that they have a long hike ahead. If you ask if everyone had breakfast on an expedition day and the students avoid eye contact, then they probably slept in and didn't have time to prepare anything.

■ **Complementing**. It is best to try and affirm verbal instruction with non-verbal cues, thus aligning what you're saying with how you are saying and reinforcing your message. If everyone in the group is sitting, perhaps stand up and somewhat lean over the group to say, "We will be rising at 4am for an Alpine Start!" If someone did a great job rigging a bear bag line maybe touch someone on the shoulder and say "Thanks, that was a great job".

■ **Substituting**. This is where no words are spoken. I remember doing a Nick the Greek (safety briefing) on a day when Petzoldt had decided that he had talked too much and promised to say nothing for a while. The group was brainstorming the odds of accidents the following day when we were to climb on the Wigwams Ridge. No one was bringing up lightning. He got hold of a large rock, stood in the middle of the group and held it up in the air like Moses, which immediately elicited conversation about lightning. Also, remember some of Greenaway's (1996) techniques for debriefing, like the morale graph where students get in a line and stand how they feel or where you might ask them to re-enact an incident without words.

■ **Regulating**. Anyone in the group can regulate, or control, the conversation by touching someone's arm to signal that they need to stop, and/or with hand gestures that say, "Give me more", "Time-out", or "Stop". Conversation is often regulated by the common norm of raising a hand to answer a question. Sometimes a rock or object is used to monitor interruptions if the discussion gets out of hand; the only person who can talk is the person holding the rock or object.

■ **Accenting/moderating.** The verbal message may be changed or moderated. Emphasizing a particular word can reinforce your message. For example, "We will NOT be missing breakfast tomorrow morning!" The intonation strengthens the message for this expedition group responsible for cooking their own breakfast. Shaking a clenched fist while you say it would communicate that you are angry as well (perhaps because they slept in the day before). Do you want that message to be received? If not, then watch what you do with your hands.

Petzoldt-isms

Instructors from The Wilderness Education Association (WEA) and no doubt from the National Outdoor Leadership School (NOLS) use Petzoldt's sayings to illustrate points. Petzoldt had such a force of personality that his ideas and corresponding sayings still resonate through both NOLS and WEA, organizations that he was instrumental in establishing. Other people, such as John Jackson (1973), quoted in Cockrell (1991) have come up with valuable sayings: "Have the right person, the right people in the right place at the right time with the right knowledge and the right equipment." (p. 19). Petzoldt developed and used this technique very effectively. It provided an easy way to boiler-plate, or strengthen, various ideas or fundamental principles of an organization that can be used by other instructors. Here are some of his sayings.

"Know what you know and know what you don't know." This saying means know your limitations. WEA leadership courses in the Tetons taught leadership through backpacking and spring mountaineering. The mountaineering was mostly to show students what they didn't know, such as knowledge of ice axe techniques, glissading, and avoidance of moats, etc. Students on these courses were expected to recognize that they wouldn't have the skills to necessarily lead mountaineering after that initial course unless they were already established mountaineers. It would limit their leadership to backpacking as they 'knew what they knew and knew what they didn't know' about working on snow or with technical mountaineering. They would need to get considerable more experience and training before considering that kind of leadership.

"Rules are for fools." This relates to judgment, Paul's most important and emphasized concept for the outdoors. Organizations that employ young and inexperienced instructors may have more rules than ones that employ seasoned instructors. Paul was against hard and fast rules along with rote learning of what to do in the outdoors. He often used to say, "We aren't preparing people for Jeopardy, the TV Show." Things change so much with things like weather, snow, water levels, and group dynamics, so hard and fast rules don't always apply.

"Chew the cud -- have a cow-like nature." On expeditions, people can sometimes get very tense as there is often no way to get away from the group and if there are some conflicting personalities, then this can heighten friction between group members. On extended NOLS, Outward Bound (OB), and WEA expedition style courses, this can be common. Hence, Paul suggested that expedition members try and develop a cow-like nature and chew the cud, rather than react forcefully to others' behavior and comments. Not that inappropriate behaviors should become the norm; they should be dealt with through effective feedback techniques (see the group dynamics chapter). He also suggested that it wasn't a good idea to get into arguments about religion or politics on expeditions. Those beliefs are deep seated, and the chances are that no-one is going to change those beliefs, so why encourage open conflict about those issues?

"Look at the Las Vegas odds like Nick the Greek." Paul viewed much of his decision-making through the Nick the Greek (king of gamblers), 'Las Vegas Odds' lens. In the outdoors, safety is not a given, so we should always be considering the 'odds' when we decide to make the climb (or turn back), run the rapid, or ski the drop. He often used this premise for safety briefings, saying, "Let's do a Nick the Greek" when embarking on something new, like an introductory rappel lesson. This would initiate a brainstorming of where Nick the Greek would place his bets on where accidents could occur along with the judgment factors during the activity. This got everybody thinking about the safety aspects, which was far more effective than listing off a set of rules for students to try and remember. Using "Nick the Greek" honors Nick's ability as a gambler to weigh the odds. As outdoor instructors, we can never assure absolute safety in the environment we work in. Petzoldt wanted us to use the Las Vegas odds regarding making safe choices (bets) in our decision-making.

"Me no lost, teepee lost." This statement referred to not being entirely sure of one's position exactly although knowing roughly where one is and to not get in a panic about it. This could be used literally in regard to navigation or figuratively in regard to being in a philosophical argument. The saying comes from a story he used to tell about cowboys. Paul never gave much credit to cowboys for judgment such as insisting on wearing cowboy hats in winter and getting frostbitten ears. We really never do see pictures of cowboys wearing woolly hats and balaclavas, do we? Anyhow, the story goes that two cowboys met up with an Indian who looked lost and one said, "I thought you guys never got lost". The Indian replied "Me no lost – tepee lost". This statement was probably also lost on the cowboys. Instead of disappearing into long division, we can say, "I can think my way out of this and find where I am as I am not truly lost."

"Meet at the old oak tree." This refers to being in the woods where there are hundreds of old oak trees. In other words, when you make an arrangement be precise so that there will be no confusion. This had special meaning to me having spent some of my childhood playing in the famous Major Oak, or Robin Hood's Tree, near Edwinstowe, Nottinghamshire. Unlike this tree, the "old oak tree" could refer to any oak tree. Two friends of mine, ropes course facilitators who regarded themselves as communication professionals, decided to meet for dinner at Pizza Hut in Bryson City, NC. There happened to be two Pizza Huts in that town and they each went to a different one. If you can make a mistake with two Pizza Huts, imagine the possibilities of confusion with the hundreds of oak trees in Sherwood Forest or the North Carolina woods.

"Be other directed." This was in Paul's mind the "raison d'etre" for being a leader. It meant looking after others. It could make the difference between being certified as an outdoor leader or not by Paul. Even if someone was a very experienced outdoorsman but was selfish and unconcerned about others in the group, they would not get a leader's certificate based on this premise. Towards the end of each week on the five - week courses, students would start to run out of some items of food, so we used to compile all the food onto a tarp and then have everyone pick from the piles of food that were laid out. Sometimes, a student would hide behind some bushes and eat the rest of their cheese instead of adding it to the tarp – a surefire way of illustrating selfishness.

"Eat like Indians." When you are part way through your supplies, you have to decide whether you will portion out food to get through the rest of the trip or "Eat like Indians" – eat normally and go hungry at the very end. This decision sometimes has to be made on expeditions. The saying refers to the old times when food was sometimes plentiful and at other times scarce. Indians didn't really have much of a choice, so when there was food it was eaten. This Petzoldt-ism was, again, not intended to be racial. All of Paul's references to Native Americans were positive. His references were about their use of good judgment,

"White man fire." The large bonfires that people love to make when camping Petzoldt called "White Man Fires". The idea was that 'white folks' had no sense of reason when making large bonfires and should really only make small fires, just big enough for a specific reason, like cooking. Nowadays the necessity of a fire of any kind is often questioned. They are rarely needed. If there is a lot of downfall and great care is taken to make sure that it is safe and will not start a forest fire and any disturbed ground is repaired, a small fire could be considered. Many a tent, nylon jacket, pants and boots have been ruined by wearing them by a fire or by trying to dry them out by a fire. And don't even think about ever trying to dry a down sleeping bag by a fire. For instructional courses, down bags are too hard to dry and so are not recommended. Using a fire to dry modern clothing is not recommended either except for extraneous circumstances.

"This is a Maasai Chief decision." Sometimes the leader has to make an unquestioned decision. Paul referred to this as a Maasai Chief Decision. In the past, questioning such a chief was not an option for the Maasai. The leader can delegate decision-making, but cannot delegate responsibility so the designated leader has the prerogative to make such a decision. It may be unpopular but because the responsibility rests on the leader's shoulders and they will have to answer for any subsequent consequences - designated leaders may take the option to do this. Paul would preface such a decision by saying "This is a Maasai Chief Decision." – in other words, don't question it. Occasionally he used it to assert his leadership. There will always be some contention for the leadership in a group. Paul was very insistent on preventing this *"Don't lose the leadership of the group"* was always stressed. If someone started to chip away at his leadership, he would make a definite effort to stop it, one way being to make a decision relating to that person that was a decision-not-to-be-questioned.

"A promise made is a debt unpaid." - Robert Service. Paul used to say "If you take someone on the course, then you have the responsibility to look after them." If you say that you will do something or take someone on your course then you can't ignore subsequent issues – so it becomes a promise. "A promise made is a debt unpaid." Paul could recite Service's entire poem (*The Cremation of Sam McGee*), which made for a powerful effect. Do not promise things that may not be possible. I remember trying to adapt a kayak paddle to a wonderfully enthusiastic woman who was a hemiplegic. She had been promised that she could kayak the five-day trip down the Vermillion River in Minnesota. We adapted the paddle, but neither she, nor any of us could paddle one armed for more than ten minutes. This created great disappointment even though we adapted a canoe paddle and enabled her participation on the trip in the front of a canoe.

"If they say they've climbed the Matterhorn – take an extra rope." - Glen Exum. Often times when someone has had a taste of an activity, they feel over-confident and they think they know far more than they actually do. Clients of the Petzoldt-Exum Guide School who had climbed in Europe, where the guiding style didn't involve any teaching, came off as 'know it alls' because they had climbed the Matterhorn, but were, in fact, a danger to themselves as they really didn't know what they were doing and so had to be watched more closely. Glenn suggested that you needed an extra rope to keep them safe. The warning here is to beware of students that are being loud about their accomplishments as they may have no real understanding of the judgments that are necessary, nor the activity concerned.

Mental Imagery

Using truisms and sayings like the above examples can help students to better see issues more clearly. For physical skills we can use a different kind of mental imagery. Imagine you are on the Chattooga River in a boat. It is a bright sunny day and the river is running at a comfortable level for you. The water is absolutely clear, and you can see the rocks all the way to the bottom of the river and the "Fools' Gold" shining on the sandy riverbed. There is a strong smell of pine as the river pushes you down through the wilderness. You are approaching second ledge, slipping through the rocks just upstream and heading for river left. You can hear the waterfall. You did this run a couple of weeks ago and so it is still fresh in your mind. You have to aim some yards from the left bank, there are some low hanging branches – but stay right enough to stay away from them; the sound is loud now, there is what looks like steam rising from the edge of the drop and no view of what is happening right below the horizon line. Your heart rate has picked up considerably, the boat in front of you disappears and you are hoping that you are positioned right now as it is too late to change course, so you power the next few strokes. You can see the edge and you are on it in a nanosecond giving one last strong pull to try and sail over the edge. You drop into the hole and it's all froth and sparkling whitewater as you pop up to the surface, through the hydraulic and on downriver to join the other boats in the river right eddy under a giant rock.

While reading the above passage you were creating, or re-creating (if you have run this rapid before), an image with many of your senses, visual, auditory, olfactory, and kinesthetic, as you moved through the scene. Vealey and Greenleaf (2010) define mental imagery as "…using one's senses to re-create or create an experience in the mind" (p. 268). It can be powerful enough to illicit physical effects like firing neurons in muscles and increasing heart rate, so athletes use the concept of mental imagery to improve performance, which enables additional practice beyond the actual physical practice - though it can't replace real practice. The ski racer for example, could imagine the complete downhill run and replay it many times, on the chairlift going back up, in the car (as a passenger), on the way to or from the slopes, in an armchair, in bed, or in a special sensory deprivation flotation chamber. Meta-analysis of research on mental imagery has shown that using mental practice is more effective than not using it for improving a motor skill (Hinshaw, 1991). Athletes in competition and training use imagery for much more though – for improving confidence, self-motivation, improved cognition and strategies, problem solving, and controlling emotional states.

Most writing and research on mental imagery is about athletes' training and competition. Can we take the relevant parts of this concept to improve outdoor instruction for recreational participants? An understanding of the various associated constructs will help to see how this could be done. First though, further conceptualization of what it is will set the stage. Vealey and Greenleaf (2010) suggest that it is a *polysensory* experience that should involve all the relevant senses (visual, auditory, olfactory, tactile, gustatory [taste], and kinesthetic). So, besides the visual, participants could be playing or re-playing the sounds of skis on snow, the smell of the river (hopefully not the Pigeon in Tennessee!), the taste of salt when surfing, and the feel of muscles moving in climbing. For some things, several senses could be a distraction so involving *relevant* senses is key to maximizing the effectiveness of the imagery. There are different terms associated with mental imagery – mental practice, mental rehearsal, visualization, and some writers, like Orlick (2007) have suggested that the term mental imagery be replaced by movement, action, or performance imagery; it is a polysensory experience, not just a visual snapshot.

However, Coffey (personal communication, May 26th, 2011) does use what he calls snapshot visualization, where he suggests the instructor pick three or four points (for a more complex run in kayaking) at which the student imagines a virtual snapshot of themselves, and stroke placement, edge, balance, and vector (direction of momentum) or turn. Run through the move verbally, then physically. This technique gives a way to address key issues within certain runs and allows more clarity as the student isn't trying to formulate the entire move in their head. The entire move will come later as they start to imagine more snapshots until it eventually becomes a "broken minds-eye video".

What is the perspective of the imagery? Is the visualization internal, from your own viewpoint, or external, from a third-person perspective? Are you visualizing from the first-person position, seeing it from in your boat, or are you viewing it as if from the lens of a camera looking at you? Both perspectives can be used. Horn, Morris, Spittle, and Watt (2005) explain that each one can be helpful in different ways; internal because of the resemblance of the physical performance, external because spatial effects and correct movement execution. Some athletes switch between the two in their mental imagery. Both could be used when teaching an eddy turn on a river, which requires an understanding and visualization of the positioning of the boat in relation to the eddy line and the power to push through it. In this case, some instructors show positioning by using a model boat on a sandbank with rocks and sticks to represent features. Downriver in a safe place above the eddy, talk through a first person (internal) script to stress the kinesthetic aspects of the move (see Figures 16 and 17 for examples).

Example Internal Perspective (Eddy Turn)

Figure 16. An Eddy Turn

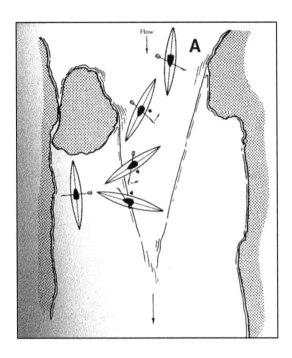

Reprinted from *Canoeing In Australia* by M. L. Phipps, & D. Stone, 1976, Lilydale, Australia: Pioneer Design Studio Pty Ltd. Drawing by Fred Schmidt. Copyright 1976, by Maurice Phipps and Douglas Stone. Reprinted with permission.

After a demonstration upstream, and possibly a video that morning (external perspectives), you are in your kayaks a few yards above the eddy in a quiet spot by the bank. You have the students close their eyes and guide them through the eddy turn in their mind's eye by saying the following:

Imagine you are paddling down towards the eddy on river right. You look right, across to the top of the rapid (Point A on Figure 16), aiming for the very top of the eddy with several powerful forward strokes, lifting your right knee a little. You see the eddy line and push through it with hard strokes going fast. As soon as you cross the eddy line, you change your lean and lift up your left knee hard, keeping it up until the boat is facing totally upstream well inside the eddy.

Repeat this exercise/script a couple of times, then have the students mentally rehearse it a couple of times. Now do it.

Example External Perspective (Rock Climb)

Figure 17. A Lay-Back Climbing Move

You are doing some practice bouldering, teaching a lay-back climbing move to beginner students. You are facing a corner, which has a nice edge. While the students watch, you demonstrate the technique and climb the boulder using the edge, explaining when you are pulling with your arms and when you are pushing with your feet, and then you talk them through the move.

Look at the edge and, in your mind, picture yourself reaching up and grasping it with both hands. You are leaning back so your arms are straight. Now you are starting to walk up the other wall with your feet until your legs are horizontal. You are now pushing with your feet and pulling with your arms. You move one hand up a little higher on the edge, and then the other hand. You move your feet up a little again. You keep doing this to the top of the corner.

Repeat this exercise/script a couple of times, then have the students mentally rehearse it a couple of times. Now do it.

The external perspective can be seen using video, which, thanks to modern technology, is becoming easier to use and offers immediate feedback. Filming a series of students' ski-turns and then showing them at the bottom of the slope to critique performance is now possible on an iPad, along with software enabled graphics on the screen.

The sport psychologist, Suin (1976) referred to his procedure for mental practice as Visuomotor Behavior Rehearsal (VMBR). He explained the procedure as more than sheer imagination, but a "…well controlled copy of experience…" (p. 41). VMBR is a popular technique involving the polysensory nature of mental imagery that is used by sports psychologists. What are some other concepts that can help us as outdoor instructors? Let's look at the PEETLEP model.

The PETTLEP Model

The PETTLEP model, proposed by Holmes and Collins (2001) optimizes the efficacy of the interventions that could assist with the development of motor imagery scripts (mental verbalizations of the imagery). It includes: *physical* (motor skills, arousal or relaxation techniques), *environment* (for athletes – personalized scripts, videos etc.,), *task* (nature of the skill, performer ability and perspective), *timing* (imagery performed in real time), *learning* (review of imagery to reflect new skills), *emotion* (the necessity of emotion), and *perspective.*

The following example illustrates how one might use this model. In this example, assuming students have managed some river rolls and built up enough skill to try a class three rapid, they might try running Wesser Falls on the Nantahala River. Wienberg and Gould (2003) gave details of what to expect in the PETTLEP elements that we will analyze to illustrate the complex nature of what could be used, and what may need to be omitted, in developing mental imagery for the students. Figure 18 shows a diagram of the rapids at Wesser Falls. A mental imagery exercise follows.

Figure 18. Wesser Falls

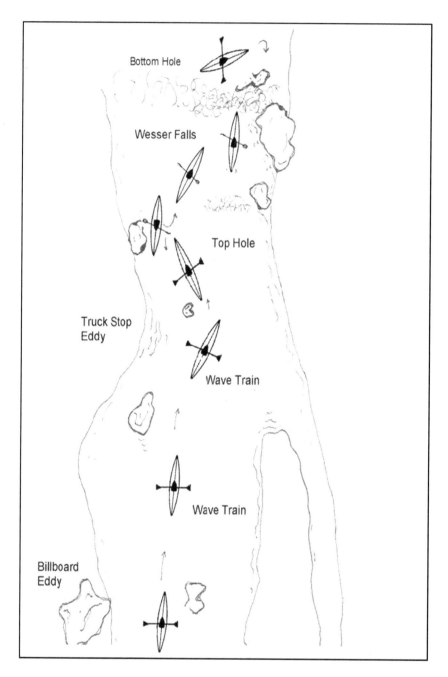

Physical. In this case visualization of specific motor techniques are needed, including a left eddy turn and a quick turn left immediately above the bottom hole. Arousal levels will need to be lowered after looking at the falls using some kind of relaxation imagery. Relaxation is also needed riding the waves down to Truck Stop Eddy on river left above the main drop.

Environment. As an instructor, as opposed to a professional athletic coach, you don't have the physical and psychological backgrounds of the students standing in front of you. You only have your observations based on their verbal and non-verbal communication as you look at the rapid as a group. From these observations, you can develop a script for them to deliver back at the top, out of sight of the rapid.

Task. The imagery will begin in this case by viewing the falls and other boaters running the rapid from an external perspective – looking down on the rapid and seeing how it is run. This brings up a problem in that imagery can produce both positive and negative results. They could see some "carnage" with other boaters flipping and swimming. If that image prevails, then they are more than likely to do the same. As the script is developed – it must focus on the positive by suggesting how to get by the top hole by just mentioning passing it rather than describing its holding abilities. At least these falls don't have names like Jaws, Doo Doo Hole, the Cruncher, Hell Hole or the Bull, all of which increase the arousal levels of anyone doing them for the first time. Even though the imagery right now, looking down on the rapid, is external, the script could be given in first person when at the top and out of sight of the rapid.

Timing. While for athletic competition this is usually very important, some slalom kayakers do speed up the imagery to emphasize the idea of pushing as fast as possible, (White & Hardy, 1998). In this teaching situation, absolute accuracy in the timing isn't so critical except for the eddy turn and the turn below the top hole.

Learning. Running the falls a second time could require a change, say in the timing to head across to Truck Stop eddy. Reviewing the first run could enable changes in the imagery for the second run. Individuals may be different, so a bit of time spent individually with each student may be worthwhile before the second run. After the second run, have the students repeat their script a few times before they try again.

Emotion. Here, initially there would be fear, which would need to be controlled so the students can relax going into the rapid. Afterward, if the run was successful, there would be elation, so for a second run, elation could be added to the imagery.

You have walked back up to the top of the rapid near the raft take-out area. You sit the students in their boats on the bank away from the hubbub of other people as best you can, sit down in front of them, and 'walk' them through the rapid using the relevant elements of mental imagery. For this event, we need visual, tactile and kinesthetic imagery. The script that you give could look like the following:

We are all in a big tight knot, but the rope is relaxing and gradually coming loose, our breathing is becoming relaxed, the knot is undone, and we are loose, relaxed and ready to go.

You are paddling down river left, small waves, relax your grip on the paddle some as you head through the bigger waves and on past Billboard Rock. Keep relaxed, nice big waves ahead but stay left. Look up and left for Truck-stop Eddy and paddle hard across to it. Big sweep stroke on the right, lean left and grab the eddy with a bow rudder. Take a little time to relax.

Turn in the eddy and paddle out of the back of it aiming to the middle of the river, a couple of hard forward strokes to just below the top hole, big reverse sweep on the left, then forward sweep on the right to turn down river. Paddle through the bottom hole and eddy turn on the right.

You could go through this, two or three times, then have the students in the first person rehearse it, 'seeing' Billboard Rock, Truck-stop Eddy and the top hole and 'feel' the relaxed grip, the relaxed run through the waves, the turn into the eddy, the turn below the top hole, pulling hard through the bottom hole and turning into the right eddy at the bottom. Ta da! Voila! or as the Brits say, "Bobs' your uncle!"

This may be more effective than just 'going for it' after a look at the falls, which to quote another British saying – could result in an "epic" with several swimmers. You would of course be running the rapid at the front of the group with an instructor at the back and would re-group in Truck Stop. While waiting in Truck Stop, the students could be rehearsing the last drop.

However, it could conversely be more successful to minimize the whole imagery by just taking a quick look at the falls, then running it with a minimum of fuss, just emphasizing going for Truck Stop eddy. It would depend on the arousal levels of the students – would detailed imagery techniques reduce the arousal or increase it? It could depend on the student, their skill level, and prior experience. More research on imagery and teaching is needed to help in situations like this. There are times when mentally visualizing exactly where you will turn say in a peel out into a fast jet on a river is crucial. Having seen someone omit to do that at the bottom of Tablesaw Rapid on the Ocoee resulted in a vertical pin on the 'landing pad'. This type of visualization is useful also in skiing, pinpointing in your mind's eye where the turn will happen.

Epics or as they are called in America, 'yard sales' where several students end up swimming with gear all over the place, may be a result of several things like poor progression of environment and or skills, but the possibility of student failure is increased by imagery conjured up with names like Decapitation Rock or Hairy Hack Falls. I remember taking British Physical Education teachers, usually a very rowdy lot to the River Ure in Yorkshire and we, as instructors, responded (badly) to their cockiness by building up "Hairy Hack Falls." On the way there it was very, very quiet in the van. At the end of the trip there was more boisterousness than you could believe but I know that we didn't increase their chances of doing well on Hack Falls and did increase the chances of an 'epic' or 'yard sale' at the bottom of the falls. Of course, the same anxiety levels can also be produced by over-the-top skiing, climbing and caving names. Notable examples from my past have been Spiral Stairs (skiing), Cenotaph Corner (climbing), and Hydrophobia Passage (caving), though for the most part, names of climbs are usually more esoteric. One instructor I know refers to Tablesaw rapid as the "Fluffy Bunny" instead to reduce anxiety levels. The thing to remember is that if the climb, ski slope or rapid does have an intimidating name, then don't mention it until afterwards if you want to create positive mental imagery, and, hold off on the stories of prior mishaps wherever you are going. Don't even show videos of hair-raising stuff the night before, lest the students think that may be the type of thing they will be doing in the morning.

The above examples have illustrated imagery type – where you are seeing yourself do the activity along with the feel of the activity. Horn (2008) suggests three categories, *imagery type* (the content), *imagery function,* which is the purpose (skill acquisition, modification or motivation), and *imagery outcome* (improved focus, confidence, strategies, skill, motivation, etc.) Scripts can be designed for all of these functions. Horn states that the most common type that has been measured in research is cognitive specific (the specific skill), but others involve strategies, progress toward goals, mastery and control, arousal and anxiety, healing and injury, and metaphorical imagery. She uses an example of runners imagining running on eggs to promote being light on their feet. Ski instructors use the metaphor of holding a large beach ball to enable the correct arm position while skiing. Staying in the 'box' is sometimes used for the same purpose in kayaking.

The ability to generate mental imagery varies and individual differences show in the actual imagery produced by the same script. Part of this is a result of perception. "People constantly process information from the world around them at the perceptual level, but the information that enters their consciousness is selected by their attention…" (Horn, 2008, p. 309). In other words, people can be more or less accurate in their perceptions and more or less able to focus their attention. However, mental imagery should be thought of as a skill in itself where improvement can be made through practice.

Sometimes mental imagery occurs spontaneously from unconscious memories. The climber that has taken a bad fall in the past may experience a negative mental image when repeating that climb in the future. This would require some powerful positive mental imagery to overcome this. If you are demonstrating a skill poorly as an instructor, then the immediate image received could have a similar effect. If you get "sewing machine" leg on a rock climb while demonstrating to students this would almost certainly produce the same outcome from the students.

Although mental imagery is used a lot by athletes and coaches in competitive events, it is used less in outdoor instruction. Outdoor instructors can use many of the elements described above. Perhaps three really important areas to assist our students would be to use it to control arousal levels, focus attention, and assist with complex motor skills.

Summary

Communication encompasses many things including: climate, clarity, timing, noise, role modeling, non-verbal cues, active listening, truisms, and mental imagery. An understanding of all these can help the instructor communicate effectively. This assumes that the student is ready to take in the information. Each student is affected by their readiness to take in information at that particular time and place which is affected by their arousal level. The next chapter reveals how to affect optimum arousal levels in learning.

References

Argyle, M., Salter, A., Nicholson, H., Williams, M., & Burgess, P. (1970). The communication of inferior and superior attitudes by verbal and non-verbal signals. *British Journal of Social and Clinical Psychology*. 9, 222-231.

Berne, E. (1964). *Games people play*. New York: Ballantine Books.

Blanchard, Ken. 1985. *Leadership and the one-minute manager*. New York NY: Harper Collins. p. 38.

Cockrell, D. (1991). *The wilderness educator: The Wilderness Education Association curriculum guide*. Merrillville, Indiana; ICS Books, Inc.

Cook, M. (1997). *Perceiving others: The psychology of interpersonal perception*. NewYork NY: Metheun & Co Ltd.

Darwin, C. (1998). *The expression of the emotions in man and animals*. London: Harper Collins. (Original publication 1872).

Drury, J., Bonney, B. F., Berman, D., & Wagstaff, M. C. (2005). *The backcountry classroom*. 2nd Ed. Helena, Montana: Falconguide.

Ekman, P., & Friesen, W. V. (2003). *Unmasking the Face: A guide to recognizing emotions from facial clues*. Cambridge, MA: Malor Books.

Gibb, J. R. (1961). Defensive communication. *Journal of Communication*. 11(3), September.

Griffin, E. (2009). *A first look at communication theory* (7th Ed). Guilford, Connecticut: McGraw Hill.

Haggard, E. A., & Isaacs, K. S. (1966). Micro-momentary facial expressions as indicators of ego mechanisms in psychotherapy. In L. A. Gottschalk & A. H. Auerbacki (Eds.), *Methods of Research in Psychotherapy* (pp. 154-165). NewYork: Appleton-Century-Crofts.

Hall, E. T. (1966). *The hidden dimension.* Garden City, NY: Doubleday

Hinshaw, K. E. (1991). The effects of mental practice on motor skill performance: Critical evaluation and meta-analysis. *Imagination, Cognition and Personality.*11, 3-35.

Holmes, P. S., & Collins, D. (2001). The PETTLEP approach to motor imagery: A function and equivalence model for sport psychologists. *Journal of Applied Sport Psychology.* 13, 60-83.

Horn, T. S. (2008). *Advances in sport psychology* (3rd Ed,). Champaign, Illinois: Human Kinetics.

Horn, T., Morris. T., Spittle, M., & Watt, A., P. (2005). *Imagery in Sport.* Champaign, Ill: Human Kinetics.

Jackson, J. A. (1973). *A few thoughts on party leadership.* Unpublished manuscript. PlasY Brenin, N. Wales: N. M. C.

Johnson, D. W. (1981). *Reaching Out: Interpersonal effectiveness and self-actualization.* Englewood Cliffs, NJ: Prentice Hall.

Knapp, M. L., & Hall, J. (2007). *Nonverbal communication in human interaction* (5thEd.). Boston, MA: Wadsworth.

Melamed, J., & Bozionelos, N. (1992). Managerial promotion and height. *Psychological Reports.* 71, 587-593.

Neill, L. (1997). Gender: How does it affect the outdoor education experience? In *Catalysts for Change: Proceedings of the 10th National Outdoor Education Conference* (pp. 183-102). Sydney, Australia: The Outdoor Professionals.

Orlick, T. (2007). *In pursuit of excellence: How to win in sport and life through mental training* (3rd Ed.). Champaign, IL: Human Kinetics.

Petzoldt, P. K. (1995). *Teton tales and other Petzoldt anecdotes.* Merrilville, IN: ICS Books, Inc.

Phelps, F., Doherty-Sneddon, G., & Warnock, H. (2006). Functional benefits of children's gaze aversion during questioning. *British Journal Developmental Psychology.* 24, 577-588.

Phipps, M. L., & Stone, D. (1976). *Canoeing In Australia.* Lilydale, Australia: Pioneer Design Studio Ltd.

Suin, R. M. (1976). Visual Motor Learning Behavior for adaptive behavior. In J. Krumboltz & C. Thorenson (Eds.). *Counseling Methods* (pp. 360-366). New York: Holt, Rinehart & Winston.

Thorenson, P. (1972). Defense mechanisms in groups. In J. W. Pfeiffer & J. E. Jones (Eds.), *The Annual Handbook for Group Facilitators.* La Jolla, CA: University Associates.

White, A., & Hardy, L. (1998). An in-depth analysis of imagery by high-level slalom canoeists and artistic gymnastics. *The Sport Psychologist.* 12, 387-403.

Whiting, H. T. A. (1975). Lecture notes from *Psychology and Physical Education*, University of Leeds, UK.

Vealey, R. S., & Greenleaf, C. A. (2010). Seeing is believing: Understanding and using imagery in sport. In J. M. Williams (Ed.), *Applied Sport Psychology* (pp. 267-299). New York, NY: McGraw-Hill.

Wienberg R., & Gould D. (2003). *Foundations of sport and exercise psychology* (3rd Ed.). IL: Human Kinetics.

Chapter 4

Arousal

Arousal, the degree to which the cortex of the brain is activated, is of particular interest to the outdoor instructor. It can be thought of as a continuum from sleep to extreme excitement. An over-aroused student could be extremely excited or 'freaked out', while an under aroused student might be falling asleep in class. Arousal level affects performance. The optimum level is somewhere between high and low, but differs depending on the task, and the individual, and personality affects arousal as well (Whiting, 1976).

Imagine beginning a rappelling lesson after the students have hiked up a steep trail to the top of the cliff where the rappel rope is set. The students have seen the drop-off and are assembled at the top, ready to clip in and rappel over the edge. Step into the shoes of each participant – some may have done this before with a scout group and may feel a little anxious, some may be sensation seekers raring to go, and some may be quaking, thinking there will be a good chance that they may fall to the bottom. For perhaps two of these different kinds of students, any detailed instruction may well go unheard, which not only creates a safety problem but can also affect the learning of rappelling as a skill. If the students are scared, fear leads to high arousal, sometimes beyond reasonable limits, making teaching impossible as the individual reverts to instinctual behavior such as freezing (becoming immobilized), flight (wanting to leave) or fight (becoming combative). A suggestion has been to add "fright" to fight, flight, and freeze (Bracha et al., 2004). Petzoldt told stories of times when guiding clients off the big rappel on the Grand Teton, that occasionally when the weather was really bad, a client would be so immobilized at the sight of the rope blowing back up to the top when it was thrown off – that they just about forgot their own name. Changes in arousal levels affect us both psychologically and physiologically. Psychologically, fear can produce a panic attack, while overcoming fear can produce a natural high. Physiological changes include increases in sensitivity of sense organs, changes in tonus of skeletal muscles, vegetative changes (body processes that maintain life), heart rate, respiration, and brain wave patterns.

It is easy to see then that if students are over aroused, as in the above rappelling example, the teaching will probably be ineffective. An unfortunate outcome of such an experience could be that they may be put off rappelling and rock climbing for good. This, in Dewey's (1963) terms, is miseducation; something that outdoor instructors should always try to avoid. The instructor can effectively teach, and positively affect learning when optimum arousal in the students is achieved. The Yerkes-Dodson law predicts an inverted U-shaped function between arousal and performance (Yerkes & Dodson, 1908). This means that the optimum amount of arousal, or the optimum point for learning, is mid-way between being over or under aroused. This has been supported by correlation studies over the years (Anderson, 2000).

So, looking back at the rappelling class, some judgments must be made on the past experience of students and the kind of students you have. For a first rappel, a 'ground school' where knots and harnesses and climbing calls can be introduced in camp or somewhere away from the cliff. A short and easy angled rappel can follow, where the rope, rappel devise and safety rope are introduced. When the students are comfortable with all the new skills, they are set to do a more challenging rappel. Remember that if you are an accomplished climber, what you personally feel to be challenging may be too much for your students, and as we don't want to be miseducative, then it may be that you have to ratchet the challenge level down considerably, especially for beginners.

If you are teaching a more mundane class where you are all sitting in a circle discussing a topic, there is less likelihood of over arousal – more likely the opposite especially if it is after a big lunch or late in the day. Anyone sleeping is the biggest "tip off", but yawns chit-chatting and restless behavior are also signals that the students may be under aroused. However, novel (new) information can lead to higher arousal, applied interestingly by way of metaphor, myth, or by relating personal or vicarious experiences with which the students can identify. Petzoldt had an uncanny ability in doing this and he developed many 'Petzoldtisms' or truisms that other instructors could use who didn't have the past experiences that he had. The communication chapter includes a list of Petzoldt's sayings along with explanations.

One example of a Petzoldtism is 'words mean nothing'. If an instructor started to drone on about the breaking strengths of the ropes, carabiners, etc., and the students were itching to climb, it was obvious that those superfluous words "meant nothing" as the students were thinking about getting on the climb. That little truism can help instructors temper explanations to a reasonable amount. "Words mean nothing" and other Petzoldtism's can be related more to communication however and so are explained more fully in the communication chapter. Another piece of advice that Paul stressed was to teach only what students needed to know. Consider a map and compass session. This could be very involved and complex but is best broken into smaller lessons using the scaffolding techniques discussed earlier.

Estimate just how much the students need to know, say, to get to the next campsite. Orient the map with the compass, and then put the compass away. Introduce the map features that they will encounter (not a lecture on every feature on every map they may possibly find in the future). Perhaps draw contour lines on someone's fist to help with topographical features – it is good 3-D imagery and can be used later on the trail – a handy visual aid, so to speak! Teach specifically to the trip they will be doing that day, distance, elevation ups and downs, and forks in the trail (the only other time at this stage of the game that they will need the compass is to check that any turn off is going in the correct direction). This is all they need for an introductory lesson – no handrails, no shooting bearings, no grid and magnetic bearings, no 'dog-legs', no triangulations etc. Just teach what they need for the first hike in about twenty minutes but then on the hike, reinforce the points that you have taught. Giving a two-hour map and compass session will result in the students being bored and frustrated with too many new concepts too soon, what technically is too much 'novel' or new information. This principle applies to other activities such as knots just before climbing or cooking just before they cook a meal.

Sometimes a complex technique is best left initially with no explanation. I remember Petzoldt in 1983 telling me to teach his Sliding Middleman Ice axe and rope technique. He said, "Just demonstrate it, don't try and explain it." After placing the three climbers on the slope, I just gave minimal directions like walk forward, then took the front person's axe and just placed it in the correct position, then did the same for the other two people in the climbing team. After two or three goes through the system, the team had it. Everyone else just watched the demonstration, and then had a go with some coaching to correct mistakes. If I had tried to explain it fully before they all started, everyone would have been totally lost. In fact, I did try and explain it on a plane to a co-instructor who still laughs at the attempt. We have persevered however, so the Sliding Middleman technique is not lost and described it in *Paul Petzoldt's Sliding Middleman Snow Technique* (Phipps & Murdock, 2014). If you are in an armchair, you can read it and look at the pictures, view the video and you will have plenty of time and a chance to puzzle it out – maybe, or maybe you may need a demonstration. If you have a group standing on the snow, just have someone demonstrate it!

Frustration can affect arousal levels to such an extent that the activity is best left alone for a time. An example of this is when the student experiences what is called a psychological set and needs to re-program his or her thinking. Teaching kayak rolling often exemplifies this, as someone can be so desperate to learn that there is over-anxiety and the student tries too hard. This can result in a mistake, like pulling down on the paddle instead of sweeping it across the surface for a sweep roll, and this faulty technique starts to get 'grooved in'. Often a break lowers the arousal level and enables more normal learning. This may mean a small break for ten minutes watching others or just paddling around the pool or lake or it may mean giving it up for another day.

Sometimes a new approach is needed to break the set. Analogies and 'gymnastic thinking' on the teacher's part can get the student to think differently - not just re-stating the instructions (remember, just repeating "Bend your knees" and "Lean forward" isn't very effective for skiing either), but by trying to paint a mental picture. To get the student to sweep in the sweep roll when upside down, prior explanation may have been to "Pretend you are the billboard "paster" and you are reaching up and sweeping the top right corner of the billboard – not the bottom right corner." This may psychologically enable the student to adjust the sweeping action. Perhaps physically guiding the paddle using kinesthetic learning where the student can feel the movement can overcome the set. Usually this would be done several times to enable some 'muscle memory'.

To revisit the skiing problem of not leaning forward, the instructor could do the same kind of guidance by the instructor pulling the ski pole so that the skier is pulled into a position that actually is leaning forward enough or asking the student to push their shins forward against the boot – rather than just re-stating "Lean forward". Physical guidance allows the learner to feel what the movement should feel like which is called proprioceptive feedback. Analyzing the problem and using creative teaching can overcome most negative sets. Video is also really effective as it allows the faulty technique to be seen by the performer and this seems to have more persuasion than any amount of verbal instructions.

Using different methods of teaching provides novelty in the process. Variety is stimulating for students and keys into the different learning styles – question and answer, problem solving, conceptual, experiential, individual, and cooperative approaches could be used at different times. Combining approaches can be successful, having small groups solve a problem such as planning for an expedition or doing a Tyrolean Traverse is far more effective than a presentation or demonstration alone. The more active the students are in the learning process, the more likely they are to understand and remember. Another Petzoldtism illustrates this point, "We are not training people for Jeopardy." The point here is that rote memorization is discouraged, (though there has to be some to learn new terms). Petzoldt, in *The New Wilderness Handbook* (1984), suggested seven different teaching methods: Memorization, Demonstration, The Organized Class, Trail Teaching, Grasshopper Teaching, Opportunity Teaching, and Quality Judgment.

His least favored style was memorization, where the instructor just presents information. This method could be the most boring but of course can be enhanced as mentioned above with stories and metaphor. Students do have to learn the names of new things like knots, techniques like 'peel-outs' or concepts like 'active-listening' so there has to be some memorization. Demonstration is common as many outdoor skills are physical – from lighting a fire to performing a canoe stroke or the sliding middleman ice axe and snow technique. Some outdoor concepts such as environmental ethics require discussion, so you may be sitting in a circle in an organized class. Doing a lot of "circular discussions" can become, well – circular, where you may end up going "round and round" if there isn't good facilitation. Limit too much sitting and 'jawboning' by using what Petzoldt called the 'grasshopper' method. This method looks like opportunity teaching – where an incident like having to treat a blister is turned into a lesson on exactly how to do it, prevent it, and manage it. Grasshopper teaching is where the group alights on what may look like random new skills needed in succession. In actuality – it is well-planned instruction where the instructor has chosen a place to enable the need for several new skills to unfold. Teton Canyon has two campsites that illustrate this well. On my initial course with the Wilderness Education Association (WEA), we started in one where there was a spring fed stream and repairable fire pits were necessary, then after two nights and two days of basic camping instruction, a move to the new campsite that provided new techniques. This campsite had established fire rings, so an alternate fire practice could be used. The new water source was a large river, which had to be crossed the following day, requiring river crossing skills and Tyrolean Traverse skills.

So, it seemed that the instruction followed a pattern of opportunity teaching – but in fact it was well-planned grasshopper teaching. This kept the arousal levels more optimal than had we just sat and discussed each topic. Some discussion ensued after each new activity so the "whys" were addressed, which brings us to Paul's favored style – the quality judgment method. Developing judgment was what Petzoldt was best known for and he gave an example in *The New Wilderness Handbook* (1984) on lighting a fire to show how more effective learning is when a student understands why for example twigs need to be very small to light, rather than just having students memorize "Do this first, and then this etc." He described instances where, after a fire lighting demonstration class that hadn't addressed the judgment factors, some days later – students were trying to light a fire with large sticks and came to the conclusion that just memorizing information without understanding the "whys" was pretty ineffective.

Making sure that there is de-briefing time after activities whether it is during, or immediately following an activity or is at the end of the day or even the start of the next day is very important to discuss the judgment factors. The specific activity will determine the best time to do this – remember the sliding middleman snow technique, where the detailed explanation is best left until afterward the activity. Also remember that the students will be doing most of the skills that you are teaching them on their own after the training course that they are taking so they really do need the judgment factors.

Paul's remaining teaching method is trail teaching. His main point with this was in regard to planning. If you are backpacking or mountaineering and you plan long days on the trail, then there is no time for teaching while on the trail. Granted there are some 'grunt' days necessary on an expedition course, perhaps the summit day, or a re-supply day, but if the course is an 'education' course, then there should be time to teach about plants, animals, topography, map reading, compass, GPS skills, trail techniques like rests, rest steps, rhythmic breathing, and a host of other things. If the students' noses are 'to the grindstone' and they are 'head down' on the trail all day, it is an experience but has limited educational value. So, two miles may be more than enough. With a large group, a ten-mile day can take ten hours – so when will you teach if you plan long trail days? It can be seen that a major focus of Petzoldt's teaching methods was to enable effectiveness in the teaching and learning by using a variety that would affect arousal levels positively.

Do be careful, however in reverting back to just naming trees, bugs, flowers, etc., which can be very boring for young students and teenagers. The conceptual approach is helpful to avoid this and useful in the classroom and outdoors. It starts with specifics and deals with a concept. The important thing is to be at the students' level of understanding. Aid in conceptualizing can also be provided by advanced reading or experience. Relating to concepts that the students know something about helps to keep their interest levels up. Lewis in his article "Nature City" (1975) used this approach, comparing communities in the outdoors using analogies relating to the experiences of his inner-city students. He effectively stimulated their arousal levels by relating to what they knew, for example:

Did Nature City have garbage men? If so, who were they and where would we find them? This was quite a question. I suggested we begin finding out by examining the layer of leaves on the ground, removing leaves one by one. Soon we discovered some leaves with holes in them. How did they get there? "Bugs ate them." "And worms!" We continued removing leaves and began to find insects. "Man, look at that bug!" "Kill it quick!" I stopped the execution. Wait a minute – why should we kill it? Was it hurting us? What was it doing? There was a thoughtful pause. "I guess he is eating the leaves and stuff on the ground." So, who was he in Nature City? "The garbage man" came the chorused reply. From that point on, everyone's eyes were focused on the miniature world found on the forest floor, where we discovered a whole host of nature's garbage men working on leaves, twigs and rotting logs. (p. 19)

Clearly, Lewis also used the correct channel of communication for his students, keeping their arousal levels more optimal. Putting information into context, in this case the environment, makes it more relevant;

just naming bugs, plants, and trees can have a negative effect on arousal levels. Optimum arousal, then, assists motivation in the learning process.

References

Anderson, J. R. (2000). *Cognitive psychology and its implications* (5th ed.). New York, NY: Worth Publishing.

Bracha, H., Ralston, T. C., Matsukawa, J. M., Matsunaga, S., Williams, A. E., & Bracha, A. S. (2004). Does "fight or flight" need updating? *Psychosomatics, 45,* 448-449.

Dewey, J. (1963). *Experience and education.* New York, NY: Collier Books.

Lewis, C. A. (1975). Nature city: Translating the natural environment process into urban language. *Morton Arboretum Quartely, 11*(2), 17-22.

Petzoldt, P. (1984). *The new wilderness handbook,* New York, NY: Norton.

Phipps, M. L., & Murdock, T. (2014). Paul Petzoldt's sliding middleman snow technique. *Journal of Outdoor Recreation Education and Leadership, 6*(1), 68-76. http://dx.doi.org/10.7768/1948-5123.1205

Whiting, H. T. A. (1976). *Lecture notes: Psychology and physical education.* Leeds, England: University of Leeds.

Yerkes, R. M., & Dodson, J. D. (1908). The relationship of strength of stimulus to rapidity of habit formation. *Journal of Comparative Neurology and Psychology. 18*(5). 459-482.

Chapter 5

Motivation

"Don't give your students sunburned tonsils."

- Paul Petzoldt

Motivation is an important factor in learning; no progress is made unless there is incentive. It provides a driving force for our behavior by selecting a course of action from alternatives, determining the amount of vigor that we apply, and influencing persistence and determination. Motivation in people depends on the strength of their motives. Motives are sometimes defined as needs, wants, drives, or impulses within an individual. Motives are directed toward goals, which may be conscious or subconscious (or in Jung's terms, unconscious).

Maslow's Motivations

Maslow (1943, 1970) suggested a hierarchy of needs (shown in Figure 19) that influence motivations.

Figure 19. Maslow's Hierarchy of Needs to Self-Actualization

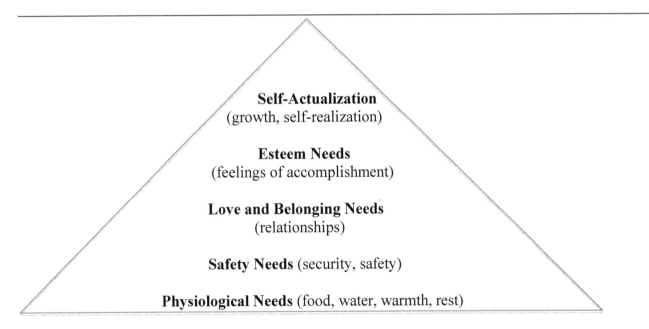

Education is usually associated with growth needs (the top of the triangle). In order for self-actualization/ self-realization and learning to occur, the needs at the bottom of the triangle (physiological, safety, love and belonging, and esteem) have to be met first. This is of particular importance in the outdoors. Safety and physiological needs on an adventure course have to be met. The students have to be suitably clothed and fed and feel comparatively safe. Shelter is a psychological as well as a physiological need; knowing that you can get back to a warm climbing hut, or mountain center may positively affect motivation to persevere on bad weather days more than just a tent or tarp. The tent itself can have an effect – are you wading through deep snow to get back to a nice, big, four season dome, or are you "squished" into a small, three-season shelter that may collapse under heavy snow? It is easy to see here how good equipment can affect motivation.

The number of tent mates also makes a difference. I remember a time when one of the women in the group who was tenting on her own because of university rules about co-ed sharing, irreparably broke a pole on a hoop tent and had to move in with three guys in a big dome. The experience became far more enjoyable for her with the added social interaction for the rest of the trip. Co-ed sharing is however a sensitive issue and I have witnessed the opposite effect on motivation because of an over-eager male wanting to share a tent with a particular female who absolutely did not want this. This was on a course where it was acceptable for co-ed tenting on adult courses. For motivation reasons, on five-week long WEA wilderness courses, everyone changed tent partners each week so no-one 'got stuck' with a particular person that they may not be able to get on with for the whole course. For the above incident, we allowed the two women on the course to stay together for the second leg of the trip and the guy in question decided he wanted to leave because he was heart-broken! Interpersonal relations are important and building relationships on a course is extremely important – but "special "relationships are very damaging. Establishing a group norm of 'no special relationships' can prevent awkward issues like others in the group being apprehensive about talking to the 'partners' for fear of jealousy, the partners getting into spats, and the partners showing too much love and affection. It is far better to deal with this issue at the beginning of a course or trip during group norms/expedition behavior setting rather than let it emerge as an issue to deal with, as it can be a very difficult issue to resolve.

Married couples bring their own relationship problems with them so beware of that when signing them up on a course. 'Special relationships', especially when they are brand new are very powerful and can override good judgment that affects everyone in the group. The relationship aspects of group dynamics can make or break a course and if the relationships go downhill, then the task quickly follows so making time to do appropriate relationship building and following up with group maintenance is critical to keep motivation high. This also requires knowledge of group dynamics and how to use appropriate leadership styles for each and every different situation. Information on leadership and group dynamics including the setting of group norms can be found in later chapters. Remember motivation is a key factor for doing Human Factors Research at NASA. They understand that in aerospace situations where there is often a time constraint to resolve a safety issue, problems can be resolved if everyone on the team can give unhindered input. Outdoor pursuits – especially mountaineering are analogous to this.

Caring for the group dynamics, however not only increases safety, it increases the enjoyment of the trip or course – yet it is sometimes totally ignored. An extreme example of where a leader affected good group morale was Shackleton's epic journey in the Antarctic where the group survived months on the ice, an unbelievable sea crossing to South Georgia and a difficult mountain range crossing without losing a participant. Huntford (1985) in his account of the 1911- 1912 race for the poles in *The Last Place on Earth*, compared Shackleton to Scott, the expedition leader racing Admunsen to the pole. Some years earlier, when Shackleton was subordinate to Scott, they had difficulties on board the Discovery on that earlier expedition as Scott needed the rigid naval hierarchy and seemed incapable of sensing the psychological undercurrents, which rule human behavior. Shackelton had the talent to get and maintain respect from his group, creating an atmosphere conducive to team building and maintaining his leadership without undue use of coercive power. Huntford (1985) referred to this type of leader as the psychological leader. Shackleton pulled through tremendous adversity while still taking care of all his men on his epic journey, but Scott was beaten to the Pole by Admunsen and died with some of his men while trying to return to his base. These are extreme examples, but the message is the same for us all and outdoor instructors should strive to be the psychological leader, recognizing the 'undercurrents' of group dynamics.

Another motivator to remember is shelter during outdoor teaching sessions. If it is a 'sitting' session, sites that provide shelter from the elements should be chosen. If it is a cold morning, some physical exercise may be necessary before teaching. If it is cold, then perhaps a 9 a.m. start to a class would be more effective than an 8 a.m. start. Teaching may be more productive in the morning when arousal levels are higher than in the afternoon when travel or a siesta may be more appropriate. Of course, this has to be balanced out with traveling at appropriate times for the environment as travelling on afternoon snow wouldn't make sense or travelling in the heat of the day in a desert or other hot climate would be unsafe.

The next level of need is the need for esteem. How can we affect this? Think of the way that you give feedback to your follower(s) – how you say something is as important as what you say. Are you being positive or negative in your leadership style? Sometimes you have to be autocratic, but this doesn't mean using demeaning behavior. How often do you give out praise? Is the only time you address the group to criticize? That can be referred to as the 'seagull' style of leadership where followers only know the leader is there when unwelcome criticisms (deposits) land on them - which is very de-motivating. Followers can take a lot of praise so be liberal with it so long as it is genuine. Meet one-on one with individuals in the group to discuss their issues. This can be done as part of individual conferencing, where the instructor meets with individuals frequently to discuss an educational topic, for example, decision making using a daily journal (Grube, Phipps, & Grube, 2002; Phipps, 2009). This can be used for personal discussion time with the student as well which shows that you care and if sensitive feedback with appropriate praise is also given, you are addressing esteem issues as well (see chapter 1).

Using soft and hard skills to assist Maslow's motivators. Interpersonal leadership skills have been called the "soft" skills (Phipps & Swiderski 1991; Priest & Gass, 1997; Swiderski, 1987). Research by Clarke and Phipps (2010) investigated the soft and hard skills of teaching concerning perceived importance and performance of these two skill sets.

The "Soft Teaching Skills", or interpersonal skills of instruction, were described as:
- Sensitivity toward students
- Sensitivity toward differences
- Attentive listening
- Dealing with group problems
- Being supportive of students
- Being respectful and polite

The "Hard Teaching Skills" or technical skills, were described as:
- Skilled and demonstrating skills well
- Logistics
- Gauging the correct level of challenge
- Explaining skills well
- Using a variety of teaching strategies
- Diagnosing and assisting different skill levels

The importance-performance research revealed that student perceptions for both skill sets in the study were good and the needs of students were being met overall, but it also pinpointed a particular class where the students were very de-motivated by the lack of soft skills of an instructor. This research also showed that female instructors scored slightly higher than the male instructors. One might expect female instructors to be more in tune with the interpersonal skills. More instructor effectiveness was shown in the Phipps and Claxton (1997) study at the Nantahala Outdoor Center for female instructors, where the perceived overall effectiveness was higher than that of the male instructors. Perhaps this was due to the female instructors' comfort levels with the interpersonal skills. Little research has been done to establish the differences between male and female instructors, needless to say though, the soft skills are a very important component of teaching and it may be that males have something to learn in that regard. Some insights are given later in the "Male and Female Vive La Difference" chapter. It seems that the soft skills are harder to learn than the technical skills, which means more effort is needed to gain these skills rather than abandon them.

The use of the terms hard and soft skills in the outdoor education has provoked some controversy, more I believe due to misunderstanding than reality. The terms are also being used now as a matter of course in business and in higher education. In outdoor education, the terms started to be used many years ago as a way of distinguishing two very different skill sets. This was about the time when personal computers were first becoming popular – around the time of the introduction of the Macintosh. This was when terms like software and hardware were being used more often. Swiderski (1987) first defined the soft skills. This author, having completed some research on the teaching of soft skills teamed up with Swiderski to write the chapter, "The Soft Skills of Outdoor Leadership" in the book *Adventure Education* (Miles & Priest, 1990). Never in our deliberations did we connect hard and soft to male and female characteristics as our view was analogous to the computer, the hardware being technical and the software being more process oriented. However, the gender controversy still persists. Warren (2009) refers to Van Nostrand's (1993) ideas about language that marginalizes or invalidates women's experiences. Jordan (1996) takes issue with the terms hard and soft skills and Warren uses this as an example of marginalization and invalidation of women. The initial articles were written by men and then further modified by men (Priest & Gass, 1997) who discuss hard, soft and *meta* skills. They define meta skills as combining hard and soft skills into a workable design and include "... leadership style, problem-solving and decision-making skills, experience based judgment, effective communication, and ethical behavior" (Priest & Gass, 1997, p 76). What are male theory builders projecting in their terminology? Are there unconscious projections? Is the use of these terms derogatory? Do they produce a language bias? Is the bias positive or negative? The soft and hard skills terms are terms that a great many people have latched onto to summarize very different skill sets that are very important for outdoor instructors to recognize. Employers also recognize them in hiring practices so a recognition of the differences that enables instructors and prospective instructors to improve whichever skill set has a deficiency can be a good thing. Perhaps emphasizing that the terminology came from computer terminology can help re-frame what the meaning of hard and soft skills is really all about and that may reduce any de-motivating aspects of the use of language in this case.

Maslow's triangle of needs suggests a hierarchy where each of the different needs - physiological, safety, love and belonging, and esteem have to be met in order for psychological growth and learning, or in his terms – self-actualization to happen. The major premise of Maslow's position on personality and motivation is that personality develops as a result of an active effort to realize or actualize inherent potentialities. When this theory is applied to education, it can be said that people are motivated to learn in order to meet their potential, thereby fulfilling their needs (Bunting, 1980). This reminds us of the importance of the individual in education; we have individual learning styles, potential, and motivation. So, we need to integrate into our program, mechanisms, that will enable this individuation to take place. Individuation is a term used by the Swiss Psychologist, Carl Jung when referring to personal growth (Mattoon, 1981).

Jung and Motivation

The very motivation to venture into the outdoors pertains to both the student and the instructor. William Siri, in his introduction to Hornbein's *Everest the West Ridge* (1981), refers to "The Primitive, often brutal struggle to reach its top is an irresistible challenge to our built-in need for adventure" (p. 16). We are not all climbing Everest, but we are motivated by the same underlying challenges. Does the combination of fear, sense of awe and satisfaction for being in challenging outdoor situations emanate from one's inner self? Jung's Analytical Psychology would explain that these feelings could rise from the deepest layer of the unconscious, the *collective* unconscious. Jung divided the psyche into the conscious and unconscious. The ego is the center of consciousness and the personal unconscious stores psychic material of our personal past. Deeper in our unconscious is the reservoir of collective images not dependent on personal experience. Because of its non-personal bias, Jung characterized the collective unconscious as the 'objective psyche' (Mattoon, 1983). He also suggested that the contents of the collective unconscious are evolutionary:

> In view of the structure of the body it would be astonishing if the psyche were the only biological phenomenon not to show real traces of its evolutionary history, and it is altogether probable that these marks are closely connected with the instinctual base. Instinct and the archaic mode meet in the biological conception of the 'pattern of behavior. (Mattoon,1983, p. 71)

The collective unconscious is a reservoir of latent images, usually called primordial images (Hall & Nordby, 1973). The contents of this reservoir are instincts and archetypes. Jung et al. (1964) distinguished between instincts and archetypes:

> What we properly call instincts are physiological urges, and are perceived by the senses, but at the same time, they also manifest themselves in fantasies and often reveal their presence only by symbolic images. These manifestations are what I call the archetypes. (p. 58)

> Jung is quoted in *The Masks of God: A Primitive Mythology* by Joseph Campbell (1959).

> An archetype "...is a memory deposit, an engram derived from a condensation of innumerable similar experiences.... the psychic expression of an anatomically physiologically determined natural tendency". (p. 31)

Jung's archetypes then are patterns of thought that lie in what he calls the *Collective Unconscious* and are shared by all of us, as compared to the personal unconscious that contains information experienced by the individual. So, what patterns do we all need to be concerned with? For outdoor enthusiasts, this author suggested four that particularly stimulate the instinctual and archetypal layer of the psyche – *the hero, the child, the journey,* and *the spirit* (Phipps, 1985). Archetypes "… give a predisposition to an image" or a way of thinking (McCully, 1971, p.53), and "Archetypal images have served as building blocks for consciousness" (Mattoon 1983, p. 301). If they affect our thinking so strongly, we should look at them in detail as they powerfully motivate us – even though we may not realize it.

The Hero

The hero archetype helps in developing the ego, providing the strength to cope with life's tasks. We all identify with heroes and the participation in adventure gives us this chance to feel like one. A teenager returning from an Outward Bound course may feel this. The recognition gained by one's peers, parents or teachers is their projection of the hero archetype. It is important to realize that this 'hero worship' is a projection and if one feeds off this, it can either strengthen the ego or it can lead to an inflated ego, and eventually, a hero complex. To some degree, accepting the projection may be deserved if the individual feels that he or she has achieved something the general population has not.

Inflation is less likely if there is an awareness of the hero archetype and hero projections. However, if the archetype becomes inflated and the individual starts to believe he or she is the hero, then connectedness is lost, and they are 'in the clouds', so to speak, awaiting the inevitable 'fall' or deflation when the true realization comes. The true hero then remains grounded, accepting appraisal but does not inflate his or her ego. In many ways adventure pursuits offer a chance to become, in a small way for many of us, a hero – which gives extra strength and confidence. Over confidence, however, breeds not only contempt from others but because it is unconscious, the individual is unaware that they are in the grip of an archetype. It is also a recipe for disaster and the common belief 'it will never happen to me,' until the metaphoric fall of the hero archetype coincides with the literal fall of the over confident climber.

The effects of the hero archetype are visible in Western Civilization through our adulation of modern heroes in sport, athletics, and pop cultures as well as outdoor pursuits, like climbing Mount Everest. Even our lifestyles, especially for men, are often geared towards this reach for the top, be it in sport, cultural activities, or business corporations. We can't all be at the top and even if we get there, we have to come down again. This is often a painful process so perhaps we should utilize the child in us to transform the way we view our recreation and lifestyles – to counteract the powerful hero archetype.

The Child

This refers to the child in us who enjoys the intrinsic values of play for the intrinsic values rather than the extrinsic rewards such as projections, psychological strokes or even material rewards. If an activity is done for enjoyment or excitement this is an internal reward. If it is done to impress other people, it is external in that the reward comes from their projections on you as a "winner".

The seriousness of an expedition can be broken down by playing in a swimming hole or by sliding down a snow slope. As a balance to the hero archetype, the intrinsic play of the child archetype is an important factor. However, childishness, if inappropriate, can also be negative. Von Franz (1981) related to this in her description of the *puer aeternus* or eternal boy. She describes people, mostly men who have not succeeded in maturing:

There is a terrific fear of being pinned down, of entering space and time completely, and of being the specific human being that one is. There is always the fear of being caught in a situation from which it is impossible to slip out again. Every just so situation is hell. At the same time, there is something highly symbolic – namely, a fascination for dangerous sports, particularly flying and mountaineering – so as to get as high as possible, the symbolism of which is to get away from the mother; i.e., from the earth, from ordinary life. (p. 2)

We can use the child within us to play more for play's sake and for pure enjoyment. Conversely, moderation might be needed as in the case of the *puer aeternus* and in everyone's ability to contend with 'ordinary life'.

The Journey

Our ordinary or not so ordinary path through life can be regarded as a journey. This strong archetype influences us, from the aboriginal 'walk about' to a major Himalayan expedition. Many adventure activities involve a journey and, as in life, it seems less satisfying to retrace the steps of the journey. To do either a traverse of a mountain or a through trip in a cave is far more inviting than to do a trip and reverse it. Caving trips hold a special fascination as caving is a journey into the underworld, the dark and the unknown, all adjectives that are sometimes used to describe the depths of the psyche, the unconscious. The primeval images and the daemonic world of the darkness beneath the surface is the world of myths, fairy tales and classical mythology but the darkness beneath is also the world of the speleologist. In dreams, a cave can be the symbol of the unconscious.

Caving does satisfy the curiosity to go beyond the visible horizon. It is a real journey into the unknown, where one is an explorer, a true adventurer, not knowing what is around the next bend, or what is at the bottom of the vertical drop until one gets there. The motivation to go into a cave seems to change with age, it is hard to hold back many youngsters from wanting to explore a cave but for adults it is often hard to get them anywhere near it unless of course they are already avid cavers. Many people question the sanity of cavers struggling through systems deep underground for pleasure. Their satisfaction could be partly the challenge but significantly, perhaps, it is an unconscious motive too.

The journey archetype represents our journey through life and actual journeys like expeditions are powerful in this regard. Inclusions of memorable events such as summiting a mountain, doing a rappel, completing a through trip through a difficult cave adds power if the participant experiences a peak experience in Maslow's terms. As instructors, we can plan in such experiences and support students through what often is a tough experience that enables the individuation or growth to occur.

A key motivator in our outdoor journeys and experiences is when an experience is that powerful that you may feel that you are losing yourself in the intensity of the activity. Csikszentmihalyi calls this 'flow' and is quoted by Allen (1980) in *High Adventure Outdoor Pursuits*.

Flow is described as a condition in which one concentrates on the task at hand to the exclusion of other internal or external stimuli. Action and awareness merge so that one simply does what is to be done without a critical dualistic perspective on one's actions. Goals tend to be clear, means are coordinated to the goals, and feedback to one's performance is immediate and unambiguous. In such a situation a person has a strong feeling of control – or personal causation – yet, paradoxically, ego involvement is low or nonexistent, so that one experiences a transcendence of self (ego) and sometimes a feeling of union with the environment. The passage of time appears to be distorted, some events seem to take a disproportionately long time, but in general, lows seem to pass by in minutes. (p. 70)

Allen (1980) also quotes a climber describing a flow situation.

The task at hand is so demanding and rich in its complexity and pull that the conscious subject is really diminished in intensity. The corollary of that is that all the hang ups or complexes that people have or that I have as an individual person are momentarily obliterated… It is one of the few ways I have found to live outside my head. (p. 70)

Looking at Maslow's theory (1970), this kind of experience would be termed a peak experience. In Jung's terms, it would be a numinous experience. These experiences help in our journey through life. They help us to self-actualize according to Maslow or individuate according to Jung. In outdoor instruction, it is far more possible for our students to experience this kind of instruction where the learning experiences are very powerful compared to regular classrooms. Can we try and build in such experiences? Is it worth doing a peak on what is primarily an education course? The boost and zest it can give is well worth it as long as it is appropriately done and is not too fearful an experience for the student, as in that would then become miseducative. It could be a rapid stretch of river, a challenging rappel in a cave, or a mountain peak. Careful judgment has to be made concerning the group's abilities.

I remember well summiting Table Mountain after an ascent with a student group, having negotiated more snow than we had ever seen up there – vast drifts, all kinds of snow conditions, and use of the sliding middleman snow climbing technique. You have no idea the view that is going to hit you until you summit. The Grand Teton, the Middle Teton, the South Teton, and Mount Owen all appear at once in all their winter finery. This was a peak experience or numinous experience for everyone in the group. That moment is forever burned in their memories. The technical snow-climbing going up there on the climb may better describe the 'flow' experience. On another occasion after a group was showing signs of fatigue having spent too many climbing days in succession with alpine starts, we decided not to do Battleship Mountain which could also have been a Peak Experience but could alternatively have resulted in a bad mishap. Sometimes making that kind of decision can be very hard especially when the group is involved in that decision.

How do the experiences help in the individuation of the person? It could be attributed to transcendence, where you may be transcending the multiple structures of the psyche that are unbalanced. This transcendence may help when one has feelings of unequilibrium as for the period of time during the flow experience, there is a sense of wholeness. The principle of entropy as adapted by Jung states that the distribution of energy in the psyche seeks an equilibrium or balance among the structures of the psyche. Inequities in the system produce tension and can give the person the feeling that they are being torn to pieces by these inner conflicts. Risk activities offer a progression towards equilibrium, not permanent perhaps, but with the embodiment of total concentration, a balance is achieved for the moment bringing some equilibrium to the system.

Individuation is the striving toward wholeness in our personal growth and adventure activities often demand the total involvement of individuals. Lester (1980) the psychologist on the 1963 American Everest expedition discussed this in his comparisons of the Americans and the Sherpas.

Experiences show movement from multiplicity to unity and toward the elimination of disharmony that is said to be the goal of all mystical activity… inner conflicts provided the particular motivation for that straining… a strong yearning toward the ideal of wholeness, the integration or transcendence of a multiplicity of selves. The respect for and idealization of the Sherpas was rooted in this, the impression that integration without the straining felt by the climbers (Americans)[6]. It seems, paradoxically, this straining toward wholeness, in itself reflects the inner division from which the climber seeks to escape; he seems often to be trying to 'lose' himself by strenuously asserting himself. This poignant conflict is one source of the inner drama inherent in mountaineering, the drama outside the equally real adventure of the external events. (p. 68)

---

[6] 'Americans' added to this quote to clarify as nowadays Sherpas are regarded as climbers if not *the* climbers on many expeditions.

Outdoor courses involving adventure activities are often very powerful experiences, so as instructors, we should capitalize on this to help our students through the actual journey that they are on – on the trail, in the bush, on a mountain, on the ocean, a lake, river or cave – as well as helping them as they individuate on their journey through life. Jung's numinous experiences and Maslow's peak experiences may be perceived as psychologically transcendent but also as spiritual.

The Spirit

The physical, the emotional, the intellectual, and the spiritual can represent the four functions of the psyche. The spiritual is the anchor securing us to life (Unsoeld, 1974). Early man arrived at a feel about the world and was more part of the environment; this feeling was demonstrated well by the American Indians who lived closer to nature. Modern man has alienated himself from nature and increasingly from his fellow men with the trappings of modern society – air-conditioned houses, computers, cars etc., all of which provide barriers to feeling close to nature.

Willi Unsoeld (1974) in his famous speech in Estes Park, Colorado in 1974 advanced the suggestion by Theodore Roszak that the world is a seamless robe where you can't take hold of any part of the fabric without "shaking the whole business." Roszak details these ideas on eco-psychology in his book, *The Voice of the Earth* (1993). His epilogue suggests that Jung's individuation may be the adventure of a lifetime "But the person is anchored within a greater universal identity. Salt remnants of the ancient oceans flow through our veins, ashes of expired stars rekindle in our genetic chemistry," (Roszak, 1993, p. 319). Capra (1982) in *The Turning Point* explained the turnaround scientists made with research into atomic physics and their view of the connectedness of everything in the universe. Unsoeld (1974) went on to say:

> For primitive man things were alive or infused with life and were viewed religiously as some ultimate worth. With modern man, we have lost this; this religious view of nature. (p.18)

He saw the continual mystery of the wilderness as directly correlative to the mystery of the sacred. Secondly, the numinous quality of the wilderness, the 'overpoweringness' relates to the religious or sacred. The third quality is the essence of fascination, the attraction in the mystery and the power. "It's an enormous fascination and the very apex of this line of experience is the vision of totality; sense of all" (Unsoeld, 1974, p. 20).

Mystical experiences have often been referred to by mountaineer writers and on the 1963 Everest Expedition on the West Ridge, of which Unsoeld was a member - one of the climbers stranded at 28,000 feet described such an experience to Lester (1980) the psychologist of the expedition.

> When we bivouacked that night, I was much clearer in the things that counted to me, I could see my body lying on a rock and snow, but it didn't matter. I cared not if I came back, for life had been found which transcended mere physical survival. I knew that we would survive anyway…I felt I could peek into the other side of life and understand death. There was no space, no time, and no sense of losing life. It did not matter whether this type of life was lost or not, for life as I knew then transcended all physical manifestations of the body. I was looking over the arête into the other side of the universe and could more fully view the life I was still part of. I was wafted into the ethereal space about me. This is not a pessimistic view of death, but an extremely optimistic view of life in its richest sense. I knew who I was and I knew what I was. (p. 102)

The outdoor environment seems to provide a key to unlocking the unconscious yet provides humility in the face of our known universe as individuals can feel powerless in the face of storms, rivers and mountains. This intertwining of religion or spirituality and nature places man in a cosmic perspective. Unsoeld (1974) asked the interesting question, "Why don't we stay in the wilderness?" (p. 20). He invited us back to the cities where "The final test is whether your experience of the sacred in nature enables you to cope more effectively with the problems of man. Seek ye first the kingdom of nature that the kingdom of man might be realized" (Unsoeld, 1974, p.20). If our roots and the roots of our religions lie back in the mists of time to the primordial environment when we were programmed with primordial responses, is it any wonder that if these images and fears are deep in our unconscious that we seek rejuvenation in the mountains, the wilderness and on the seas?

Implications of Jung's Concepts for Outdoor Instructors

Understanding our own basic drives is important and is especially so for outdoor instructors. It has been asserted that an important value of outdoor recreation is that it aids in self-actualization. That capacity is increased if peak experiences are possible. Allen (1980) explained "Self-actualization, which Maslow called the goal of identity, involves accepting one's inner self, fully realizing one's capacities and then actualizing them" (Allen, 1980, p.71). Allen goes on to say "The cognitions of peak experiences include "Total attention, enriched perception, disorientation of time and space, resolution of internal conflict and complete (but temporary) loss of fear and anxiety…. peak experiences and growth towards self-actualization are thus mutually facilitative" (p.71).

Jung's concepts of individuation and numinous experiences anticipated Maslow's (1970), self-actualization and peak experiences (Hilgard, Atkinson, and Atkinson, 1979). According to Hilgard, Atkinson, and Atkinson (1979) Jung was to some extent a predecessor of the humanistic psychologists. Jung not only recognized the importance of personal growth and self- realization, but also understood the powerful effects of unconscious influences. With regard to one's inner self and fully realizing ones' capacities, his developments concerning the unconscious are particularly relevant. Campbell (1959) quoted Jung on this:

The young man (or woman) can have only an incomplete understanding of himself and others and is therefore imperfectly informed as to his and her motives. As a rule the motives he acts from are largely unconscious. Subjectively of course, he thinks himself very conscious, and knowing, for we constantly overestimate the existing content of consciousness, and it is a great and surprising discovery when we find that what was supposed to be a final peak is nothing but the first step in a long climb. (p.165)

Mattoon (1981) also quoted Jung, adding:

Whoever makes progress along the path of self-realization must inevitably bring into consciousness the contents of his personal unconscious, thus enlarging considerably the domain of his personality. (p. 23)

For self-actualization or in Jung's terms, individuation, Jung's psychology is of particular importance - understanding our unconscious drives can enable us to try and use the effects of the archetypes such as the hero to build youngsters' egos but to contain it when necessary. When planning a mountain trip – plan for the students - not for the personal desires of the instructor. It's not about you when it is a teaching situation, it's about them so be 'other-directed' and plan for them. Don't as an instructor choose a rock climb that is too difficult for the students but will gain 'admiration' for the instructor. As Petzoldt would say – "Don't give the students sunburned tonsils!" (as they gawp up at you climbing an impressive pitch). For people already involved in outdoor pursuits the influence of the hero archetype needs careful appraisal as to whether it is inflating or strengthening the ego. The hero archetype is so strong in western society, using it needs special care and often it should be balanced with the use of the child and spirit archetypes – doing things for fun and more spiritual reasons. These aspects of Jung's psychology focus strongly on the "self". Much research in outdoor education has been about the self - - concept, esteem, confidence, efficacy and image. These aspects of the self are commonly used in outdoor instruction, often as goals (for example to increase self-concept), so let's investigate these more closely.

Self-Concept

Self-concept is the way people view themselves. "Self-concept is acquired over the years by experiencing how other people react to you" (Schoel, Prouty, & Radcliffe, 1988, p.13). Increasing students' self-concept is something that many outdoor programs and instructors maintain they do. "Participation in outdoor activities has usually been considered a method of enhancing or strengthening one's self-image" (Ewert, 1989, p. 49). Outdoor instructors can increase motivation by teaching in a way that strengthens self-concept. Put downs and over criticism can be exchanged for frequent praising and recognition for students who are achieving and meeting group norms. This applies to all courses, not just 'affective' courses for youth-at-risk. Motivation is the key to learning anything whether it is group-skills, interpersonal skills or physical skills. So, even if you are a mountain guide hired to get someone from one point to another, think about how you are affecting your clients' self-concept in what you say and how you say it, what you do and how you do it. Self-concept includes the following self–perceptions or self-beliefs whose meanings are interconnected and sometimes overlap.

1. Self-esteem
2. Self-confidence
3. Self-image
4. Self-efficacy

Self-esteem. This relates to both satisfaction and confidence. People with low esteem tend to view themselves as inferior, whereas high esteem produces more confidence and self-reliance in dealing with every day events. It is an overall opinion of one's self –worth.

Self-confidence. This relates to one's abilities but is a general term addressing an overall picture of one's abilities as compared to self-efficacy that is more task-specific. John Graham (1997) in the preface to his book, *Outdoor Leadership: Technique, Common Sense & Self Confidence*, describes the Giraffe Project "…which moves people to stick their necks out for the common good" (p 7). The project honors "Giraffes" who stick their necks out throughout the world. To stick your neck out suggests that you have sufficient self-confidence to deal with whomever or whatever would stand in your way.

Self-image. This is how you see yourself--your self-worth, which is also less context-specific than self-efficacy. The two concepts are not necessarily related – one can have good self-image while having a low self-efficacy regarding being, say a skier. Conversely, one could be an excellent skier but have low self-worth. According to Perera (2015), self-image includes what you think you look like, how you see your personality, what kind of person you think you are, what you believe others think of you, how much you like yourself or you think others like you, and the status you feel you have.

Self-efficacy. This relates to what we can and can't do. Outdoor pursuits offer opportunities for everyone to gain success as long as the correct activity level is chosen by the instructor. "… Self-efficacy is a cornerstone of many outdoor pursuits programs" (Ewert, 1989, p.93). The construct of self-efficacy was developed by Bandura (1977). Pajares (1996) explains the concept; "How individuals interpret the results of their performance attainments informs and alters their environments and self-beliefs, which in turn inform and alter their subsequent performances" (p. 544). Pajares (1996) also made the point that students are more likely to select challenging tasks, be persistent, and successful with high self-efficacy:

> Efficacy beliefs help determine how much effort people will expend on an activity, how long they will persevere when confronting obstacles, and how resilient they will prove in the face of adverse situations - the higher the sense of efficacy, the greater the effort, persistence, and resilience. Efficacy beliefs also influence individuals' thought patterns and emotional reactions. People with low self-efficacy may believe that things are tougher than they are, a belief that fosters stress, depression, and a narrow vision of how best to solve a problem. High self-efficacy, on the other hand, helps to create feelings of serenity in approaching difficult tasks and activities. (pp. 544-555)

When looking at the possibility of success, students weigh many factors (see Figure 20). According to Bandura (1994), the instructor can influence the students' internal machinations on their self-expectation in four ways:

1. *Performance accomplishment* – mastering experiences and developing resilience through sustained effort persevering through setbacks and difficulties. By sticking it out through tough times, students can emerge stronger. Past successful attainments and transforming experiences provide strong persuasion.

2. *Verbal persuasion* – students' beliefs can be strengthened if an instructor tells them that they can do something to push them through self-doubts. This is also called social persuasion.

3. *Vicarious experience* – seeing others succeed who are perceived to be similar in ability. Seeing others fail can lower a student's self-efficacy. Seeing more accomplished performers succeed does not have much influence (as in expert demonstrations by the instructor -- which give a picture of what to try, but don't affect the students' self-perception that they can do the same thing).

4. *Emotional arousal.* – requires reducing stress to change negative emotions. Students being tense, mentally and physically can reduce them to 'nervous nellies' with poor performance. Enabling performance accomplishment through good scaffolding techniques and good sequencing of activities that build in increments can alleviate emotional arousal. 'Psyching up' students with horror stories about 'Hairy Hack Falls' or showing hair-boating videos the night before a class could produce mental and physical tenseness that can negatively affect learning. If a student does not have self-doubts, high states of arousal could be energizing.

Bandura's theory is illustrated in the following Figure 20.

Figure 20. Bandura's Theory of Self-Efficacy (1977)

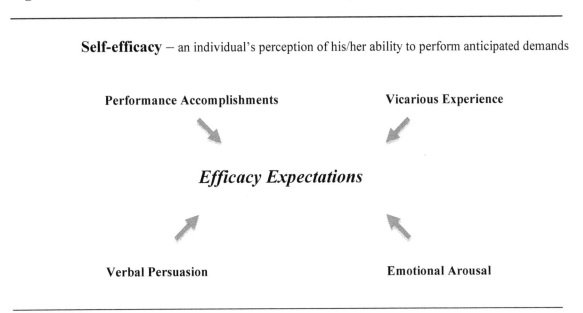

Self-efficacy – an individual's perception of his/her ability to perform anticipated demands

Performance Accomplishments   Vicarious Experience

Efficacy Expectations

Verbal Persuasion   Emotional Arousal

Fear is often the factor that prevents a feeling of self-efficacy along with doubt, anxiety, and dissonance (Ewert, 1989). Dissonance is discomfort through having two conflicting thoughts at the same time. We may believe that we cannot lean back to go over the rappel but know also that we have to do this to avoid slipping. Overcoming the doubts, anxiety, and dissonance can produce peak experiences, or a flow experience, which aids in the self-actualization process, positively affecting self-esteem, self-confidence, self-image, and self-efficacy. The outdoor instructor should therefore strive to enable all these positive self-perceptions wherever possible.

Competent feelings that are engendered, such as success on a ropes course or an expedition, can carry feelings of self-reliance over to other situations. "Indeed, this ability to carry over feelings of competence to different situations is one of the most important outcomes on many outdoor programs" (Ewert, 1989, p.93). Ewert also advised that specific "performance based" standards lead to higher performance and so goal setting is important.

Motivation is affected by many things as described above. They include safety, physical, mental, social, conscious, unconscious, and self-perceptions. However, sometimes motivation is affected by maturity, or the lack of it. One would hope that our students are hungry for knowledge, but this is not always the case.

Mature and Immature Learners

Blanchard, Ford, and Strong (2007) address the motivation differences between mature and immature learners. They point out that the immature learners lack foundational skills and knowledge, whereas the mature learners have this and could prefer problem solving approaches to the learning rather than a direct approach. Mature learners may be more motivated by choosing the method of learning. They may also be more self-directed as opposed to immature learners who may be more dependent on the instructor.

Maturity relates to motivation and the "readiness to learn". It is often apparent in different situations. On the crag, river or snow slope our students are usually ready. In the classroom, their readiness varies and if it is not there intrinsically, then instructors have to inject motivation through the various techniques described in this chapter. Often it is necessary in the classroom to identify why the theory being presented is important and to sometimes enforce learning through extrinsic means such as exams and tests. Assessing through observation and grades can also encourage learning motivation for subjects that are not as exciting as skiing and climbing. The National Outdoor Leadership School (NOLS) in fact does give grades to students who attend their courses. Assessing the students can boost effort from immature learners, but overdoing this for mature learners could also be de-motivating.

There are individual differences in students' learning abilities. Age, developmental maturity and gender can all affect readiness levels so some differentiation in meeting the different needs which could be called 'age' and 'stage' is important to engender responsible learners (Beames, Higgins, & Nicol, 2012). These authors also stress the importance of students taking the responsibility for their own learning. For less mature learners, linear learning (learning through testing) is often resorted to if the students won't read or do pre-class assignments (McKeachie, 1969). Regular quizzes and tests become the norm. This is unfortunate but sometimes it is the only way to ensure assignments are completed.

Non- Linear Learning as a Motivator

According to Jernstedt (1980) it is not what the teacher does but what the teacher encourages or enables the student to do that determines what is learned. This approach taps into intrinsic motivation, which is far more powerful than external motivators, such as punishment or examinations. Intrinsic motivation also encourages non-linear learning through curiosity. Linear learning is directed at what is desired by the teacher, to gain a grade or to pass an exam. Linear learning could sometimes be likened to digging a ditch with your brain cells and is just plain hard work – but sometimes the metaphorical ditch digging has to be done. For example, when learning the medical information for a Wilderness First Responder course, at some time you have to put in the hard work of memorizing and understanding complicated information.

Students experience non-linear learning when they satisfy their own curiosity (McKeachie, 1969). One way to achieve this is to enable students to experience the curiosity of discovery by choosing their own research (applicable for professors teaching outdoor education courses, environmental educators, camp instructors, etc.), to the extent that is possible to be in keeping with course goals. This would be associated with a course, but if the student has substantial choice of what he or she pursues, the motivation will be more intrinsic and not imposed. Non-linear learning assumes that the student is a mature learner.

Fun and Enjoyment

There should be some fun and enjoyment on any course – as the saying goes "All work and no play isn't fun for Jack or Jill". Fun and enjoyment were always a part of the WEA courses that I taught with my co-instructors. Appropriate humor, role modeled by instructors at appropriate times can set the tone. Planned activities like pot luck dinners, talent shows, campfire games, songs and skits can all lift morale. Be careful with "mind games" like "three points of contact" where one has to guess who is "it". It is fun for everyone who "gets" it, but not for those who don't. After a while if some folks are in the dark on these guessing games, I let them in on it. We have even had "costume" parties on expeditions where students have made hats out of rolled up insulation pads, masks out of bandannas etc. There are many group games that can be played so researching some is worth the effort, especially if you have a long expedition course that happens to have lot of bad weather. Fun and Enjoyment is a large part of motivating a group, especially for expeditions.

References

Allen, S. (1980). Risk recreation: A literature review and conceptual model. In J. Meier, T. Morash, & G. Welton (Eds.), *High adventure outdoor pursuits* (pp.52-81). Salt Lake City, UT: Brighton.

Bandura, A. (1977). Self-efficacy: Toward a unifying theory of behavior change. *Psychological Review, 84*(2), 191-215.

Bandura, A. (1994). Self-efficacy. In V. S. Ramachaudran (Ed.), *Encyclopedia of human behavior* (Vol. 4, pp. 71-81). New York, NY: Academic Press.

Beames, S., Higgins, P., & Nicol, R. (2012). *Learning outside the classroom: Theory and guidelines for practice.* New York, NY: Routledge.

Blanchard, J., Strong, M., & Ford, P. (2007). *Leadership and administration of outdoor pursuits.* State College, PA: Venture.

Bunting, C. (1980). Wilderness learning and higher education. *The Physical Educator, 37*(4), 172-175.

Campbell, J. (1959). *Masks of God: Primitive mythology*. New York, NY: Viking Press.

Capra, F. (1982) *The turning point*. New York, NY: Simon and Schuster.

Clarke, G., & Phipps, M. L. (2010). An investigation into the technical and soft skills instruction using an importance-performance analysis. *Unpublished study*. Cullowhee, NC: Western Carolina University.

Ewert, A. W. (1989). *Outdoor adventure pursuits*. Worthington, OH: Publishing Horizons.

Graham, J. (1997). *Outdoor leadership: Technique, common sense and self-confidence*. Seattle, WA: The Mountaineers.

Grube, D., Phipps, M. L., & Grube, A. J. (2002). Practicing leader decision-making through a systematic journal technique: A single case design. *The Journal of Experiential Education, 25*(10), 220-230.

Hall, S. C., & Nordby, J. (1973). *A primer of Jungian psychology*. New York, NY: Mentor.

Hilgard, E. R., Atkinson, R. C., & Atkinson, R. L. (1979). *Introduction to psychology*. New York, NY: Harcourt Brace Jovanovich.

Hornbeim, T. F. (1981). *Everest the west ridge*. Seattle, WA: The Mountaineers.

Huntford, R. (1985). *The last place on earth*. New York, NY: Atheneum.

Jernstedt, C. G. (1980). Experiential components in academic courses. *The Journal of Experiential Education,* 3(2), 211-219.

Jordan, D. J. (1996). Snips and snails and puppy dogs tails…The use of gender-free language in experiential education. In K. Warren (Ed.), *Womens' voices in experiential education* (pp. 205-211). Dubuque, IA: Kendall/Hunt.

Jung, C. G., Von Franz, M. L., Freeman, J., Henderson L., Jacobi, J., & Jaffe, A. (1964). *Man and his symbols.* New York, NY: Dell.

Lester, J. (1980). A psychologist on Mount Everest. In J. Meier, T. Morash, & G. Welton (Eds.), *High adventure outdoor pursuits* (pp. 91-106). Salt Lake City, UT: Brighton.

Maslow, A. H. (1943). A theory of human motivation. *Psychological Review, 50*(4), 370-96.

Maslow, A. (1970). *Motivation and personality.* New York, NY: Harper.

Mattoon, M. A. (1981). *Jungian psychology in perspective.* New York, NY: The FreePress.

McCully, R. S. (1971). *Rorschach theory and symbolism.* Baltimore, MD: Williams and Wilkins.

McKeachie, W. J. (1969). *Teaching tips: A guide for beginning college teachers* (7th ed.). Toronto, ON: D. C. Heath.

Miles, J. C., & Priest, S. (1990). *Adventure education.* State College, PA: Venture.

Pajares, F. (1996). Self-efficacy in academic settings. *Review of Educational Research,* Winter, *66*(4), 543-578.

Perera, K. (2015). More-Selfesteem.com. Retrieved from http://www.more-selfesteem.com/selfimage.htm.

Phipps, M. L. (1985). Adventure – an inner journey to the self: The psychology of adventure expressed in Jungian terms. *Adventure Education, 2*(4/5), 11-17.

Phipps, M. L. (2009). Using situational leadership theory in decision-making. In R. Stremba & C. Bisson (Eds.), *Teaching adventure education theory* (pp.195-205). Champaign, IL: Human Kinetics.

Phipps, M. L., & Claxton, D. (1997). An investigation into instructor effectiveness using experiential education constructs. *Journal of Experiential Education, 20*(1), 40-46.

Phipps, M. L., & Swiderski, M. (1991). The soft skills of outdoor leadership. In J. Miles & S. Priest, (Eds.), *Adventure education* (pp. 221-232). State College, PA: Venture.

Priest, S., & Gass, M. A. (1997). *Effective outdoor leadership in adventure programming.* Champaign, IL: Human Kinetics.

Roszak, T. (1993). *The voice of the earth.* New York, NY: Touchstone.

Schoel, J., Prouty, D., & Radcliffe, P. (1988). *Islands of healing: A guide to adventure based counseling.* Beverly, MA: Project Adventure.

Swiderski, M. (1987). Soft and conceptual skills: The often-overlooked components of outdoor leadership. In G. Robb (Ed.), *The bradford papers,* (Vol. 2, pp. 52-63). Martinsville, IN: Bradford Woods Center for Outdoor Education.

Unsoeld, W. (1974). *Spiritual values in the wilderness.* Paper presented at the 1974 Experiential Education Conference at Estes Park, Colorado.

Van Nostrand, C. H. (1993). *Gender-responsible leadership.* Newbury Park, CA: Sage.

Von Franz, M. L. (1981). *Puer aeternus.* Santa Monica, CA: Sigo Press.

Warren, K. (2009). Outdoor leadership with gender in mind. In B. Stremba & C.A. Bisson (Eds.), *Teaching adventure education theory: Best practices* (pp.232-240). Champaign, IL: Human Kinetics.

Chapter 6

Perception

"All our knowledge has its origins in our perceptions."

- Leonardo da Vinci

"Me no lost – teepee lost."

- Paul Petzoldt

Perception is the way people receive and process information. We all see things differently, but there is often a consensus of opinion. The more ambiguity or novelty, the more likely there are to be different interpretations or misinterpretations. In Paul's quote above, he told the story about some cowboys coming across an Indian looking for his camp. They said to him "I thought you guys never got lost." He replied, "Me no lost, tepee lost." People really do see things differently.

I got in a situation one time when a student and I had stashed some bikes in the woods, then bush-pushed to see some waterfalls. I had been there many times before and so didn't take a map or a compass. On the return, we started "jaw-boning" (talking about nothing in particular) until we realized that we weren't where we were supposed to be and this was in the middle of some rough terrain with a lot of Rhododendron to negotiate. The question came up "Are we lost?" I remembered Paul's saying and thought "Me no lost - bikes lost". We knew that we were in between two specific creeks and so heading downhill we would hit one of them – which we eventually did to follow one down to the confluence of the streams where the bikes were located. In this instance there were two different perceptions of who or what was lost as my student for sure thought we were lost.

Sometimes misinformation or ignorance can cause misperceptions, which can be dangerous and cause safety issues. I remember once jumping into the outdoor swimming pool at the center where I was working – fully clothed and in my climbing gear. I happened to be the nearest person to a student who had gone under water in the deep end. After I lifted him out I asked, "What happened?" He said that he had asked one of the other kids if it was deep at the far end and the other kid (who didn't know) had said, "No". So, the unfortunate student had tried to put his feet down in the deep end.

I have had students in the mountains of Wyoming ask each other whether they thought they needed down booties and river shoes after we had checked their gear. They perceived that they didn't need them, and so left them. They were subsequently referred to as "men on the move" while we camped on the snow, having wet their boots in river crossings and then had no change of footwear on the snow. This was spring mountaineering and so was very uncomfortable, but their perceptions definitely changed as to the need for the booties. This happened even though the need was explained, but as Petzoldt said "Words mean nothing". Often perceptions can only be changed through experience. As instructors, we have to make sure that the experience, though uncomfortable, is not dangerous. A winter experience would require that the students return to town to get some booties - which could shorten the expedition. Another time I remember sliding down Hardies Horror, a small slot in Dowber Gill Passage, a famed cave in Yorkshire where four of as were having a common adventure. It was a squeeze for me and 'Big John' was next so I yelled back "Take your sweater off John – it's really tight". Well, John's perception was that he would be OK with his sweater on. The slot leads down to a small ledge for your feet and a small stalagmite for a handhold, then a traverse to the side away from a fairly large drop into a pool. John became wedged and nicely stuck in Hardy's Horror and at that moment probably had a "one on one" with his perception! This was unsettling for him and the two cavers behind him who knew that they didn't have the strength to return back the way we came in, as it is a very strenuous cave. The slot is bell shaped so when John shouted "I'm breathing all my air out", I yelled back, "Don't miss the ledge and stalagmite". Of course, he missed both and plummeted down making a big splash. Fortunately, having great strength, he managed to 'back and foot' out (a caving technique to climb a rift passage). He nearly got a Darwin Award for that mishap. So why didn't he take his sweater off? I guess his perception differed and we didn't have a consensus of opinion. This can truly be a problem in adventure activities.

Sometimes perceptions are false because of a lack of knowledge. There is a killer hydraulic on the Chattooga River at Woodall Shoals. It looks benign to anyone not educated in river hydrology or uneducated in how many deaths have occurred there. For the unaware person it looks like a fun drop that you could raft or tube easily. To avoid the hydraulic, you can run the river on the far right. One time I referred to this as "the chicken chute". When the kayaker following me dropped over this "chicken chute", her eyes widened as she dropped over the edge of quite a big steep drop into a fairly big (but not killer) hydraulic, then into an eddy. "Some chicken chute," was the response. Her past experience of chicken chutes was different. I should have said that it was about a 12-foot drop and there would be a big hole but not a "keeper" to get her perception closer to reality.

Perception and Psychological Sets

Sometimes there is a blockage because the student or teacher can see only one interpretation. This is called a set. An example of a set could be the old environmental ethic (non-protective) of 'four wheelers' who cannot 'see' the value of non-motorized travel to protect the environment. A lot of Leave No Trace principles along with environmental education and eco-psychology would have to be successful to change the 'four-wheeler's set and encourage a change of viewpoint to the ethics of protection. Sets are based on past experience; we never come to an experience completely naïve. The student or teacher may be tuned in to a different wavelength. Group discussions are valuable for exposing students to different opinions and wavelengths. The teacher can also look for other points of view. Sometimes students get hung-up on the way that they may have learned something in the past, which they refer to as the 'best way'. Petzoldt discouraged this and any instructor referring to a 'best way' as it may be the best way in one situation – but not in another. Wagstaff (2000) described an incident where a student chose to do small group cooking for a climbing outing because he had learned this way on an expedition course. Well the climbing outing was a weekend that allowed only enough time to teach climbing, so the group didn't have good food because there wasn't time to teach cooking. Small cook groups are probably better on a extended expedition courses, but it could well be better to have someone cook for the whole group if you are concentrating on an activity with no time for cooking lessons. Discouraging the perception that there is a 'best way' can be done by linking judgment to your methods in processing sessions continually looking at the judgment factors of what you are doing.

When receiving information, we also tend to be selective because of our limited capacity and because some information may be irrelevant. Selective attention can be conscious or unconscious and is affected by our emotions, physical homeostasis, memory stores, and intensity of arousal. Imagine an instructor explaining how to run the Lost Guide Rapid[7] on the Pigeon River in Tennessee. If you are a kayaker you could miss the very large hydraulic by hugging the right bank, dodging the large rocks below the hole, and then negotiate another hole at the end. Suppose someone in the group recently had a scary experience in a hydraulic. They may only hear "hydraulic" and not "rocks to dodge". Coming up on the

---

[7] The Lost Guide Hole has now disappeared due to a flood.

rocks then may be a complete surprise because their attention has only selected "hydraulic". A trip up the Grand Teton many years ago with my wife before we were married entailed a question about which route to climb. I answered that the Exum Route was longer. There were three of us on the rope and we eventually had to queue at the rappel, which took a very long time, so her perception on a long climb changed. Subsequent references to long climbs or long days elicited, "Tell me more!"

As people perceive things differently, this affects their learning styles so looking back at Kolb's (1984) learning styles in chapter 2, it can be seen that using different teaching techniques can assist with different perceptions. Remember Kolb's styles were: *Accommodating, Diverging, Assimilating, and Converging*. Each different type of learner would have a different perception of how best to learn.

Problem Solving

Kolb (1984) relates the above learning styles to problem solving as well as learning. He encourages the development of all the styles for everyone rather than having someone think, "Hey I am a thinker, so don't expect me to get things done." Kolb, Rubin, and McIntyre (1984) explain problem solving in relation to the styles:

> The accommodator's problem-solving strengths lie in executing solutions and in initiating problem solving based on some goal or model about how things should be. The diverger's problem-solving strengths lie in identifying the multitude of possible problems and opportunities that exist in reality "compare model with reality" and "identify differences". The assimilator excels in abstract model building that is necessary to choose a priority problem and create alternative solutions. The converger's strengths lie in the evaluation of solution consequences and solution selection. (p. 39)

If a group has all the different styles with a multitude of perceptions, and a good facilitator to be able to bring out everyone's strengths, then it could be a very strong team. The development of a good team would also require that everyone perceives interdependence and sharing different perceptions as important. Everyone in the group must also perceive that they need to rely on each other. Another concept to help with interdependence is distributed leadership, suggested by Johnson, Johnson, and Smith (1998), where anything that is done to move the group forward in either task or relationship is a leadership role which can be done by anyone in the group, not just the designated leader. This perception can really move a group forward but there are many complexities to leadership and to this type of cooperation (further explained in the group dynamics chapter).

Problem solving in a group requires that someone emerge as the facilitator. Imagine a ropes course initiative. Problem solving initiatives are designed to promote intra group communication, collaboration, and teamwork. So, the person in the leadership role shouldn't initially take charge by giving orders but suggest a way to get everybody's input. There may be many ways to solve a problem. Using everyone's ideas and abilities makes problem solving more effective. For example, at Cal Poly I was working with a group of students trying the 'Amazon Raft' initiative. Most of the students were Parks and Recreation Majors and they were very relationship oriented, but definitely not engineers. Being an engineering school, we asked, "This looks like an engineering problem – does anyone have those skills? This question immediately located an engineer in the group and the problem was solved by crafting a suspension bridge to the 'shore'. There are ways to make sure that different perceptions are given. Rod Neubert (personal communication, 1988) from Cal Poly (San Luis Obispo) used the pneumonic PROCESS:

P = Make a *Plan*
R = Decide on different *Roles*
O = Does everyone have *Ownership* of the plan?
C = Have you *Communicated* clearly
E = Are you *Evaluating* as you go? Do you need to change to plan B?
S = Are you being *Sensitive* in giving any suggestions?
S = If all the above is being done, then there should be *Synergy* and the group will
 be functioning as a team.

I usually add another S for safety (always be looking for safety issues). Newly formed groups usually have to be told to use a circle to make their plan, so everyone can see each other for good verbal and nonverbal communication and more accurate perceptions of ideas and how the ideas are being received. Initially I use a piece of plywood with the PROCESS notes as a 'cheat sheet', until the group launches into using it spontaneously. I have had past students tell me that they actually used it to get their truck out of a ditch. Another time they should have used it when they dragged a tree out of the river that was creating a strainer just below their favorite kayak play-spot. The rope snapped, and someone could have been injured. They didn't perceive that and didn't put a damper on the rope. I am sure that they didn't circle up either to process what they were about to do or do a "Nick the Greek"! Transfer of learning sometimes doesn't happen. Perhaps they all should have had a small visual aid card to carry around in their wallets.

Visual Aids, Visualization, and Perception

Visual aids can help get everyone on the same page. In the classroom (outdoor instructors do use classrooms sometimes), Power Point presentations with pictures, videos, and sounds reduce misperceptions of what something actually is, for example a parallel turn in snow skiing, compared to an explanation describing it. In an ordinary lecture the student's imagination may conjure a different image or meaning than the deliverer intended. However, a Power Point presentation can make the learner passive, and less imaginative. It can also be stultifying, boring and sleep inducing, especially when the lights are out in a classroom. Technology can definitely aid in giving the correct perceptions, but should be used expertly to maintain those optimum arousal levels. Students should be given just enough information, with an appropriate mix of graphics and video, and the presenter engaging without just reading what is on the screen.

When going into the field I sometimes take something like the above-mentioned PROCESS board or a card with the Situational Leadership Model™ pre-drawn on it. Drawing contours on a fist to illustrate topography in 3-D has already been mentioned and of course we have the real thing to look at when we are in the field. Constant comparisons of the map to features "look at the map, now look at that cliff and compare the steepness to the contour lines and how close together they are. How far is it from point A to point B? When you have walked it, refer to it immediately and say, "That was a mile." Thus, they perceive what a mile looks like and how it feels. We should constantly help participants hone their ability to align their perceptions and reality. In addition to navigation, it can be done for time control. Related to time control, the instructor might ask students how long they think it will take to pack up camp and be ready to 'hit the trail'. Their estimations will likely vary from 1 to 3 hours. When everyone is packed up and ready to go, compare the actual time to the estimations so the students' perceptions are checked and modified. Modified perceptions lead to learning judgment.

Another way to make people think differently about time, energy and miles was Petzoldt's (1976) suggestion that we use energy miles to plan trips. Paul suggested adding 2 miles to the actual distance for every thousand-foot climbed for trail hiking. He gave an example of a group starting out at noon to hike to

Surprise Lake from Jenny Lake in the Tetons – only four and a half miles… but three thousand feet in elevation gain. It was dusk before they reached Surprise Lake; add some bad weather and a wrong turn on the way back and part of the group arrived back in camp, covered in beaver pond moss, for breakfast the following morning – instead of for dinner the prior evening. "They were only going to stay for a week and it took them more than two days to get rested up" (Petzoldt, 1976, p.27). So, Paul would have said that the trip to Surprise Lake was ten and a half *energy* miles, not just four and a half miles. He used energy-related miles in his guide book, *Teton Trails* (1976) to give a more accurate perception of how much energy would be required to do the hike as people knew how much energy they used for a mile on the flat, then, they needed to add in more energy for elevation gain. Subsequent physiological research showed that Petzoldt's estimated increase in energy was fairly accurate (Troy & Phipps, 2010).

Using energy as modifier is a good way to do trip planning, so the perception that you can do a ten-mile day with a group of beginners while climbing one or two thousand feet, can be dispelled. In reality with a group that needs to adjust boots, packs, navigate, take frequent rests to drink, eat and adjust clothing, a ten-mile trip could easily take ten hours. Not the Marines, the Rangers, the Special Air Service, but we aren't leading them, as outdoor instructors, we are usually leading youngsters, so we need to perceive what they are capable of – not what we as instructors are capable of, in our planning. Many outdoor instructors are in their twenties and are at their peak in regard to strength, so you have to put yourself in your students' 'shoes'.

An occasion on a WEA Teton Expedition Course illustrated this. Petzoldt used to call super-fit young people who couldn't slow down 'racehorses' and on this occasion decided to 'handicap' the racehorses by asking the women to bring all their food in their food bags to the evening meeting. At this meeting, he told the 'racehorses' to pick up the food bags and carry them for the rest of the trip. This sounds very sexist, but Paul had noticed that the women in the group were struggling because of the weight (WEA groups did carry very heavy packs on the five-week expedition courses where we were doing spring mountaineering, including 14 pounds of food each – 2 pounds per person per day) and the 'racehorses' were not offering any help. Paul was pretty blunt as he sometimes could be and set up quite the dynamic whereby some of the guys started to ask whether they were going get a meal when we got to the 'cave'! I tried to address the conflict that was getting worse by the minute – but "We don't want to open that can of worms" was the response, so we let it fester for the day as we climbed over Table Mountain with full packs and then on down to a campsite.

That night, we dug up the conflict and Paul changed everyone's perceptions. He likened the 'gals' to sports cars who use a small amount of gas, the 'guys' to 'limos' who use lots of gas. He explained that as we shared all the food at the end of each week, then we would find that the gals' food bags would be still half full, and that the guy's bags would be nearly empty so in reality the gals were carrying the guy's food. This was true but the 'racehorses' had not considered it. We used to carry fourteen pounds of food per person for a week. The last two days we would put all the food on a tarp as individual cook-groups would be short of different ingredients – then we could all still pretty much eat what we wanted which offset bartering which produces bad group dynamics. On collecting everyone's food bags, sure enough, the women's bags were still half full and most of the men's bags were very nearly empty. For the rest of the course, the women gave half their food to the men to carry - as the men would be eating it anyway. This change of perception made for a more equitable sharing of loads, and the racehorses found it easier to go slower. This sounds like a massive generality, so it is important to point out that some women are very strong, like a co-instructor of mine whose backpack sometimes weighed nearly as much as she did and she could still go all day. Some women eat a lot too, but most don't. Making sure that perceptions match reality can change how the group thinks.

With creative thinking, there are many ways to use visual aids in the field. Topographical features can be made in mud or sand and cord can be placed around the features to represent contour lines. River techniques like eddy turns, peel outs and ferries can be taught by constructing a small-scale river in the sand with rocks, twigs and lines drawn to represent the banks, eddy line, and hydraulics. A small plastic kayak from the Dollar Store or a 'Kayak Joe' refrigerator magnet can be used to show where to hit eddies, what angle to use for ferries etc. A caving trip can be drawn out in mud to illustrate important points in advance of starting a trip. Whatever visual aid is used which may include more and more technical gadgets, the goals of the course should be considered to determine how gadgetry will affect the impact of the trip. If the aim is to get away from that type of the urban lifestyle with all its technology, then leave it behind.

Case Studies

Focused discussion about case studies can bring out different perceptions. In a nine-year study of a college level curriculum, Raiola (1996) found that case studies consistently ranked as useful, exciting, and important methods for helping the students understand and grasp the concepts of judgment/decision making and the impacts of leadership styles" (p.63). A case study that I use in an Avoidance of Survival Situations Class looks at the couloir on Symmetry Spire in the Tetons where several people have met an untimely end in a moat (under the snow water hazard). A waterfall, hidden under the snow can't be seen, so if you don't know about it, you could plunge straight through. The students are asked to discuss the case study, which involves students on a geography field trip falling into the moat. The discussions then revolve around the hazards of couloirs to preparations for such a venture, knowledge or lack of knowledge about mountaineering, equipment carried, or rather in this case not carried (ice axes), and of course Petzoldt's saying "Know what you know and know what you don't know." This elicits a change in perception about couloirs and moats, but also about going into an unfamiliar environment. The fact that this case study is real makes the discussion more meaningful and is more likely to change the students' perceptions of mountaineering, the importance of proper preparation choosing an appropriate route, and going with someone who knows what they are doing.

Role-Playing

Role-playing can be another way to achieve a more correct understanding. This can be used effectively for group dynamic issues. Conflict resolution can be acted out, where students illustrate different conflict styles. An exercise like going through a hypothetical conflict such as "Stranded in the Desert" as suggested by Johnson and Johnson (2000) where different conflict styles are actually being used can be done. The follow up to that is usually for everyone to give everyone else anonymous notes describing individual's conflict styles observed (placed in a hat, then distributed by instructors). The students look at these notes to see how other people in the group perceived them in this hypothetical conflict. This is a perception check for everyone to see how other people perceive them and the perceptions often do not match. This gives room for discussion about how to act in conflict to be recognized for a particular style. More detail on how to do this exercise is given in the Group Dynamics Chapter. This new perception of oneself viewed through this exercise may be illuminating to the person and is an example of the revealing of an unknown aspect of oneself as in Luft and Ingham's (1955) *Johari Window* (see Figure 21).

Figure 21. The Johari Window

	Known to Self	**Not Known** to Self
Known to others	1. *open*	2. *blind*
Not known to others	3. *hidden*	4. *unknown*

The Johari Window is a model used to illustrate a person's self-awareness. The four types of awareness are *open, blind, hidden,* and *unknown,* shown in the quadrants above. The open window (1.) refers to what is known; what you know about yourself and what others know about you. The blind window (2.) refers to what is known by others but is unknown by you. The hidden window (3.) refers to what others don't know but you do. The unknown window (4.) refers to what is unknown to you and others. An exercise like 'Stranded in the Desert' can allow one to see into the unknown window – something about yourself that you didn't know. In this case, it would be how you are perceived in a conflict situation. I remember doing the exercise myself, thinking I was exhibiting wise and group centered behavior, while the group gave me feedback that I had personal agenda! This revealed something that I wasn't aware of and could work on correcting. Another 'unknown' about oneself to learn is your favored leadership style, so you can check yourself and choose the correct style for the group rather than the one that is easy for yourself but may be damaging your communication with followers.

What about the other three types of awareness? Window number one, the open window, refers to things that you know about yourself and you open the window to share this information to the extent you wish. Sharing information develops trust but sharing too much information too soon can damage relationships. On expedition courses instructors usually push people to share some by having three-minute self-introductions, which allows everyone to get to know each other better. Three minutes for twenty-year -olds is a long time so we open up for questions if they 'dry up'. Of course, appropriateness is a key word in this endeavor, so facilitation may become necessary. We used to do 20 minutes on our five-week expeditions and that is a long time to self-disclose. On expeditions, we have found it a good idea to downplay religion, politics, and really personal information. No one is going to change anyone's mind about religion and politics so encouraging argument on these topics could be counterproductive unless that is part of the course goals.

Window number three, the hidden window, refers to information that you know but others don't. You need to reveal intimate details with care and trust only after you have allowed enough time to be able to trust whomever you share with. This can strengthen bonds and can break bonds. Open this window with great care.

Window number two, the blind window, is what others can see in you that you are unaware of – your blind spots. You may reveal this information unwittingly through verbal and non-verbal behavior. If you are uncomfortable with something, your non-verbal behavior might communicate that discomfort even if you have agreed to something. It may be something frivolous like agreeing to sing at a campfire while your arms are folded tighter than a double fisherman's knot. However, it may be something serious where you are agreeing to run a rapid that you think is too difficult for you and you are saying "yes" but inferring "no" with the look on your face. This is when the instructor may bring up your "challenge by choice" agreement. This window can be wide open showing some kind of complex that you may have. Are you aware that you have a "god" complex or a martyr complex or some other complex? Often times we are unaware of a complex but everyone else can see it as plain as day. A trip to Freud's couch or a Jungian analyst would reveal it but that isn't a requirement (to have been for analysis) for acceptance onto an outdoor course. Damaging behavior that is sometimes caused by complexes would have to be dealt with and in less time than Freud or Jung ever had, so we are often containing behavior as instructors not trying to make any cures.

Window number four, the unknown window, represents unknowns for both the self and others. The Johari Window then reveals peoples' awareness --which affects peoples' perceptions. The instructor can monitor the opening and closing of the windows to help develop relationships and communication in the group. Someone may be perceived in a totally different light for example after an introduction. In the case of mental health problems - personal or interpersonal, the instructor needs to assess their own qualifications in relation to the goals of the course -- which would be either educational, recreational or for the *qualified* person - therapy. If we are not qualified to do therapy, we should develop ways to back out of situations that may emerge where it is needed but where we may do more damage if we try. We have to back-up to recognize that our skills may well be limited to education and recreation. The problem may have to be contained behaviorally until the person can seek qualified help. Ringer and Gillis (1995) outlined eight levels of psychological depth and maintained that the deeper levels require intervention by qualified therapists. This may mean an evacuation.

Exercises and inventories can aid in revealing unknown aspects like conflict styles and leadership styles, and so can be very useful when trying to teach such behaviors. Another inventory that reveals something unknown to the individual (like the decision making process, personality traits, learning styles, complexes, conflict styles, leadership styles, etc.) is the *Myers-Briggs Type Indicator* (Myers & Briggs, 1975) that measures Jung's *conscious* functions.

Jung's Conscious Functions

An understanding of Jung's Conscious functions can help the instructor to see that there are different decision-making styles, attitudes, and feelings in people. Understanding these differences can then be very useful. Extroversion, introversion, thinking, feeling, sensation and intuition are conscious attitudes and functions (Jung, 1921). Preferences for these functions shape different personalities. These personality types are measured in *The Myers-Briggs Type Indicator* test (Myers & Briggs, 1975). Each different type experiences, perceives, and interprets situations differently. The test delineates six sets of dichotomies. The preferences for them are shown below.

Attitudes ---------------------	**E**xtraversion	**I**ntroversion
Perceiving Functions -------	**S**ensing	**IN**tuition
Judging Functions ----------	**T**hinking	**F**eeling

The first letter of each type is used to abbreviate the sixteen distinct types (except *iNtuition* to avoid confusion with *Introversion).*

Information processing
S (sensing) type prefers facts
N (intuition) type prefers ideas, the unknown

Decision-making
T (thinking) type prefers objective logic, analysis and detachment
F (feeling) type prefers values, and personal beliefs.

The attitudes extraversion and introversion separate into preferences for action, people and things (external) versus ideas and reflection (internal). The functions are all used in different situations, but one function is more dominant.

Myers and Briggs added a lifestyle dimension to the dichotomies, judgment/perception. They held that the Thinking and Feeling functions were more likely to be used by *judgers* and the *sensors* and *intuitives* would be more likely used by the perceivers. The judgers would be logical and more closed in their thinking. The perceivers would be more open to keeping decisions open.

J (judging) prefers life to be planned, stable and organized, with quick decisions
P (perception) prefers flexibility, going with the flow and spontaneity, with lots of input.

The four letters are put together to show your personality type code. For example, an INTJ show preference for Introversion, iNtuition, Thinking and Judging, they use the other functions but prefer INTJ (Teamtechnology, 2009).

It may be a critical decision to decide on changing the focus of a well-established program where the instigator of that decision is a judger and suddenly came to that conclusion. Other members of the group who are perceivers would need more information and more time for some critical decisions. It is important to allow for the perceivers to get on board by giving lots of information and some time.

There are many instances that aren't as critical when you may think "Ah, they are a different type to me, so they have a different thought processes and perhaps I should step back and accommodate." You could be planning a ski trip to the Alps where there are a myriad of ski resorts and after a quick Google you have found the one because you are a "judger" Your co-instructor, however is a "perceiver" so you...allow for much more input.

Cultural Differences

Cultural differences can bring a host of misunderstandings. This can be in the form of direct miscommunication, and regarding the communication climate of the group. Let us look at some examples. Let's say that you are addressing a group with mixed nationalities. Should you begin with a joke to break the ice? It may work if the groups' first language is the same but even then, Spanish is different in Nicaragua than in Spain, English is different in Yorkshire than in London, not to mention the many regional differences in the US. The joke then may result in blank stares or quizzical looks from any foreign language students as idioms fly right past anyone not fluent. So, while humor is important, with people from diverse cultures, it becomes much more difficult and could even be offensive. Although jokes are problematic, fun and enjoyment are important as well so go ahead and try but do be sensitive. Sensitivity is necessary in other forms of verbal and non-verbal communication as certain words and gestures that may be acceptable in one culture may not be to another. Some words have totally different meanings. For example, you wouldn't want to ask Australians what team they root for. If you have a diverse group, do some homework before teaching begins. Homework is also required for instructors travelling or taking groups overseas to determine acceptable behavior so that the local population is not offended by what they perceive to be rude and offensive behavior.

Taking students from our regional public university in North Carolina to Idaho over the years has necessitated some advanced preparation as we outfitted at an outdoor center belonging to a Mormon University. This meant no wearing of shorts, smoking or drinking coffee or alcohol – some of which are our norms, but we substituted long pants and hot chocolate while at the camp and smoking and alcohol was prohibited anyway. Their students (trainee instructors for the camp) and ours were from very different backgrounds, but while we outfitted, and they prepared for their summer positions we shared meals and integrated extremely well, which was helped by our advanced preparation.

Some perceptions of acceptable culture may have to be addressed as some students may arrive with a preconceived notion that they can act like cave men with deteriorations in sanitary and communicative behavior – not bathing, swearing, off-color jokes, etc. The verbal problems often begin with inappropriate jokes or language which needs to be "nipped in the bud" very quickly so poor norms are not developed. Of course, addressing this while developing group norms before the expedition or very early on can prevent the cave man culture. It is common for some folks to just want to quit bathing which may be acceptable for them but wouldn't be for everyone else, especially their tent partner. To cover these behaviors, I usually insist that we all behave in a more civilized manner while on the expedition than when at home. As this was deemed so important, WEA created a rubric to illustrate expected hygienic practices.

Rubrics

As perception of expectations can be a problem in any area of a curriculum, rubrics are often developed. A rubric helps to break down the expected task or behavior into details. This enables the student to know what the instructor expects. It could be related to a required skill, like map and compass reading, or to a behavior norm, such as hygiene. An example for this is given in the Evaluation and Outcomes Assessment chapter.

Simulations

For complex events, simulations can change perceptions enabling good reality checks. They are often used in rescue scenarios. Wilderness First Responder training usually includes a complex response where multiple injuries and evacuations must be considered. This provides a more life-like experience that can be de-briefed thoroughly to deal with misperceptions. For accuracy purposes regarding the feedback, a video of the event gives a true picture of what happened. Rescue simulations on swift water rescue courses provide far more realistic perceptions of rope lengths, river width, and power of the water.

Perceptions of Your Teaching

Your perceptions of your instruction may not be the same as your students' perceptions. For example, you may think that you are giving the right amount of activity, but they may disagree. How would you know whether to modify what you are doing? If the group is mature and has an open communication climate, then it could be brought up in debriefing discussions. Most likely it wouldn't automatically be brought up. A way to check would be to use the Instructor Effectiveness Check Sheet (IEC), which allows you to go down the list to see what aspects of instruction you have covered. To get feedback on the students' perceptions, after some instruction has taken place, they could complete the Instructor Effectiveness Questionnaire (IEQ) -- a companion instrument that allows them to rate what you have covered and their perceptions of your effectiveness. The IEC and the IEQ are detailed in the Evaluation and Outcomes Assessment chapter.

References

Luft, J., & Ingham, H. (1955). *The johari window: A graphic model for interpersonal relations.* University of California: Western Training Lab.

Johnson, D. W., Johnson, R., & Smith, A. (1998). *Active learning in the college classroom.* Edina, MN: Interaction.

Johnson, D. W., & Johnson, F. P. (2000). *Joining together: Group theory and group skills* (7th ed.). Boston, MA: Allyn and Bacon.

Jung, C. G. (1921). Psychological types. Classics in the History of Psychology. Retrieved from http://psychclassics.yorku.ca/Jung/types.htm

Kolb, D. A., Irwin, R. I. M., & McIntyre, J. M. (1984). *Organizational psychology: An experiential approach to organizational behavior.* Englewood Cliffs, NJ: Prentice Hall.

Myers, I., & Briggs, K. (1975). *Myers-Briggs type indicator.* Mountain View, CA: CPP.

Petzoldt, P. (1976). *Petzoldt's Teton trails.* Salt Lake City, UT: Wasatch.

Ringer, T. M., & Gillis, H. L. (1995). Managing psychological depth in adventure programming. *Journal of Experiential Education, 18*(1), 41-51.

Raiola, E. (1996). Outdoor leadership education: Review and analysis of a nine-year study of a college level curriculum. In M. L. Phipps (Ed.), *Proceedings of the 1996 Wilderness Education Associations' National conference for Outdoor Leaders* (pp. 60-83). Nashville, TN: Wilderness Education Association.

Teamtechnology.co.uk. (2015). Myers-Briggs personality type. Retrieved from http://www.teamtechnology.co.uk/tt/t-articl/mb-simpl.htm

Troy, M., & Phipps, M. L. (2010). The validity of Petzoldt's energy mile theory. *Journal of Outdoor Recreation, Education, and Leadership, 2*(2), 245-259.

Wagstaff, M. (2000). The right way: Training outdoor leaders. *The Fall WEA Legend: Newsletter of the Wilderness Education Association*, Saranac Lake, NY: Wilderness Education Association.

Chapter 7

Outdoor Leadership

"The full measure of a leader is not to be found in the persons themselves but in the colors and the textures that come alive in others because of them."

- Albert Schweitzer (edited)

The outdoor instructor is most often in a leadership role, so an understanding of leadership is very important. There are hundreds of definitions and theories of leadership, on which ones should we hang our hats? Russell's (2005) definition can give us a start: "Interpersonal influence exercised by person or persons, through the process of communication, toward the attainment of an organization's goals" (p.16). This definition includes co-leaders. Outdoor instruction often includes two co-instructors – a basic safety premise and common practice.

Co-Leaders

Co-leaders can enable more of a sense of cooperation but can also create some problems where both instructors think that each other are taking care of something when in fact neither of them are doing this. Sometimes a difficult decision has to be made, say whether to "bag" a summit bid and there may not be agreement between the two co-leaders, which may result in a stalemate. Don't forget that the ultimate responsibility for whatever happens belongs to the leader or leaders. Will one leader question the other at a later date? It is cleaner to have one designated leader who would be making that bottom line decision that could have serious consequences. That leader however, does need to take input from an assistant leader and for that matter everyone in the group to help make that decision. I like the question "Am I missing anything?" for complex situations to ask the other instructor(s) or with a mature and experienced group – everyone.

Leadership Functions

After reviewing many theories, Chemers (2000) suggested four leadership functions that are very true for the outdoor leader:

- Establish the legitimacy of their authority through being both competent and trustworthy
- Guide and support, enabling followers to contribute to goal attainment
- Enable followers to satisfy their own needs and goals by understanding the abilities, values and personalities of followers
- Use the combination of the leaders' and followers' skills to accomplish the group's mission

Leader competence refers to more than a particular activity; competence includes judgment, decision-making, interpersonal skills, program planning and management, medical skills, teaching and safety skills as well as an awareness of ethics, and environmental ethics and practices.

In "The New Ethic" chapter of Petzoldt's, *The New Wilderness Handbook* (1984) he addressed his three goals for outdoor leaders – (1) safety, (2) protection and preservation of the environment and (3) enhancement of the quality of the outdoor experience. His "new" ethic is just as relevant today as it was in 1984:

- Honest self-evaluation – don't lead in situations above your ability level.
- Honesty to others – communicate accurately what your trip entails along with possible dangers and difficult evacuations.
- Responsibility to pre-plan expedition – do thorough planning.
- Respect rules and regulations of regulating agencies like the park, and forest services or other land management agencies.
- Be a teacher of skills, environmental practices, and the beauties of nature. Be a psychologist when special problems arise like students showing off, bullying or being scared.
- Don't allow anyone to travel alone.
- Know when to turn back. (pp. 19-32)

He suggested using control plans to avoid getting into a survival situation. These control plans consisted of: Personal climate control (effects of weather), time control (for trips, camp set-up and take down, river crossing etc.), and energy control (fatigue prevention). Petzoldt's goals relate to the quality of instruction and he comments that good outdoor leaders must also be good instructors. Listening to Paul pitch WEA courses at Mankato State University in 1984, I remember a student commenting that she hated camping. He replied that she must not be doing it correctly and needed some good instruction.

So much for functions and goals, now what about a theory of leadership that will work for outdoor instructors to encompass the complexities of styles, group dynamics, communication and motivation? Last in that list, but most definitely not least is the concept of motivation. Motivation is key to not only instruction (as evidenced by a whole chapter in this book), but to successful leadership. More than many other situations, our success depends on our followers staying motivated to the task or mission, be it an expedition or an activity skill. Motivation can be effected in different ways. If we give out grades as we do for school, college, and university courses or the National Outdoor Leadership School, this is an example of transactional leadership – the better the performance, the better the grade and vice versa. A grade is a transaction and a kind of motivator for the student to do their best. Transactional leadership according to Bass and Avolio (1997) focuses on identifying mistakes, agreements, and contracts with rewards or other consequences. Contracts and agreements are often used with Youth at Risk students who know in advance the consequences of certain behaviors that would get them removed from a course. This type of motivation is extrinsic. For many students in the outdoors their preference would be intrinsic motivation – enabled by Chemer's (2000) leadership functions and Petzoldt's leadership goals listed above.

Transformational Leadership

Burns, in his classic book Leadership (1978), introduced us to Transformational Leadership and stated that transformational leaders motivate followers to transcend their own self-interest for the sake of the mission. It is inspirational, intellectually stimulating, challenging, visionary, development oriented, produces maximum performance and is charismatic. Outcomes include extra effort, effectiveness and satisfaction of followers (Bass & Avolio, 1997). Burns (1978) stated that transformational leadership develops needs from lower to higher levels of maturity and is used between followers, bottom up and top down by:

☛Raising the level of awareness of the importance of achieving valued outcomes and strategies for reaching them.

➥ Encouraging followers to transcend their self-interest for the sake of the team, and
➥ Developing followers' needs to higher levels in such as achievement, autonomy, and affiliation.

Bass and Avolio (1997) say that transformational leadership can encourage others to perform beyond standard expectations. They add though that transformational leadership does not replace transactional leadership, but rather augments it. They also add a non-leadership factor to their model --Laissez-Faire (French for "Allow to do"), which indicates the absence of leadership, the avoidance of intervention, or both. Laissez-Faire would preclude transactions and agreements, decisions would be delayed, feedback, rewards and involvement are absent, and no attempt would be made to motivate others or to recognize and satisfy followers' needs. Non-leadership or Laissez-Faire should not be used in outdoor instruction. Don't confuse letting a student group do a final expedition without instructors or a student doing a solo with this. In both these cases, students are prepared beforehand and there are some controls like pre-arranged meetings, instructions on what to do in an emergency or the prohibition of swimming. Students are carefully prepared before they are sent to make their decisions and instructors may step in if needed.

The transformational ideal of raising levels between followers from the bottom up in the group is a good one. The Johnsons (Johnson, Johnson, & Smith, 1998) from the Cooperative Learning Center at the University of Minnesota talk about 'distributed leadership' whereby anyone that moves the group forward in task or relationships is acting in a leadership role. If followers buy into this concept, then they can be encouraged to participate in positive group roles as suggested by Warters (1960). This is explained fully in the next chapter on Group Dynamics.

Transformational and transactional leadership can be a useful milieu in which we can view our leadership in the outdoors. The five transformational leadership factors according to Bass and Aviolo (1997) are:

Idealized influence through behavior – the leader is viewed in an idealized way (charismatic).
Idealized influence through attributes
Inspirational motivation – relates to shared goals.
Intellectual stimulation – is the furthering of followers' ideas.
Individualizes consideration – relates to treating each individual uniquely to develop their potential (mentoring or coaching).

Bass and Avolio (1997) detail the integration of transactional, transformational
(and laissez-faire non-leadership) into their model in their manual, Full Range Leadership Development: Manual for the Multifactor Leadership Questionnaire (MLQ). These components can all be measured in the MLQ. They give detailed information on each of the factors in an example report for "Sandy Sample" (Bass & Avolio, 1998) to lay out exactly what is being looked for in these concepts. Bass and Avolio detail regular leadership constructs. Tables 1-3 show how an outdoor leadership expedition course or how an outdoor instructor could affect these MLQ constructs to better enable both transactional and transformational leadership. More or less of the techniques could be used depending on whether the course is a leadership course compared to a skill focused, or personal growth type course.

Table 1. Transformational Leadership Techniques

Idealized Attributes
- Use logos, t-shirts, patches, hats, etc., to instill a sense of pride in belonging to the organization
- Promote other-directedness (thinking about others rather than self)
- Consciously role model as an instructor
- Emphasize acting even more civilized than normal
- Encourage good leadership practice like distributed leadership
- Encourage good followership roles when not in any leadership role
- Use students as 'Leader of the Day'
- Help with communal tasks such as bear bagging or digging snow kitchens, especially in bad weather
- Use evening discussions to allay anxieties
- Talk about student values and beliefs during self-introductions, group norm/expedition behavior setting and through discussing Petzoldt's "new ethic", the WEA way or the NOLS way or the ACA way etc., for SOPS
- Relate back to the values of the organization
- Discuss behaviors, positive and negative
- Discuss historical aspects of the expedition or course
- Discuss future possibilities
- Discuss trust through belaying each other, spotting each other, using good hygiene when cooking and food packing
- Use distributed leadership.

Inspirational motivation
- Discuss the evening before about travel or the new cave, or the new ski runs or river.
- Give a motivational presentation at the end of the course
- Push curriculum goals and physical goals only where feasible
- Provide excitement through brochures and stories
- Insist on civilized behavior early
- Confront inappropriate behavior early
- Sometimes let the group decide an issue after they have group skills to deal with conflict.

Intellectual Stimulation
- Use the "There's no 'best' way mantra" and always look for what may suit different situations
- Question the 'whys' behind decisions and teaching techniques
- Avoid normalized deviance (letting a practice that is hazardous become accepted)
- Use journal techniques to encourage alternate thinking
- Teach group skills to enable sensitive challenging of ideas.

Individualized Consideration
- Teach physical skills, leadership skills, interpersonal skills and group skills throughout the course
- Have frequent one-on-one discussions
- Cater to different needs in teaching styles and in activities and locations
- Recognize different readiness levels for different tasks and activities
- Build confidence by recognizing students' strengths and giving opportunities for them to use them
- Stop by cook groups on expeditions for informal 'check-ins', have formal one-on-ones for concerns as well as teaching, and address group concerns at group meetings
- Develop abilities along with more responsibilities in decision-making
- Purposely increase the readiness levels in tasks to enable less direction from the instructor.

Table 2. Transactional Leadership Techniques

Contingent Reward
- Assist the leader of the day where needed in exchange for efforts
- Designate roles where necessary like Leader of the Day or who may be in charge of navigation or erecting bear bags, or digging snow kitchens etc., so students know who is responsible for various tasks
- Develop both common and different performance targets for differing abilities in skill classes
- For academic courses give grades, but explain what they mean for example A-outstanding, B-good, C-average, D-poor, F- fail, or just use satisfactory/unsatisfactory grades
- Use a check sheet with some other Likert scale based on expectations but show this at the very beginning as a rubric
- Give a certificate of completion or of verification of knowledge and ability
- Give verbal praise for effort and performance
- Explain fully what the expected outcomes are at the beginning of the course or before the course
- Remind students often what the goals are (which should relate to outcomes)
- Complete mid-course evaluations. Mid-course peer evaluations are often very powerful reminders of expectations
- Use carefully developed rubrics
- Give the actual grade, certificate, praise (often given too sparsely), and even the unexpected reward like a chocolate bar after a hard day or after perseverance during bad weather.

Management-by-Exception (Active)
   Too much adherence to this type of leadership can result in it being perceived as the "seagull" style where the follower gets attention only when they do things incorrectly and are "hit" by the leader and so should be used with caution and be well balance with transformational techniques.

- Correct mistakes early but relate to judgment
- Discuss one-on-one or in a group setting, whichever is most appropriate
- Keep a track of mistakes in the case of certifying for a medical leader or instructor certificate otherwise expect that in experiential education, learning takes place through making mistakes, so on skills courses or challenge courses there could be less emphasis on all mistakes
- Point out failures in regard to standards where necessary
- Re-visiting pre-set group norms can help to resolve behavior problems
- An open communication climate should help in revealing when things go wrong. "Near misses" are an example of useful information that can help with safety
- It should be an expectation for followers to keep the leader informed about what is happening
- Besides norms or expedition behavior (which are not actually rules but agreed upon behaviors), usually there are agency policies that have to be met such as no drug use, ethical behavior etc.
- Stay within the law.

Table 3. Expected Outcomes Techniques

Using the transformational leadership techniques and transactional techniques in moderation should motivate followers to increase effort, leaders to be effective and the team to be satisfied. Some specific techniques follow:
Extra Effort
- Role modeling is a powerful motivator for this
- Don't forget rest days on expeditions to help rejuvenate students
- Arrange easier days on skills course for students that aren't used to a lot of exercise every day
- Talk up goals and tell motivational stories
- Use effective mentoring and teaching
- Have all the right things in the right amounts in the right place at the right time
- Teach the following skills well: Activity, outdoor living and group dynamics
- Change leadership styles to suit the readiness of followers. Ask what is working and not working
- Be a transformational leader.

Transformational Leadership is designed for long-term groups so some of the above MLQ factor concepts may not fit for short courses or individual lessons but most factors do fit for expedition style groups which make it a very relevant theory as an overarching philosophy. Practicing motivational leadership such as Transformational Leadership could help an individual understand one's own feelings as well as the feelings of others. The ability to do this and then use the information to make decisions is determined by emotional intelligence. Hayashi (2006) made the point in her research that "...while emotional intelligence was found to be an important facet of outdoor leadership, in order to become an effective leader, opportunities to practice utilizing it seem to be necessary to develop leadership effectiveness" (p. 108). Leaders in training then need plenty of practice opportunities such as a leader of the day and working as assistant leaders or apprentices.

As we sometimes do include certificates and grades, then this is where Transactional Leadership comes into play. The MLQ factors include the management-by-exception within Transactional Leadership which can have some benefits but the passive management-by-exception and the non-transactional laissez – faire should not be used as these are not only de-motivating for followers but are irresponsible. Don't forget that the designated leader has the responsibility for followers and completing whatever outcome is expected. The appropriate MLQ factors listed above can be used by leaders and in the development of leaders.

However, for the MLQ factors to be achieved, they do need additional methods. Examples include the correct use of leader styles -- which is paramount in motivating followers and teaching group skills - which enable a group to reach a high functioning state. The leader requires these communication and teaching skills to affect the suggested intellectual stimulation and individualized consideration in Transformational Leadership. Without the ability to successfully relate the correct leader style or assist the group to meld by using specific strategies, then these two components of Transformational Leadership would only happen where a group would naturally coalesce – a rare occasion. So, specific "tools" are required to make Transformational Leadership work. Hersey (1992) suggested:

For every job there is an appropriate tool. Hammers are great for pounding nails. You could also use a hammer to cut a two by four, but it would leave rough edges. For that particular activity there is probably a better tool. To build effectively, you need a variety of tools and the knowledge of what they are designed to accomplish. The same is true for leadership. (p. 22)

So, leadership education requires tools as well as philosophy. The corollary is true too, as leadership requires an overall philosophy or umbrella as well as the tools. Using transformational and transactional strategies in conjunction with tools such as Situational Leadership™ and The Group Dynamics Teaching Model (see following chapter) could be a more effective way to learn about and apply the soft skills of outdoor leadership.

In the past, many outdoor leadership courses taught leadership through opportunity teaching – when problems arose, trainee leaders were then taught how to 'fix' them. This doesn't correspond to Transformational Leadership as documented above and doesn't enable offsetting problems or preparing students with skills to deal with problems when they arise. Research by this author (Phipps, 1986) suggested that a systematic approach to teaching leadership is more effective. The approach suggested was called Experiential Leadership Education and included using an inventory to illustrate to trainee leaders their favored and non-favored styles, and leader effectiveness; a journal to document decisions they are making, analyzing them using a leader style theory such as Situational Leadership™ and conscious use of a group dynamics teaching model. Subsequent research (Grube, Phipps & Grube, 2002; Irwin & Phipps, 1994; Phipps & Hayashi, 2005) analyzed this systematic approach and found it to be effective.

Leadership Style

Using the most appropriate leadership style is critical for motivation purposes. If a highly experienced group is being ordered around by an autocratic instructor, it can de-motivate followers. The same is true if a leader is being non-directive with a group of beginners. The old terms describing leadership styles (autocratic, democratic, and laissez-faire) give the wrong messages. Sometimes a leader has to be autocratic and so that is an acceptable term, but democratic can infer voting. Voting means that some people will not buy into the decision. I would prefer that if a group decision has to be made then ownership by everyone is necessary, so time should be taken to reach consensus. This requires both time and skills in interpersonal interactions (group skills). Systematic leadership teaching would include dealing with communication skills early, in preparation for the moments when they will be needed. If a group votes, then there are some members who have not bought into the decision and may not go along with it, either outright or in passive-aggressive ways. Laissez-faire or non- leadership is not the same as the overall leader delegating decision-making to the group. Sometimes the leader needs to delegate decision making but the follower(s) need to always keep the designated leader apprised of what is happening. They may be intent on making a disastrous decision and be unaware of it – for example something political within the organization of which they know nothing, or like digging fire-pits on Indian lands or changing route plans on a federal permit. As the designated leader cannot delegate responsibility, then the followers should always keep that person in the loop. This is very different to laissez-faire where the group and leader are not communicating. The laissez-faire, democratic and autocratic group of styles is outdated and not appropriate for the outdoor field.

A well-established leader style theory that is used in business, the military and the outdoors is Situational Leadership™. There are two situational leadership theories (I and II). Situational Leadership I™ was developed by Hersey and Blanchard (2001) and it uses the styles telling, selling, participating and delegating predicated on the readiness level of the follower in a particular task. Blanchard later developed Situational Leadership II™ using the styles, directing, coaching, supporting, and delegating predicated on the developmental level of followers (Hersey, Blanchard, & Johnson, 2001).

Most outdoor research has been completed using Situational Leadership I which includes the idea of developing followers. The style use does match group development theory as will be illustrated later. The Situational Leadership Models are shown in Figure 22.

Figure 22. Situational Leadership Models

Situational Leadership	**Situational Leadership II**
Determine the Followers Readiness	Determine the Followers Developmental Level
Readiness Level 1 (R1)	Developmental Level 1 (D1)
Readiness Level 2 (R2)	Developmental Level 2 (D2)
Readiness Level 3 (R3)	Developmental Level 3 (D3)
Readiness Level 4 (R4)	Developmental Level 4 (D4)
Match these styles to the above R levels	**Match these styles to the above D levels**
Telling for R1	Directing for D1
Selling for R2	Coaching for D2
Participating for R3	Supporting for D3
Delegating for R4	Delegating for D4

Looking in depth, Hersey and Blanchard's Situational Leadership I model (2001) bases style selection, telling vs. selling vs. participating or delegating on the followers' readiness level. Readiness refers to the followers' willingness and ability in a specific task and can be R1, R2, R3, or R4. Readiness levels in relation to specific tasks are as follows: R1 followers are not ready, unable and/or unwilling; R2 followers are willing but not able (they often think they are); R3 followers are able but somewhat unwilling, perhaps lacking in confidence; R4 followers are willing and able. The key then to using the model is to first determine the readiness level, and then match the style as represented in the model above. So, R1s would prefer telling (directions are given, leader centered with low relationship), R2s would prefer selling (directions are given with reasons, leader centered with high relationship), R3s would prefer participating (both group or individual and leader input into the decision, group centered, with high relationship), and R4's would prefer delegating (leader delegated the decision-making, group centered with low relationship). Let us look at rock climbing as an example activity requiring leadership that is situational.

If you are introducing rock climbing to students who have never climbed on a 30-foot top-rope site you would assume their readiness level as R1 - they don't have the ability to tie the correct knots, put on the harness safely, and they don't know the climbing calls. In this case, your style selection would need to be telling; your instruction must be very directive. Most, if not all, RI students prefer direct instruction rather than being left floundering around not knowing what to do. After students feel comfortable with basic climbing techniques, they may be introduced to a new task or skill, such as rappelling. This could move the students into a classic R2 position; they might think they know more than they actually do and become less willing to listen. In this situation, the instructor really needs to watch them closely. Instead of just being directive (telling), the instructor should add in more dialogue related to the reasoning, or the 'whys' of certain rules, practices, and techniques. For example, the instructor might discuss where to stand on the top of the cliff (and why), why the anchor may be set up differently (to enable a lower if necessary), why one should not descend too fast, or why to double check that clothing and hair are tucked away from the rappelling device. In this example, you would now be selling the decision-making; the students may be overconfident about their abilities as they have had some experience, but they don't know enough to ensure they can keep themselves safe. Overconfident students don't know what they don't know.

After a couple more days of instruction, you might ask the students to set up anchors. They may feel a little insecure in trusting their own decisions and judgment about where and how to place them. Students lacking confidence, the R3 category, would need you to participate in the decision-making. By the end of the course some students may gain the competence to make decisions on where and how to properly set anchors, belay, use good judgment in which climbs to do, and demonstrate all the required site-specific techniques. If they truly are able and willing, then you can delegate decision-making to these R4s. Keep in mind though that good R4s should keep you informed, as you are still the designated leader.

If you were to move on to a new, multi-pitch climbing site using skills previously learned, new skills would be also be required. If the cliff is 500 feet high the students may consider themselves as R1s. It's likely there will be some R2s as well. So, while being directive (telling) you should also use the selling style to make sure students understand they don't know what they don't know in this new situation. If you had moved onto a snow slope and started an ice axe arrest lesson, then it would be very obvious that you need to go all the way back to telling R1s in a completely new task.

When the task changes, then the readiness level can change. The readiness level can also change if followers are doing the same task and someone becomes de-motivated, or if some negative group dynamic affects the group as a whole. The model is based on motivation so as an instructor, you are trying to push the students along to be R4s wherever is reasonable. This may not happen during one course where difficult technical skills are required. If students are going on to do or teach the activities when they graduate from your course, then enabling them to reach R4 status is ideal. Otherwise, make sure they know they are not R4 and they should seek a mentor and more experience.

For things like camping skills and trail hiking, then a goal can be to get students to be competent at making decisions by the end of the course. Some programs include student expeditions where the instructors are not present. These are done at the end of the program after the students have learned the required skills. Judgment as to whether the students are really R4s should be applied before allowing them to venture off on their own as you then, as the instructor, are definitely delegating decision-making.

If there are mixed abilities in a group, such as in the climbing example above, then in general they need to be pegged at the lowest readiness level in regard to climbing site and route choice. However, if there are a couple of experienced climbers in the group, they could be given some extra responsibilities like belaying, or checking knots which would increase their motivation.

As an instructor, you will need to select different leadership styles to fit the group's needs. You need to assess the ability and willingness of the followers in the particular task then use the corresponding leader style. Perhaps the most difficult part of the Situational Leadership Model is in its actual application. Many people have a favored or comfortable style. Many instructors are very relationship oriented, thus selling and participating come easy. It is often very hard to delegate (don't forget that we are talking about delegating decision-making - not task). If a group is truly R4 in their ability, it would be very demotivating to never let them make decisions. Using an uncomfortable style is like practicing a new skill; it's always hard in the beginning. Remember, Hayashi (2006) suggested that practice is what helps develop the emotional intelligence that is often needed to become an effective leader.

The other aspect of application is how the leader style is communicated as this could be done positively and negatively. If there is an open communication climate in the group and everyone understands that you are using the Situational Leadership Model, followers can communicate their perceived abilities with regard to decision-making using the readiness level terminology. For example, the instructor may delegate the task of the rigging of a bear bag line to some of the students and they may say "We don't feel like we are R4's on the butterfly knot yet, can you check us on that?" It is clarifying for the students to let the instructor know to what extent they need help rather than if they just say "I/we still can't tie this knot." On the flip side, they may assert, "We're R4s on this" (let us do it on our own).

Encouraging students to take more initiative in doing things independently is what we are often trying to do so making the communication easier to enable that helps to move them along. Do make it known though that in the event you have to step in to change what they are doing, you, as the designated leader, have the final say. Stepping in may require a selling style or, if time doesn't permit that, then a telling style followed-up later by some selling. There is often contention for the leadership in groups. As the instructor, you are usually the designated leader, so maintain the leadership of the group. This may require a telling style and a "Maasai Chief" decision as explained in the communication chapter earlier.

Your style execution should be accurate. Whatever the students perceive your style to be is the style being used. If you think you are selling but they think you are telling, then you are telling. A common misperception is delegating (of decision-making), where you think you are delegating as the leader – but they don't think you are, so using the term delegating can clarify what you are doing like "I am delegating the decision on when to get up tomorrow to the group". Letting them know that you are increasingly delegating more decision-making to them keeps their motivation high. Don't forget to use delegating in relation to decision-making as it gets confusing if you use it in relation to delegating tasks (which can be the telling style).

It is very important to be positive when communicating the style. To deliver the style you have to talk to an individual or group unless you are delegating when you may say nothing as in when you get to a campsite and say nothing about where to set up tents because the students know what to do. All the other styles could be related in a positive or negative way. You could be directive or demeaning when telling, explaining or preaching when selling supporting or patronizing when participating or entrusting or dumping when delegating (Hersey, Blanchard, & Johnson, 2001). Think of positive ways to say what you want the students to do. Negative delivery of your leadership style will result in negative perceptions from the followers and could lead to negative group dynamics. Communication of the style then is the trickiest part of using Situational Leadership. A good way to think about the whole process is to think, "diagnose, adapt and communicate": diagnose participants' readiness levels in the task, adapt to changing situations with the appropriately matched style, and communicate the style accurately and positively (Situational Leadership Course Director, Escondido, July, 1996).

Situational Leadership enables an instructor in a leadership role to communicate and influence the group or individual followers in a way that keeps motivation high. It also matches group development theory. There are several theories of group development that suggest groups go through different stages, including Tuckman (1965), Tuckman and Jenson (1977), Lacoursiere (1980), and Jones (1973).

Models of Group Development

While Tuckman's (1965) model (forming, norming, storming, performing and transforming or adjourning) addresses adjourning, which is important for instructors to carry out for transference of learning, re-entry into social groups after an expedition, and because returning to regular life after an expedition can be problematic. Lacoursiere's (1980) model (orientation, dissatisfaction, resolution, and production), was the development impetus for the Situational Leadership II™ model (Hersey, Blanchard, & Johnson, 2001). Jones' model openly addresses conflict, which is important to bring up with students. Conflict is natural in groups and should be thought of as a "conflict of ideas" in relation to the group task(s). Inter-personal conflict is different and is addressed in the next chapter on group dynamics. If the group expects conflict and they are taught how to deal with it, then they are more likely to work through it. Jones (1973) suggested the following stages:

1. Dependence - the group is being orientated.
2. Conflict - the group is getting organized.
3. Cohesion - the group is getting tasks done.
4. Interdependence - the group can problem solve.

The readiness levels of the Situational Leadership Model™ correspond with these four stages of group development so the leader can match the styles to the group in the different stages. The leader must then judge the stage that the group is in. Initially the group is in an orientation stage. Imagine students jut arriving to the first class or to the first day of an expedition style course – they have to have some kind of orientation and basically be told expectations, goals, mealtimes, where the bathrooms are, what the agenda is etc. The telling style is usually what they want at this stage.

After a while when the students are feeling more comfortable with the activity, then they may want some input. They may have done things in a different way with other organizations that they may be affiliated with which brings up conflict of ideas. The instructor, while still making the call on decisions can help the group work through these types of conflict by using the selling style. Saying why you are doing things is selling and keys into the quality judgment method of teaching. The instructor's leadership mode while doing this is still leader-centered as it was in telling, regarding the decision-making but is more relationship oriented. At this point students should have been taught skills to deal with conflict such as conflict styles, giving and receiving feedback, and conflict management. Group building activities like initiatives and team games should be done at this time. Some groups do not get past this stage. If the students have the group and interpersonal skills and have been prepared to work through the expected conflict, then they will progress to the next stage - cohesion.

When the group is cohesive and getting on well together, they are more likely to be getting the tasks done (in Jones' terms – data flow). The instructor at this stage should remain high relationship oriented by using the participating style. Often the group may still need a little guidance. At this point both the group members and the leader will have input so the decision-making has moved to be group centered rather than leader-centered. The instructor is however trying to push the group along to the next stage of interdependence and problem solving.

If the group can get to the interdependent stage, they are willing and able in the task, have excellent group skills to deal with group dynamic issues and really do know what they are doing. This is when the leader can delegate decision-making and so be using the delegating style. Imagine a high function group being ordered around and told what to do all the time – at best this would produce eye rolling, at worst a mutiny, and in between lots of negative behavior like passive aggressiveness. The followers would be R4s but as such should not think of themselves now as totally independent of the designated leader – remember that person has the responsibility that cannot be delegated. So R4s should keep the designated leader in the loop on whatever is happening. Figure 23 shows Jones' (1973) model of group development and the Situational Leadership styles.

Figure 23. Jones' Model of Group Development and Situational Leadership™ Styles

Group Development

3 **Cohesion** **(Data Flow)**	**2** **Conflict** **(Organization)**
4 **Interdependence** **(Problem Solving)**	**1** **Dependence** **(Orientation)**

Matching Leader styles

Style 3 **Participating**	**Style 2** **Selling**
Style 4 **Delegating**	**Style 1** **Telling**

Reprinted from An Assessment of a Systematic Approach to Teaching Outdoor Leadership in Expedition Settings p. 44, by M. L. Phipps, 1986, University of Minnesota, Dissertation Abstracts 862263. Copyright 1986 Maurice Phipps.

Teaching Leadership

Teaching leadership involves both theory and practice. The starting point needs students to look into the Johari Window and learn their own biases, like their favored leadership style, so that they can also practice their less favored styles. The Experiential Leadership Education Model is experiential and systematic, and provides a way for students to learn about themselves, learn about theories, practice the theories, and then get feedback from the group about how their leadership affected the group dynamics. The method utilizes a profile consisting of:

1. Scores from a test instrument showing student their dominant and supporting styles.
2. Scores from a test instrument showing their style adaptability leader effectiveness.
3. Data gained from experience, actual decision-making recorded in a journal related to a theory such as Situational Leadership™
4. Perceptions of group process from a group dynamics questionnaire.

If the leadership course is one week or more, then the inventory or test instrument, such as the LEAD-Self Inventory (1993) (measures how one uses the different styles) or the Expedition Style Leadership Analysis (ELSA) (Phipps & Phipps, 1992) should be given before any theory so it measures the students' actual styles rather than memorized theory. A pie chart illustrating their strengths and limitations can be stuck into the back of a decision-making journal to remind them to practice all the styles. A presentation on Situational Leadership™ can then be made with directions on how to complete the journal pages (see Chapter 1 for an example) as suggested by Phipps (1999) and Grube, Phipps, and Grube (2002).

In the field, the instructors can meet with students regularly to discuss their journal decision-entries. This keeps the students on track as clarifications can be made and discussion can be had concerning correct use of styles or whether enough relationship decisions are being made. The journals can be used in the evening to illustrate actual decision-making being made in the group. Even if a student is not leader of the day (LOD), they can record important decisions that they see (the four most important decisions per day is a realistic goal) and say what they would have done. This way, the instructor can better understand the students, and the students are more likely to think about the leader decisions all the time – not just when they are the LOD.

To be able to find out what is happening within the group, the students can be given The Group Dynamics Questionnaire (Phipps, 1986, 1992). This can be found in the appendix. It can be used as a measure of the group climate and bring out specific aspects of group dynamics that may need dealing with. Often times it brings up misconceptions that are easy to straighten out. On longer courses it can be used several times.

This data can be "eyeballed" in the field or for a university or other academic course could be measured and analyzed using charts and graphs in a personal leadership analysis. This kind of analysis is documented in detail in a leadership chapter "Using Situational Leadership Theory in Decision-making" (Phipps, 2009) in the book *Teaching Adventure Education Theory*.

Summary

The outdoor instructor is often placed in a leadership role. Having an overarching theory such as transformational leadership along with an understanding of concepts like transactional leadership and Situational Leadership™ can enable instructors to make better decisions. The various theories are complex and so need to be taught systematically rather than just through a scattering of theories and opportunity teaching. Both understanding the big picture of how leadership affects motivation and the specific techniques to get the group and individuals to be high functioning is key to enabling successful leadership. This is all tied together with day in, day out decision-making. Add the complexities of group dynamics and it can be seen that a haphazard method of learning leadership would be ineffective.

References

Bass B. M., & Avolio, B. (1997). *Full range leadership development: Manual for the multifactor leadership questionnaire.* Redwood City, CA: Mind Garden.

Bass, B. M., & Avolio, B. J. (1998). *Multifactor leadership questionnaire report: Prepared for "Sandy Sample".* Redwood City, CA: Mind Garden.

Burns, J. M. (1978). *Leadership.* New York, NY: Harper and Row

Chemers, M. (2000). *Leadership research and theory: A functional integration.* Group Dynamics, 4(1), 27-43.

Grube, D., Phipps, M. L., & Grube, A. J. (2002). Practicing leader decision-making through a systematic journal technique: A single case design. *The Journal of Experiential Education,* 25(10), 220-230.

Hayashi, A. (2006*). Leadership development through an outdoor leadership program focusing on emotional intelligence* (Unpublished doctoral dissertation). Indiana University, Bloomington.

Hersey, P. (1992). *The situational leader.* Escondidio, CA: The Center for Leadership Studies.

Hersey, P., Blanchard, K. H., & Johnson, D. E. (2001). *Management of organizational behavior: Leading human resources* (8th ed.). Upper Saddle River, NJ: Prentice-Hall.

Irwin, C., & Phipps, M. L. (1994). The great outdoors and beyond; common threads in leadership training on land in the air, and in space. In L. McAvoy (Ed.), *Proceedings of the Research Symposium for the Coalition of Education in the Outdoors* (pp. 43- 52). University of Minnesota.

Johnson, D. W., Johnson, R., & Smith A. (1998). *Active learning, cooperation in the college classroom.* Edina, MN: Interaction.

Jones, J. E. (1973). Model of group development. In J. E. Jones and J. W. Pfeiffer (Eds.), *The Annual Handbook for Group Facilitators* (pp. 159-176). La Jolla, CA: University Associates.

Lacoursiere, R. B. (1980). *The life cycle of groups: Group developmental stage theory.* New York, NY: Human Service Press.

LEAD-Self. (1993). *LEAD–Self: Leadership style/perception of self.* Escondido, CA: Center for Leadership Studies.

Petzoldt, P. (1984). *The new wilderness handbook.* New York, NY: Norton.

Phipps, M. L. (1986). *An assessment of a systematic approach to teaching outdoor leadership in expedition Settings.* (Unpublished doctoral dissertation). University of Minnesota, Minneapolis.

Phipps, M. L. (1992) The group dynamics questionnaire. In D. Cockrell (Ed.), *Proceedings of the 1992 WEA National Conference.* Pueblo, CO: University of Southern Colorado.

Phipps, M. L. (1999). Practicing leader decision-making through a systematic journal technique. In E. Raiola (Ed.), *Proceedings of the National Conference for Outdoor Leaders at Brevard.* Nashville, TN: Wilderness Education Association.

Phipps, M. L. (2009). Using situational leadership theory in decision-making. In B. Stremba & C. A. Bison (Eds.), *Teaching Adventure Education Theory: Best practices* (pp.195-205). Champaign, Il: Human Kinetics.

Phipps, M. L., & Hayashi, A. (2005). Application of leadership theories: Examples from the Western Carolina University 2004 Teton course. In M. L. Phipps & A. Hayashi (Eds.), *Proceedings of the 2005 National Conference for Outdoor Leaders* (pp. 104-113). Indiana University, IN: The Wilderness Education Association.

Phipps, M. L., & Phipps, C. A. (1992). Expedition leader style analysis (ELSA) in experiential leadership education. In R. Cash & M. L. Phipps (Eds.), *Proceedings of the 1991National Conference for Outdoor Leaders: Public, Commercial, and Non-profit partnerships in Outdoor Recreation* (pp. 47-55). Gunnison, CO: Western State College of Colorado.

Russell, R. V. (2005). *Leadership in recreation* (3rd ed.), New York, NY: McGraw-Hill.

Situational Leadership Course Director (1996). Applying situational leadership lecture. Escondido, CA: Center for Leadership Studies.

Tuckman, B. W. (1965). Developmental sequence in small groups. *Psychological Bulletin,* 63(6), 384-399.

Tuckman, B. W., & Jenson, M. C. (1977). Stages of small-group development revisited. *Group and Organizational Studies,* 2(4), 419-427.

Warters, J. (1960). *Group guidance: Principles and practices.* New York, NY: McGraw-Hill.

Chapter 8

Group Dynamics

"Group Dynamics in the Outdoors – a Model for Teaching Outdoor Leaders" was originally published by M.L. Phipps, 1985, in R. Waters (Ed.). *Proceedings of National Conference in Outdoor Recreation at Bozeman, Montana.* Adapted.

"Take care of each other. Share your energies with the group. No one must feel alone, cut off, for that is when you do not make it."

- Willie Unsoeldt

Group dynamics play a very influential role in outdoor and adventure groups. The National Aeronautics and Space Administration (NASA) studies this as Human Factors research for safety reasons (Kanki, 1991). Negative group dynamics not only affects the quality of an experience, but it can also affect safety. It can increase tensions in a group, which can lead to careless, passive aggressive and aggressive behavior. This could lead to accidents and put the success of an expedition in jeopardy.

Physical and technical training for an expedition is usually a given but training for the soft skills that affect group dynamics is frequently omitted. Prior to an expedition, ongoing group processing training could contribute to group harmony. For educational expedition courses, training as you go would be the mode. For serious expeditions (scientific or lengthy, sponsored expeditions, as opposed to friends going out together), taking along compatible members is often considered. For professional trips, a selection process regarding membership and leadership is helpful. To steal terms used informally by NASA in their past selection process for missions, related to soft skills, do members have the "right stuff" the wrong stuff" or the "no stuff"?

For short courses (averaging 3-10 days), some aspects of group dynamics education could be selected that would most benefit the course, but all courses can benefit from the inclusion of group skills and group processing (assessing how the group is functioning). This chapter will detail a group dynamics teaching model that can be used for expeditions or parts of the model can be used for short courses.

Groups in the outdoors often experience conflict. In an expedition setting, where there are few ways to "escape" from the group, feelings become intensified and incidents can be magnified out of all proportion. The success of many otherwise well-planned trips have been jeopardized by the lack of education (of the instructor and the participant) in how to deal with such problems. This is compounded by a lack of awareness on the part of the group members and leaders in how their behaviors affect each other. Some behaviors are conscious, and others are unconscious, but if they are brought out and discussed openly, changes can be made more easily than pushing them "under the carpet." If they are suppressed they will surface later, usually more seriously. Making group dynamics an explicit part of the learning experience from the very beginning can relieve many problems that could emerge later. This can be started at a pre-trip meeting.

The teaching model described here is intended as a flexible guide. What works with one group might fail with another. The presentation is critical: If the students see the usefulness of learning these communication skills, and practice them, it becomes an integral part of their leadership. Such a process will lead to a team of interdependent members rather than just a group of individuals! With modifications, this model could be used for shorter or longer expeditions or short courses.

The Teaching Model

Group cohesiveness is an essential key to success. Right at the start in the course introduction emphasize a "we" mentality and stress teamwork. Clearly explain the course and group goals to ensure that everyone can work towards the same ends. Include an icebreaker and brief individual introductions.

As outdoor courses involve many different educational aspects, the group and people skills need to be tailored at the right moments. For example, teaching "expedition behavior" and setting norms around expected behavior early is a good idea as this clarifies behavioral norms and brings awareness into the group that these civilities must exist. Teaching group roles is often best left to an opportune time when some of the behaviors have been exhibited and roles are unfolding. There is no best order of teaching, but a logical sequence is as follows:

1. Group development
2. Expedition behavior/group norm setting
3. Giving and receiving feedback
4. Conflict strategies
5. Conflict resolution
6. Group dynamics
7. Role functions in groups
8. Defense mechanisms in groups
9. The Group Dynamics Questionnaire

Teaching styles can include, but are not limited to, lecture, discussion and experiential work, which can be applied to situations that occur, as well as exercises and role-plays. It is important to remember that a group is made up of individuals. It is strongly recommended that the instructor get to know all the individuals in the group and facilitate them getting to know each other. A more substantial introduction from each person distributed over the shakedown period of the course will often reveal information that could help the instructor and the group understand group dynamics and/or problems later in the course. It also opens people up and increases communication in general. Frequent one-on-one student-leader meetings can also reduce tension produced by poor communication.

Understanding the following elements of group dynamics will increase students' knowledge of the internal workings of the group and give labels to behaviors (positive vs. negative). This may make changes more possible when needed. Awareness may prevent or eliminate many of the dysfunctional roles that often appear. It is recommended that the instructor include at least the first five elements of this teaching model in the shakedown period of the course so that they can be applied early.

Group Development

Groups go through an initial period where rules, roles, and rewards are all in flux. Cohesive groups are often noisy; they joke around, have disagreements, arguments and overrun time limits. Non-cohesive groups are often quiet, boring and apathetic. They seldom disagree and deal quickly with critical issues with little discussion.

Tension is always initially present and can be dealt with through smiles, laughs or jokes or can be dissipated by humor, direct comment, or conciliation. Positive behaviors can be established by being supported and eventually becoming norms. Norms are the common beliefs of the group and expectations of behavior

124

Group development encompasses a human component - establishing and maintaining relations - and a task component - the job to be done. Anticipating common group interaction problems enables the leader to prepare possible solutions ahead of time. As the stages of group development are generally predictable, they can be guided. For example, good organization and the correct leader style can ease the group through the conflict stage. The two dimensions, personal relations and task functions, combine at the different stages of group development. Four stages of group development that include both these functions were suggested by Jones (1973). There are many models of group development, but few make the distinction between the two functions. Jones' model is summarized in Table 4.

Table 4. Jones' Model of Group Development

Stage	Personal Relations	Task Functions
1	*Dependency*	*Orientation*
2	*Conflict*	*Organization*
3	*Cohesion*	*Data-flow*
4	*Interdependence*	*Problem-solving*

The stages of group development correspond with Situational Leadership theory. Matching the correct leadership style with the group stage can assist with group communication (see Leadership Chapter). Initially, personal relations show dependency on the leader who sets the ground rules. At this stage, the parallel task function is orientation of individuals to the work involved. Individuals question why they are here, what they are going to do, how it will be done, and what the goals will be.

Next, conflict develops in personal relations, and organization emerges as the task function. The conflict may be covert, but it is there. Conflicts are normal. Johnson and Johnson (1982) suggested that often it isn't the actual conflicts, but the way they are handled that creates the problems. Things can escalate easily, and conflicts come from contention for leadership, influence, popularity, and tasks besides personality issues. They are complicated by our own (leaders' and followers') unresolved problems with authority, dependency and rules. At this stage, the group has emerged through orientation and is feeling less dependent on the leader and members want a say in decisions. A desire from the group emerges to organize both tasks and relationships that create conflict as the different ideas clash.

If the group resolves the interpersonal conflicts, a sense of being a team is achieved and the cohesion enables the task and communication (data flow) to take place efficiently. Ideas are shared with feelings and feedback is given. There is sharing of information related to the task and people feel good about belonging to the group. There could be a period of play unrelated to the task, an enjoyment of the cohesion.

Interdependence, the final stage, is not achieved by many groups. There is high commitment to activities related to common goals. Experimentation with problem solving is supported and there is functional collaboration and competition. Members of the group can interact with each other as a team. They are more than just cohesive; they have no fears in sharing points of view as they respect each other's expertise. Divergent thinking is accepted and encouraged within the group. The members are truly interdependent and not reliant on a specific leader unless the task changes to something unfamiliar.

Sharing Jones' (1973) model with groups enables insight into what may be expected, and it also gives a goal to aim for – interdependence and problem solving. The model is useful for leaders as a predictor of group behavior. For the group members, it serves as a reference for certain norms. An example would be the conflict stage. If conflict is expected, then followers will be less anxious when the group starts to experience it. The correspondence of the group stages with Hersey and Blanchard's (2001) Situational Leadership styles enable the leader to more easily choose the correct leader style by judging what stage of development the group is in.

Expedition Behavior

Paul Petzoldt (1984) stressed that expedition behavior is a teachable skill. He discussed incidents where conscious control has been lost in situations that seem desperate like storms, accidents, and when food runs short. He devotes a chapter in his book, *The New Wilderness Handbook* (1984), to expedition behavior, spelling out in detail positive and negative kinds of behavior. Taking the time to talk about expedition behavior at the beginning of the course or expedition helps to set positive group norms during the orientation phase of the group's development. A comprehensive session that facilitates everyone's involvement will lay cooperatively set norms. Expedition behavior as defined by Petzoldt (1984) is:

An awareness of the relationship of individual to individual, individual to group, group to individual, group to other groups, individual and groups to the multi users of the region, individual and group to administrative agencies, and individual and group to the local populace. Good expedition behavior is the awareness, plus the motivation and character to be concerned for others in every respect as one is for oneself. Poor expedition behavior is a breakdown in human relations caused by selfishness, rationalization, ignorance or personal faults, dodging blame or responsibility, physical weakness and in extreme cases, not being able to risk one's own survival to insure that of a companion. (p.168)

An effective way to teach expedition behavior is to explain Petzoldt's concepts, "individual to individual, individual to group," etc., for appropriately chosen sub headings, then facilitate small group discussions about what would be acceptable behavior for the different types of sub groups. After this has been thoroughly discussed, combine all the smaller groups' conclusions to cooperatively lay down the group norms together. The instructor(s) facilitate but may add information that the students may not be aware of). If the group norms are cooperatively set in this manner, the members will be more likely to follow them than if they are imposed rules. Examples of group norm topics include, but are not limited to sharing food and equipment, respecting personal space in tents, courteousness at group meetings and being on time for meetings. Petzoldt gives many more examples in his chapter on expedition behavior.

The list of group norms that have been brainstormed can be copied by everyone in the group. When this is complete, ask if anyone disagrees with anything. If they don't, which is often the case, then you will have reached consensus. If someone disagrees with something, it is important to discuss it more and reach a consensus rather than have the students take a vote as you do need everyone to buy into the norms. It is everyone's job to monitor the norms. Conforming to them may or may not happen so revisiting them later is important.

Giving and Receiving Feedback

When group norms are overstepped or problems occur, feedback must be given for behavior to change. Evaluating the leader of the day is often done as a group process in reviewing the day on leadership courses. When reviewing the day, or addressing behavioral problems, some individuals receiving feedback can become defensive. Defensiveness can be discouraged by giving feedback in as positive a manner as possible. Feedback is usually more easily accepted if the communication climate in the group is positive. If feedback concerns poor expedition behavior related to one student, it could be discussed in private. Giving and receiving critical feedback should be equated with, as much as possible, providing support.

One-on-one feedback meetings with students, two or three times or more, during the course, prevents such problems as misguided goals. For example, students sometimes think they are not travelling enough if there is more concentration on teaching. Feedback for the leader of the day is often done by the group as well as by the instructor. In this situation, asking the student leader first what he/she would have done differently in hindsight reduces defensiveness as he or she can often see mistakes that have been made. These observations are then "off limits" for the rest of the feedback session. It is all the better, that students are encouraged to evaluate themselves in this way as this completes the reflection part of the experiential learning cycle.

Giving feedback requires accuracy, objectivity, and clear communication. Feedback should focus on:

1. Behavior rather than the person
2. Observations rather than inferences
3. Descriptions rather than judgment; in terms of "more or less", rather than "either/or". Rather than "You are a…! It would be more appropriate to say 'When you do/did this, I feel/felt …'"
4. Behavior related to a specific situation rather than abstractions
5. Sharing information and ideas rather than giving advice
6. Exploring alternatives rather than answers
7. The value it may have for the recipient, not the kudos sought by the giver
8. The amount of information that the person can receive.

Give feedback at the right time and place. Excellent feedback presented at an inappropriate time may do more harm than good. For example, if a person is angry and emotional, then it may be better to wait until they have calmed down. Feedback after experiential leadership situations enables learning to take place more effectively. Some groups attack, while others just give generic positive statements. Both of these styles need to be monitored and discouraged. Effective communication skills develop trust among group members and they then understand that feedback is part of the learning process. If the above guidelines are followed, and once trust develops, students accept feedback as a useful and valuable learning situation. Positive feedback is far more effective than criticism. The amount of feedback given is also critical. Students receiving feedback can manage their limits by saying "Give me more" or, "My cup is full" after having received some feedback.

Feedback on the group norms will be necessary after two or three days. A good way to revisit them is to have the students write down on a small piece of paper one thing they perceive the group is doing well and one thing that they could improve on. Their answers can be dropped into a hat and shuffled so the information is anonymous when the slips of paper are pulled out individually be everyone. The information can then be discussed, and this usually brings up the where the norms may be excelling and/or slipping.

Conflict Strategies/Styles

We assume from the group development section of this model that conflict is going to appear even after discussing expedition behavior and establishing group norms. The ability to discuss specific conflict behaviors in general, in feedback and in review sessions is essential. Johnson (1981) described an exercise, called "Stranded in the Desert", which initiates controversy and conflict. The group must resolve a hypothetical desert survival situation in which there are alternative solutions. The exercise should be given to the group to resolve without them being aware that its primary purpose is to uncover conflict styles. Give the situation explanation (see below) to each group member and a 30-minute time limit for them to resolve it by consensus (voting will prevent discussion, controversy, conflict, and learning).

Stranded in the Desert Exercise

Situation: You are one of eight members of a geology club that is on a field trip to study unusual formations in the New Mexico desert. It is the last week in July. You have been driving over old trails, far from any road, in order to see out-of-the-way formations. At 10:47 a.m. the specially equipped minibus in which your club us riding overturns, rolls into a 20-foot ravine, and burns. The driver and the professional advisor to the club are killed. The rest of you are relatively uninjured. You have no cell phone reception. You know that the nearest ranch is approximately 45 miles east of where you are. There is no other place of habitation closer. When your club does not report to its motel that evening you will be missed. Several people know generally where you are, but because of the nature of your outing, they will not be able to pinpoint your exact location. The area around you is rugged and dry. You heard from a weather report before you left that the temperature would reach 110 degrees F. You are all dressed in lightweight summer clothing, although you do have hats and sunglasses. Before your minibus burned, you were able to salvage the following items:

Magnetic compass
Large, light blue canvas
Book, *Animals of the Desert*
One jacket per person
Accurate map of the area
A .38 caliber pistol, loaded
Rearview mirror
On flashlight
Bottle of 1000 salt tablets
Four canteens, each containing two quarts of water

The group needs to make two decisions:
1. To stay where it is or to try to walk out, and
2. To hunt for food or not to hunt.

(Johnson and Johnson, 2000)

To make these decisions, it will be necessary to rank order the salvaged items in regard to their importance. In making the decisions, your group must stay together. The correct answer is not the issue at stake here, and giving one could reinforce the competitiveness of some of the students. When the time limit is over, get everyone together and give an explanation of the following styles as outlined by Johnson (1981).

1. The Turtle - withdraws from the conflict.
2. The Shark - forces and tries to make opponents accept his or her solution.
3. The Teddy Bear - smooths and avoids the conflict in favor of harmony.
4. The Fox - compromises, giving up part of his or her goals and persuades others to give up part of theirs.
5. The Owl – views conflicts as problems to be solved, confronts, seeking solutions that will satisfy both parties.

Drawing the turtle, shark, etc., in notebooks provides for some amusement and it can reduce any tension produced by the exercise. It also paints mental pictures, so students tend to use the terminology frequently after it has been introduced. Ask the students to write the names of the others in their group on the outside of small pieces of folded paper and on the inside of each piece of paper write the conflict strategy that best fits their actions in this exercise. Then, students pass the pieces of paper to the leader who distributes them to the group members. Each member should receive pieces of paper containing his or her conflict styles as seen by the other members. This enables a perception check. All of these styles are appropriate at different times; however, good judgment is necessary to choose the appropriate style at the appropriate time. If the style perceived by others doesn't match the behavior the individual thought they were exhibiting, then the individual needs to adjust his/her behavior to be more accurate. The style chosen may be affected by the necessity to keep good relations, achieve personal goals, safety factors or by doing the best thing for the group.

Conflict Resolution

If a conflict develops between two people, address the issue and set a time to talk about it using confrontation and negotiation skills. Johnson (1981) suggested a progression of definite stages in defining and resolving interpersonal conflicts. These stages are as follows:

I. **Define conflicts Constructively**
    a. Define the conflict.
    b. Define the conflict trying to describe the other person's actions toward me.
    c. Define the conflict as a mutual problem.
    d. Define the conflict to give a specific description of the other person's actions.
    e. Focus on describing feelings about or reactions to the other person's actions.
    f. Focus on how I create and continue the conflict.

II. **Confrontation and Negotiation**
    In confronting another person and negotiating a resolution to a conflict, the following steps can be taken:
    a. Confront the opposition
        1. Do not hit and run, schedule a negotiating session
        2. Communicate openly your perceptions of and feelings about the issues involved in the conflict and try to do so in minimally threatening ways.
        3. Comprehend fully the other person's views of and feelings about the conflict
        4. Do not demand change.

    The skills required are:
    1. Use of personal statements – how the conflict affects "me"
    2. Use of relationship statements – how the conflict affects us
    3. Use of behavior descriptions – behavior reference rather than personal attacks
    4. Direct descriptions – be direct and to the point
    5. Understanding responses – say how you understand explanations
    6. Interpretive responses – enquire further if you don't understand responses
    7. A perception check – give a summary of what you perceive
    8. Constructive feedback skills – see earlier section on feedback skills.

    a. Arrive at a mutually agreeable definition of the conflict
    b. Communicate position and feelings
    c. Communicate cooperative intentions

    d. Take each other's perspective
    e. Reach an agreement through negotiation
       Then
       1. Generate and evaluate possible solutions
       2. Decide together, without voting, the best solution
       3. Plan its implementation
       4. Plan for an evaluation later

(Johnson 1981)

Teaching conflict resolution is best done in the shakedown period of the course so that the skills can be used in real situations that will emerge later. An interesting way to teach conflict resolution is to have the group "invent" situations in dyads and have them role play the resolution in front of the group. For real conflicts, Johnson's (1981) plan could be used to enable the people with the conflict (usually a pair), to work through the steps. A mediator should be present to keep them on track. Sometimes misunderstandings can easily be cleared up, but deeper-seated conflicts take time, so arranging that time is important. You may not have the two folks emerge as best friends, but you may be able to continue the expedition in a civil way. On one trip, my co-instructor and I had two females really going at each other on a trip. We sent them down the trail, out of earshot of the group (about 100 yards), to work through the Johnson steps with a competent mediator (this is a must!). In this case, the mediator was a mature, 24-year-old female participant. We said, "Work through it until you have some resolution and we will cook your supper". A full two hours later they emerged, not smiling but not swearing either. We got through the next three days to the end of the trip without any more blowouts. Having practiced conflict resolution through role-plays earlier enhanced the students' ability to put it into practice.

Group Dynamics

Understanding group dynamic theory can help the instructor understand what may otherwise look like strange behavior. It can enable proactive interventions and help the group building and maintenance processes. According to Pfeiffer and Jones (1972) the group process is the dynamics of what is happening between group members while the group is working on the content or task. The group process, or dynamics are often neglected even when it causes serious problems. As it emerges, it encompasses morale, tone, atmosphere, influence, participation, style of influences, leadership struggles, conflict, competition and cooperation. Understanding group process enables leaders to diagnose group problems early and deal with them effectively. Educating the group about group dynamic theory, and showing them that this is expected development, can relieve tension. Many students naively expect that the group should be always completely harmonious. Four areas that Pfeiffer and Jones (1972) suggest covering are Communication, Task and Group maintenance, Emotional Issues, and Cohesion Building.

Communication

Without effective communication, a breakdown in the team will ensue. Communication includes expressing messages clearly so the intention is received, but also creating a receptive atmosphere dealing with conflict, affecting motivation, and using effective leadership techniques. Communication is essential and set times to enable this must be made available. A review of the day, each day, will enable consolidation of the day's instruction after students have had time to digest material, but will also enable a time to air problems and monitor the group process (how the group is working together). Some students may resist the specific diagnosis of the process. They can be encouraged to become involved through making it one of the "leader of the day" duties. During review sessions they should be encouraged to analyze the workings of the group, point out unwanted behaviors, and praise functional behaviors. This provides an experiential way of learning the different roles that group members can play, and it can also encourage generally positive behavior.

Positive communication skills are important in maintaining morale. Choosing the wrong leadership style at the wrong time can be very de-motivating for the group. Regarding group process, communication and participation are not necessarily the same. Someone with little participation may still capture the attention of the group while someone may be verbose and ignored. Influence can be positive or negative, it can enlist support or alienate

Communicating feelings is as important as communicating thoughts. The leader of the day should allow communication of feelings from all individuals and expressing feelings should be a group norm. It is a good thing to own feelings and not to make excuses for them. Refusal to include this kind of information reduces the individual's sense of worth and belonging. It can be de-motivating and lead to poor morale. Expression of feelings may be inhibited, but non-verbal communication can be seen through facial expressions, gestures, tone of voice etc. An effective way to bring up feelings and anxieties is to use the "anonymous note in the hat" exercise. Everyone in the group anonymously writes down their anxieties and places them in a hat. These are shuffled, drawn randomly out of the hat, and read aloud by individuals from the group.

Appropriate communication techniques such as effective feedback, conflict management, active listening, paraphrasing, etc., are then required to deal with these anxieties. Active listening involves showing empathy and perception checks by restating or paraphrasing what is being said (restating in a different way) to ensure accurate communication. This creates trust for the student that their anxieties are really being listened to, heard and understood.

Borman and Borman (1976) suggest some ways to meet group needs like assigning attainable goals and giving feedback to the group as a whole, as if the group is one person, using the techniques discussed earlier. They also suggest identifying personal needs and either meet them or acknowledge the impossibility if this is the case.

Task and Group Maintenance

To maintain harmonious relationships and a good working atmosphere the following functions are important: Gate-keeping (helping others into the discussion or cutting off others), clarification of ideas, evaluating suggestions, diagnosing problems, mediating arguments, and relieving tension (by joking or placing issues in perspective).

The social aspects of group involvement should not be underestimated. Socializing on expeditions can be done informally or at "banquets" (pot luck dinners). These can provide good social occasions. Combined "cook-ins," campfire style activities, songs and stories all give social outlets not directly related to the task. Special events such as swimming at hot springs, or an arranged special meal at the trailhead with plenty of fruit are all tonics for group morale. Maintaining group morale in such ways creates an atmosphere that the task is more likely to be done effectively. If relationships in a group decline, then the task often follows the relationships. Group task functions can be maintained by clarifying ideas, evaluating suggestions and diagnosing problems.

Emotional Issues

Emotional issues include power struggles, fears, wrestling with or questioning one's identity, setting and meeting goals, personal and group needs, and intimacy. For example, someone withdrawing emotionally affects the group. Dependency, fighting and dominance issues can affect relationships and communication. Such issues need to be confronted openly in front of the whole group, or privately on an individual basis. Explain that strong feelings and anger are acceptable but teach students how to use "I" statements, keep their words congruent with feelings, and talk directly about issues rather than general terms. An example of a specific, issue related "I" statement might be, "I feel frustrated when you don't help me cook dinner" vs. "You are a jerk and never contribute."

Cohesion Building

Borman and Borman (1976) suggest sharing stories as this promotes connectedness. As an expedition progresses stories will develop. Doing something exciting early in the trip, like a rappel, can jump-start the bonding process. Develop cohesiveness also by:
   a. Identify we and our, rather than they or I wherever possible.
   b. Build a tradition through 'history', and ceremony.
   c. Stress teamwork.
   d. Get the group to recognize good work and give praise for it. Give praise for students meeting group norms.
   e. Give rewards such as fruit or chocolate when possible.
   f. Treat the group as people, not as machines. People do have feelings so always make time for people to share these and make it an expectation on expedition style courses rather than have people bury them.
   g. Have an expectation of no backstabbing and model it.

Regarding atmosphere and cohesion, an atmosphere is created in the way a group works. Individuals differ in the kind of atmosphere they like; some prefer congeniality, others prefer conflict or competition. It can change from time to time from work, play, satisfaction and sluggishness to enthusiasm. There can be an air of permissiveness, warmth, or defensiveness. People could be inhibited or spontaneous.

Group Roles

Role functions in a group consist of what it takes to do the job (task) and what it takes to strengthen and maintain the group (relationship). Jane Warters (1960) described both functional and non-functional roles. Johnson and Johnson (1982) suggest that any role that moves the group forward, in either task or relationship, can be regarded as a leadership role. They call this *distributed leadership*. Using the term distributed leadership can encourage everyone to take on the functional roles necessary to keep the group moving forward in a positive way. Warters' suggested the following roles:

Task Roles
1. *Initiating activity*: solutions, new ideas, etc.
2. *Seeking opinions*: looking for an expression of feeling.
3. *Seeking information*: clarification of values, suggestions and ideas.
4. *Giving information*: offering facts, generalizations, relating one's own experience to the group problem.
5. *Giving opinion*: concerns values rather than fact.
6. *Elaborating:* clarifying examples and proposals.
7. *Coordinating*: showing relationships among various ideas or suggestions.
8. *Summarizing*: pulling together elated ideas and related suggestions.
9. *Testing feasibility*: making applications of suggestions to situations, examining practicability of ideas.

Group Building Roles
1. *Encouraging*: being friendly, warm, responsive to others, praising others and their ideas.
2. *Gate keeping*: trying to make it possible for another member to make a contribution to the group.
3. *Standard setting* (and keeping): expressing standards for the group to use in choosing its content or procedures or in evaluating its decisions, reminding the group to avoid decisions that conflict with group standards.
4. *Following*: going along with decisions of the group, thoughtfully accepting ideas of others.
5. *Expressing group feeling*: summarizing what group feeling is sensed to be, describing reactions of the group to ideas.

Both Group-Building and Maintenance
1. *Evaluating:* submitting group decisions or accomplishments to compare with group standards, measuring accomplishments against goals.
2. *Diagnosing*: determining sources of difficulties, appropriate steps to take next, and analyzing the main blocks to progress.
3. *Testing for consensus*: tentatively asking for group opinions in order to find out if the group is reaching consensus.
4. *Mediating*: harmonizing, conciliating differences in points of view, making compromise solutions
5. *Relieving tensions*: draining off negative feelings by joking or pouring oil on troubled waters, putting tense situations in a wider context.

Types of Dysfunctional Behavior
An understanding of this aspect of Waters' group roles is very important as these roles can create a negative communication climate and so should be discouraged.
1. *Being aggressive*: working for status by criticizing or blaming others, showing hostility against the group or some individual, deflating the ego or status of others.
2. *Blocking*: interfering with the progress of the group by going off on a tangent, citing personal experiences unrelated to the problem, arguing too much on a point, rejecting ideas without consideration.
3. *Self-confession*: using the group as a sounding board, expressing personal, non-group oriented feelings or points of view.
4. *Competing*: vying with others to produce the best ideas, talk the most, play the most roles, trying to gain favor with the leader.

5. *Seeking sympathy*: trying to induce other group members to be sympathetic to one's problems or misfortunes, deploring one's own situation or disparaging one's own ideas to gain support.
6. *Special pleading*: introducing or supporting suggestions related to one's own pet concerns or philosophies, lobbying.
7. *Horsing around*: clowning, joking, mimicking, disrupting the work of the group.
8. *Seeking recognition*: attempting to call attention to one's self by loud or excessive talking, extreme ideas, or unusual behavior.
9. *Withdrawing*: acting indifferent or passive, resorting to excessive formality, daydreaming, doodling, whispering to others, wandering from the subject.

Dysfunctional behavior, as described above, could be a symptom that all is not well with the group's ability to satisfy individual needs. However, each person is likely to interpret behavior differently. Content and group conditions must also be considered. For example, there are times when some forms of aggression contribute positively by clearing the air and instilling energy into the group.

Defense Mechanisms in Groups

Defense mechanisms are behaviors motivated by personal need to maintain one's position in the group. Defense mechanisms evade conflict by moving away (flight) or toward (fight) the source of the conflict, according to Paul Thorenson (1972). His categorization of these defenses applies to any group as conflict often arises along with corresponding defenses. Generally, evasive maneuvering should be confronted using effective feedback techniques. Thorenson's categories can be seen below:

Fight Defenses
1. *Competition with the facilitator*: This can be an attempt to build personal ego or avoid dealing with a personal problem. It occurs sometimes for example on "professional" courses that are for instructors already working in the field that try to justify their being on a course themselves.
2. *Cynicism*: This challenges the group's goals through skeptical questioning of genuine behavior.
3. *Interrogation*: Someone giving heavy questioning may be trying to keep the spotlight away from himself/herself.

Flight Defenses
1. *Intellectualization*: This is a way of evading giving anything away personally or emotionally. It is sometimes done in introductions (when lengthy ones are the norm) to avoid any self-disclosure. Self-disclosure done appropriately cultivates trust; intellectualizing can evade giving personal or emotional information. Encouragement of "I" statements should help discourage this.
2. *Generalization*: Impersonal statements about group behavior such as "we think" rather than "I think" means the individual may be speaking for the group without the group's consent.
3. *Projection*: One person's unconscious needs or behaviors projected onto another, he or she attributes to others traits that are unacceptable in him or herself (sometimes something one doesn't like about oneself that can be seen in another).
4. *Rationalization*: This is a substitution of less incriminating reasons to try and justify a decision, feeing, emotion, or statement rather than what is probably the correct one.
5. *Withdrawal:* Members suddenly falling silent are in flight. Individual confrontation followed possibly by group confrontation is necessary to bring such an individual back.

Group Manipulation Defense

1. *Pairing up* is sub-grouping to gain support.
2. *"Red-crossing"* is a defense of a person under fire to try and encourage mutual aid.
3. *Focusing on one issue* enables the group to spend excessive time on a person or issue to keep the action away from where it should be.

Decision Making

Decision-making is sometimes done by the leader and sometimes by the group, depending on the situation. A good leader makes a judgment about the group, the task and the environment before making decisions. Tannenbaum and Schmidt (1973) discuss that leader control conditions differ from group control conditions (See Table 5).

Table 5. Tannebaum and Schmidt's Leader and Group Conditions

LEADER CONTROL CONDITIONS	GROUP CONTROL CONDITIONS
A. Time factor and urgency to prevent an emergency	A. No time pressure
B. Emergency	B. No emergency
C. Individual knowledge – the leader knows what to do, the group doesn't	C. Group knowledge regarding the situation
D. Lack of group skills – lack of understanding of group dynamics with an inability to facilitate	D. Group skills in regard to dynamics with an ability to facilitate group discussions
E. Expectations of leader's role – the group might expect the group to be leader-centered	E. Expectations of the group – if there is not an expectation to take responsibility, followers may find it difficult to take it
F. Legal responsibility	F. Freedom of responsibility

Hersey Blanchard and Johnson (2001) further developed decision-making with their Situational Leadership model that uses task readiness levels to determine followers' optimum level for making the decisions and how much direction they need. This is detailed in the leadership chapter.

When a decision is made by a group, then it is difficult to undo without going through the whole process with the group. Undoing a group decision with a leader-centered decision could destroy trust. In outdoor leadership, a careful balance of decision-making is necessary. Sometimes decisions are best made by the group (such as developing group norms) where ownership is paramount.

The Group Dynamics Questionnaire

The Group Dynamics Questionnaire (GDQ) (Phipps, 1986) was developed for expedition groups and consists of both task and relationship questions. If the students complete the questionnaire, it gives good feedback for the instructor on how each student understands the group. A reward such as a small candy bar is most effective in getting written comments along with stressing that instructors need to know what the problems are if they are going to try and fix them. It also acts as a barometer of group atmosphere and highlights problems that may not be obvious to group leaders. Peers are often aware of undercurrents and if the information is kept confidential, problems can be brought to the surface and dealt with in a diplomatic way. The questionnaire can be administered two or three times during a long expedition course to assist the instructor in assessing the group's stage of development. Without such feedback, the instructor might not realize that some aspect of the group dynamics is deteriorating. The GDQ can alert the instructor to possible problems. The GDQ can be found in the appendix.

Summary

Being aware of the possible negative behaviors in groups and making the group aware of them can enable energy to be spent building a positive atmosphere, eventually pulling the group together into a team. Working through this teaching model should help to bring an awareness of the complex interactions that exist in groups.

References

Borman, E., & Borman N. (1976). *Effective small group communication*, (2nd ed.). Minneapolis, MN: Burgess.

Hersey, P., Blanchard, K. H., & Johnson, D. E. (2001). *Management of organizational behavior: Leading human resources*, (8th ed.). Upper Saddle River, NJ: Prentice-Hall.

Johnson, D. (1981). *Reaching out: Interpersonal effectiveness and self-actualization*, (2nd ed.). Englewood Cliffs, NJ: Prentice Hall.

Johnson, D. W., & Johnson, F. P. (1982). *Joining together: Group theory and group skills* (2nd ed.). Englewood Cliffs, NJ: Prentice-Hall.

Johnson, D. W., & Johnson, F. P. (2000). *Joining together: Group theory and group skills* (7th ed.). Englewood Cliffs, NJ: Prentice-Hall.

Jones, J. E. (1973). A model of group development. In J. E. Jones & J. W. Pfieffer (Eds.), *The Annual Handbook for Group Facilitators.* La Jolla, CA: University Associates.

Kanki, B. (1991). *Performance factors and leadership: Problem-solving, crew coordination and communication.* Paper presented at the National Conference for Outdoor leaders: Public, Commercial, and Non-profit Partnerships in Outdoor Recreation. Crested Butte, CO.

Petzoldt, P. (1984). *The new wilderness handbook.* New York, NY: Norton.

Pfeiffer, W. J., & Jones, J. E. (1972). What to look for in groups. In *The annual handbook for group facilitators.* La Jolla, CA: University Associates.

Phipps, M. L. (1985). Group Dynamics in the outdoors – a model for teaching outdoor leaders. In J.C. Miles & R. Waters (Eds.), *Proceedings of National Conference in Outdoor Recreation at Bozeman, Montana* (171-189). Pocatello, Idaho. Idaho State University Press. Also included in the 2nd. Edition of *High Adventure Outdoor Pursuits.* (Eds.) Meier, Marsh, and Welton. Columbus, Ohio: Publishing Horizons, 1987. Also in *The Wilderness Educator: The Wilderness Education Association Curriculum Guide.* D. Cockrell (Ed.). Merrilville, Indiana: ICS Books Inc.

Phipps, M. L. (1986). The group dynamics questionnaire. In *An assessment of a systematic approach to teaching leadership in expedition settings* (Doctoral dissertation). University of Minnesota, Minneapolis.

Thorenson, P. (1972). Defense mechanisms in groups. In W. Pfeiffer & J. E., Jones (Eds.), *The annual handbook for group facilitators.* La Jolla, CA: University Associates.

Tannenbaum, R., & Schmidt, W. H. (1973). How to choose a leader pattern. *Harvard Business Review*, May/June.

Warters, J. (1960). *Group guidance: Principles and practice.* New York, NY: McGraw Hill.

Chapter 9

Male and Female Differences in Teaching and Learning

Vive la Difference!

The saying goes that men are from Mars and women are from Venus—a galactic metaphor for how different their worlds are. But, Mattoon (1981) references Jung in saying they're not as different as you may think. "It is the logical conclusion of Jung's hypothesis that consciousness (predominantly feminine in women, predominantly masculine in men) must integrate much of the unconscious (predominantly masculine in women, predominantly feminine in men) in order for individuation to proceed" (p. 100). Jung then, suggested that males have a female side to their personality, the anima, and females have a male side, the animus, which resides in the unconscious. When we are instructing, would it be possible to adjust our thinking by bringing forth the attributes we may have hidden (and possibly suppressed) to better suit the needs of each student?

Little research has addressed the gender differences in instructional styles and student needs. Research at the Nantahala Outdoor Center compared female and male instructor effectiveness scores and found that the female instructor effectiveness scores were perceived to be higher than the males (Phipps & Claxton, 1997). Another study completed in Ireland and the U.S. (Clarke & Phipps, 2010), found small instructor effectiveness differences between the male and female instructors. Neill (1997) quoted results found in his ten-year study of Outward Bound saying, "The differences between participants' evaluations of male and female instructors were small. The tendency was, if anything, towards higher ratings for female instructors in the areas of *course value* and *instructor/participant rapport*" (p. 4). Perhaps some studies could be designed to tease out the androgynous traits that would improve all instructors, such as the anima (female) trait mentioned above to improve sensitivity, or animus traits to improve directness where needed. Despite having worked with many female co-instructors, because the author of this book is male it seems sensible to introduce some firsthand perceptions on instruction by some females. Having two daughters, one a whitewater kayaking instructor, and the other who was a participant on an extended expedition course and summer camps, I thought their views and perceptions from the perspective of instructor and student could reveal some gender variations within the field of outdoor instruction.

Following are some narratives on male and female differences regarding instruction and learning by Stephanie and Chelsea Phipps.

Stephanie's Observations as an Instructor

During my time as a whitewater kayaking instructor, I had the incredible opportunity to work with a wide variety of instructors and clients, and the chance to observe many different learning styles and approaches to instructing. My observations and those of my fellow instructors are exactly that, personal observations, experiences, and opinions, and should be taken as such.

Interpersonal Connections

When people sign up for a kayak lesson, they are signing up for an experience. Clients want to acquire the skill through a memorable and enjoyable process. Therefore, the instructor's job is not just the cut-and-dried delivery of facts and concepts; it is creating a connection with the client and delivering an experience. This connection is advantageous in many ways as it not only establishes trust within the relationship, (and a more comfortable learning environment) but it also increases the chances for repeat business from that client or through word of mouth. Because females generally seem to have a more innate ability to tune into people's emotions, connecting on a personal level may come easier and can be more naturally integrated into their instruction routine.

This connection with the client should not be confused with the instructor becoming a "rent-a-friend." Professional distance is essential to maintain the instructor role, separate from the role of friend or therapist. Making a distinction between caring about the client and their skill progression in the field rather than personal life dramas is important to maintaining that professional relationship. As a female instructor, I often engaged in more in-depth conversations with my female clients about their lives or daily happenings outside of our instruction time. These women came to me for instruction on a regular basis and our connection grew off the water; but on the water, instruction time was and must be used for instruction. Nonetheless, I have noted that when clients (men and women) open up about their personal life during the short instruction period, it is often used as a stalling tactic, whether it is because they are tired or uncomfortable with the task at hand. Often it is women that employ this tactic. It is important to continue to build a relationship with the client but also keep the relationship professional, so the client understands what the instructor's job is, and what it is not. This also establishes the precedent that when they are on the water, they will make the best use of their time for instruction.

Not having a connection and treating the lesson as a mere number racked up for the day or the season is detrimental to the instructional program and the psyche of the client. The entire experience can be ruined when the instructor does not attempt to connect with the client in any way. In these cases, the client does not develop feelings of trust or confidence in the instructor and, therefore, is less likely to push himself/herself in the activity. When trust is established, the instruction given holds more value and the client is more willing to be engaged.

The client, their needs, and their experience should remain the instructor's focus from the moment of their arrival to their departure. At the end of our lessons, the instructors would hike with their clients from their stopping point on the river back to the put-in to deposit boats and gear. I worked with a young instructor who would end his lesson and direct his client to walk back and de-gear alone, so he could continue paddling. What a missed opportunity! This walk back is a good time to talk with the client, to recap the lesson, or to establish goals and hopes for the next lesson. The client has paid for an instructor and should have the instructor until the lesson ends and the gear is off their back.

It is important to gauge the client's short and long-term goals before each lesson so the instructor can give them an experience that suits their expectations for themselves. There was an older gentleman who came to our program after a particular experience gave him a new lease on life. He decided to try kayaking as he wanted to cross it off his "bucket list." This gentleman only wanted to "get his feet wet" in the sport. He was not necessarily going to become a world-class kayaker who would compete in a future Olympics, so his lessons were tailored accordingly.

Whenever I received a new client I asked the same basic questions to begin the connection right when they walked in the door: What amount of kayaking experience do you have? What got you into kayaking? What are you looking to do in kayaking? What do you do for a living? These questions allow the instructor to gauge the client's knowledge, motivation, and goals and learn a little bit about the individual. Only one of these four questions do not involve kayaking, but these basic questions initiate a personal connection with the client. It is an excellent way to use time when they are getting geared-up for the lesson. Having this background information enabled me, as the instructor, to give them a lesson that met their expectations for the day, plan more lessons based on their goals, assess any of their pre-existing kayaking skills, and touch a little on their personal life and what they do on a daily basis.

Delivering Feedback

Instructors use an expression when individuals are overloaded with work or having a particularly difficult day: we reference a metaphorical cup each individual fills every day with emotional and mental baggage. This cup can fill up slowly, or quickly if the person is bombarded with new information, critique, or negativity. The cup itself is a concept that can be equated with a person's emotional capacity. When an instructor gives excessive feedback without tuning into the emotional needs of the client, the instructor can over-fill the individual's cup. This can be the breaking point for the client: a point where the individual becomes unreceptive and will not respond to any more instruction. This is detrimental if it happens early in the lesson. Feedback and constructive criticism are good only in prescribed and calculated doses based on the emotional needs of the client in question.

In my experience, my female clients tended to bring the day's stresses with them to the lesson. They came to me with cups that already had something in them. Depending on how their day had gone, it would dictate how much new information or feedback that they were able to take. Although tough days impact us all, I noted that my male clients were able to either empty their cup prior to the lesson or bring a new one. There was a notable separation between the male client's day and the lesson, whereas my female clients carried the weight of their day's cup with them. It is always a balancing act for the instructor to gauge the capacity of the individual and temper feedback accordingly.

Small doses of feedback or critique translate into setting small, achievable goals. People can get very frustrated when learning a new skill, especially when their expectations for themselves don't come to fruition as quickly as they wanted or expected. The client has the arduous task of taking what the instructor has taught them, processing it, and then translating what they just learned into physical movements. This translation, if slow, can be extremely frustrating. Because the individual is mentally aware of what they are supposed to be doing, it is tiresome when their body is not yet capable of complying. Receiving immense amounts of feedback, especially when the client is aware of what is supposed to be happening, further fuels their frustration. I have found there is usually a delay from the individual's initial comprehension of the task at hand to the actual execution. This is due to the counter-intuitive nature of the task, or because they are actively trying to train the body to do something it has never done before. This delay is typically more pronounced when instructing middle-aged or older clients. In our teen and children's camps, the younger generation were much more capable of soaking up all of the new movements. In a single example of a children's camp of thirteen kids ages 10 to 13, all but two of them had mastered whitewater-ready rolls by the end of a single week.

One of my clients stood out to me in particular because of her voiced frustration of the mind-body translation process. She was a great-grandmother in her late 60s and she had a tough time controlling her boat and making it go where she wanted it to go. This is lesson one in the grand scheme of kayaking. But she would go three or four strokes forward and her boat would spin out of her control. I had given her verbal instructions, demonstrated to her, and even guided her paddle in the necessary strokes that would guide her boat and allow her to stay in control. She kept telling me that she knew what she was supposed to do and expressed her frustration in the fact that she just could not do it. After a while, I felt like a broken record, giving her the same feedback and I could sense her increasing frustration. In her second lesson, after still not gaining much headway, she ended early out of pure frustration and physical exhaustion.

This woman taught me the great importance of giving positive feedback. As much as the instructor wants to provide constructive criticism to improve the client's progress in the field, that much 'hard' feedback can and will fill up the client's cup much faster if not tempered by positive reinforcement. There is a balance between the technical and emotional needs of the student. As instructors, we want to focus on the technical aspects of what we are teaching, but the emotional needs of the student can override those technical needs. People pay for lessons for a positive experience and they do not need or want an experience that makes them feel awful. This does not mean one should provide false positive feedback solely to make the student feel good, but one should spotlight when the student does do something correctly, and then provide constructive feedback that supports their accomplishments. Setting small, achievable goals tailored to the individual will help fuel their sense of accomplishment and progress and will enable the instructor to provide deserved positive reinforcement. I have found the use of positive reinforcement is especially important when teaching females.

The male instructors I have worked with to improve my own skills generally took a hardline approach to feedback. They tended to critique in a purely technical manner, emphasizing only what I needed to improve. At times, I truly appreciated this approach, but at other times, I felt my cup filling very quickly. When this happened, it was hard to stay positive about my skills progression. I appreciated the fact that this hardline approach to instruction was aimed at making me a better paddler without 'sugar coating' constructive criticism with positive feedback simply for the sake of providing one with the other.

Each student's ability to receive and take criticism should be assessed by the instructor, and feedback should be issued according to the capacity of the individual. As a female who has both received and given instruction, I know how important that positive feedback can be. I also know that I do not appreciate being coddled. I have been brought up in a male-dominated sport and I do not want my instructors to make allowances based on the perceived needs of my gender. But I also know that, as a female in this testosterone-driven environment, I may need a little more encouragement than my male counterparts. Getting that positive feedback gives me a confidence lift that puts me back on the same playing field as my male friends. Female students often achieve a sense of self-encouragement when they feel like they did something correct and accomplished a goal. For the instructor, half of the lesson is teaching, and the other half is instilling confidence and a love for what is being taught. A spoonful of sugar really *can* make the medicine go down.

Supportive Environment

Learning is always done best in a comfortable environment. A student of mine introduced me to her all female paddling group. This group was formed so that intermediate female paddlers could kayak together in a supportive setting and without the "machismo" attitude common to many male paddlers. None of them had much formal instruction but wanted to progress further in the sport. After discussing it, we formalized a women's clinic through the kayak department, so they could still paddle with each other in a comfortable environment, but with guidance and instruction. This clinic thrived, and attendance grew throughout the summer.

By the end of the season, I was surprised at the amount of growth shown by each woman in the clinic. They enjoyed paddling and as their confidence grew, so did their skill level. They had great personal relationships with one another, and by the end of the season we were swapping family stories and updates while we geared up for our session. We all established good interpersonal connections both on and off the water, which provided a comforting and friendly learning environment. It also remained females paddling with other females. The women were supportive of each other's mistakes and accomplishments and were never in competition with one another. Ego was essentially subtracted from the learning environment.

I grew up kayaking with a group of older men who called themselves the 'Ibuprofen Gang' thanks to their pain killer needs after a day of paddling. These men had grown past the age of machismo and had created a very similarly supportive environment for me to learn and grow as a paddler. On the ride to the river, they always asked me about school and knew a little about what was going on in my life. On the river they celebrated my successes and also provided suggestions for improvements in a supportive manner. Occasionally the adolescent-like male behavior would pop out, but it was only on rare occasions when we would hear, "Hey guys, watch this!" from one of the "gang".

This notion of showing off to impress others or encourage them to do the same puts ego into the environment. Ego can trivialize the accomplishments of the lesser-skilled paddlers and turn the focus away from the teaching process toward the exhibitionist. It has always been a pet peeve of mine when the instructor wants to show off their most complex tricks. These antics only intimidate their clients and steal focus from the student and their progression. It is not conducive to the learning process for the instructor to demonstrate his/her prowess and it is extremely off-putting to the client as they are still trying to master the most basic of concepts, thereby belittling what accomplishments the student has made.

During my women's clinics, I was very aware that these women were paddling together long before I arrived and so my presence provided a new dynamic. I cautiously provided feedback so I was not a stressful or imposing presence. Initially, I gave feedback sparsely until we strengthened our interpersonal connections and each of them started actively seeking feedback. I began slowly pushing these women outside of their comfort zones and saw them begin to push themselves. A supportive environment is one that promotes growth but feeling *too* comfortable in an environment doesn't promote growth and learning. These women came to me because they wanted to grow as paddlers and therefore it became my job to push them beyond what they were initially comfortable doing to widen their comfort zone and increase their abilities. All of my biggest personal accomplishments came during times where I felt outside of my immediate comfort zone and I was pushed to go beyond what I thought I would be capable of doing.

Comfort Zone – Pushing the Boundaries

Males are generally driven by ego and challenge. They feed off one another and have more testosterone, which seems to fuel this competitive nature. Being a spectator at a particular river feature can be extremely entertaining due to the male driven competition that will undoubtedly ensue. If, in an effort to outdo one another (or even themselves), someone gets thrashed by the feature, it is supported for what it was, a brilliant failure.

I have found that females, on the other hand, are driven by the desire to feel confident and gain mastery over new skills. Females typically err on the side of playing it safe. We can be hesitant to practice and push ourselves further as we don't want to make a mistake. This approach, at times, can hold us back. Whereas males will throw themselves into a river feature, regardless of what the consequences may be, females will take the more analytical approach in an effort to get it right the first time. Females tend to not take as many risks, even though taking those risks and making mistakes can help the learning process. Going into the feature and getting whipped around a bit can actually be beneficial as it is experiential learning in its purest form.

The female trait to "over-think" or "over-analyze," and let the possible consequences of messing up prevent experimentation and practice, can hinder our development and get in the way of our growth. Learning through the experience of messing up can strengthen confidence through the knowledge that it will not only teach us what not to do but what to do when a future mess up occurs.

Women can also be held back by their own perception of themselves. In my experience, females have a skill level that is generally above that of our confidence level. In this case, kayaking becomes a head game. One of my clients, a mother who was a Class IV boater before she had two children, panicked at the thought of running simple Class II drops. She may not have lost her skills or abilities she once had, but her confidence in those abilities had diminished.

As a female instructor in a 'man's world,' I have had occasional moments in some of my lessons where I feel I would have more respect or authority had I been a six-foot tall man. But then again, I would wager that some male instructors have had similar moments where they may have thought that it would be easier for them if they were more muscular, taller, or were Chuck Norris. As it stands, I am a below average sized, young, female, but I have never once felt inadequate in my skills or my ability to do my job. I have gotten occasional comments that I didn't appreciate, such as one from an ex-power lifter that I was teaching how to roll: "I am still getting used to getting instruction from a female." He may have just been trying to be honest with me but was nonetheless grateful for my instruction. In the end, those that judge on petty things such as gender, height, or eye-color will see past their initial judgment when they realize how much their instructor has to offer them. They may try to ignore the instruction or belittle it, but after they do it their way and get pummeled in a hole or two, they are almost always ready to come back and receive instruction.

I enjoy teaching and have been lucky to have so many repeat clients. I love to see the progress in my students' skills and have enjoyed each lesson as a new challenge and a new opportunity to pass on something that I enjoy doing every day. I enjoy paddling with both my male and female friends. I have learned to appreciate the female approach as being only *different* to the male approach to paddling and instructing; neither is more correct than the other.

Chelsea's Observations as a Student

Because my father is an outdoor instructor, my sister and I were put in boats before we learned multiplication, were put on skis as toddlers, and were rock climbing before we lost our baby teeth. Because we had no brothers or other immediate male family members other than our father, we more easily avoided facing gender discrimination in our family while growing up. Because there was no male to compete with we were unaware that males were more apt to do these types of sports. We grew up competing only amongst ourselves: two physically capable girls. My sister has always been strong and athletic, so right from the start my perception has been that females were highly competent, and I never really felt the need to compare myself or other women to males in my early years.

My introduction to the gender divide in sports didn't really come until high school. There, I learned, certain sports were for boys and others were for girls, and wherever the sports overlapped for both genders, they were still never played co-ed. The strong, male football player and the pretty, female cheerleader archetypal roles were reinforced in the social structure of my rural, small high school. But these sports were ball sports and team sports, and they seemed to fit in a separate category from the lifetime and much more gender non-specific outdoor activities I'd grown up doing with my parents. Because the separate sports for both genders were more clearly demarcated in high school, the differences in how instructions were given to males and females were easier to detect. For a couple of my years playing women's varsity soccer, I had coaches that coached both the men's and women's varsity soccer teams. Having watched and/or participated in practices for both the men's and women's teams, it was clear that the coaches employed different tactics for handling the different teams, for inspiring and motivating us, and for using discipline. I also noticed that the diverging methods for instructing did seem to be more effective for the respective genders for which they were intended. The girls on my team responded more to positive reinforcement such as cheering, positive speeches, compliments on our successes, and promises of rewards if we achieved goals. The men's team seemed to respond more to negative reinforcement such as threats of punishment, the use of discipline, or stroking their competitive natures with suggestions that what they were doing wasn't good enough yet or that their competitor might be able to beat them. When players were criticized by the coaches, the females seemed to take the criticism, internalize it and begin believing it, and then feel down on themselves as well, whereas the males would immediately set out to prove that the criticism was wrong and would talk themselves up to prove that they were better than the critique suggested. These contrasting reactions meant that the coaches approached criticisms differently per gender to achieve their intended goal; motivating the team to improve by emphasizing the positive with females, and the negative with males.

Of course, there were always exceptions among the girls on all of the sports teams on which I participated. One example was a girl on my cheerleading squad who seemed to respond only when our coach berated her constantly. At first, I worried our coach was being too harsh, but when she came into her own and improved to be one of the best performers on the squad, seemingly as a result of the harsher tactics, I realized this was what this particular girl needed from a coach to motivate her. However, despite seeing exceptions to my theories about gender differences in instructional needs, I noticed similar dynamics between instructors and students on my extended expedition course. I saw how overlooking general gender differences could hinder instruction.

It would be easy to assume that female instructors use teaching methods more adapted to female students, and male instructors use teaching methods more adapted to male students. I had four instructors on my Alaska course: three males and one female. The female and one of the males seemed to fit this assumption, but the other two males did not. The experience with them led me to believe that the teaching styles had more to do with the personality types and the leadership styles of the instructors, and less to do with their gender.

It is not advisable to make assumptions about learning style based on gender, which is a fluid construct in itself. But practicing outdoor leadership is the absolute ideal environment for using situational leadership. Every person and group should be treated based on the various combinations of personalities and leadership styles. That is not to say that gender should be ignored as a factor, it simply means that it will not mean the same thing for everyone. Gender roles often come into play, especially in groups that are very isolated, such as they are in the wilderness, but there are no rigid rules for those roles. Assuming that any one individual ought to fit into them could cause issues and unnecessary conflict.

Instructional Styles on an Extended Expedition Course

There was never a question about who was in charge on my course. The power dynamic between the four, and then eventually three instructors for the backpacking section, was so natural and down to a science that I was shocked when I learned it was the first time they had all met each other. John, Fiona, and Pete all recognized and respected that Steve's experience and prestige within the expedition agency's community afforded him a higher place of leadership among them. I perceived him as the head instructor, but for the rest of the instructors, there was a much more egalitarian order in place. Not a single person doubted Fiona's ability to perform the skills we were learning or her ability to lead us to where we needed to go. No one thought of her as less than the other instructors in any sense. In fact, our initial impression of her was more of what a "badass" she was. Learning that this woman who had no qualms about urinating out of a kayak and who normally sported a shaved head (although not on this course) attended two Ivy League universities made us more in awe of her. There was no question Fiona handled the less than pretty and less than comfortable aspects of the wilderness lifestyle with just as much ease as the males. In fact, probably with more ease because it was Pete, not her, who brought a beauty magazine on the sea-kayaking section as his one indulgence. It was also Fiona who donned the wet suit and stood in glacial waters to help us learn a kayak roll. The group members generally perceived her as a woman with strong beliefs who was passionate and completely willing to go against accepted norms.

Despite all of this, Fiona was not necessarily the most well-liked instructor on the trip. In our feedback session at the end of the course, many people brought up concerns about her not making enough effort to converse with everyone. I know one person spent the whole trip thinking she hated him. I, however, liked Fiona precisely because I appreciated how quiet she was. I know some members of the trip thought this was a flaw in her ability to instruct, but I disagreed. I thought that her being a more quiet, reserved person just meant she was better able to connect with and relate to those with similar personalities. This opinion was affirmed by one of the older students on the course when she expressed how much of a help it was for her to have Fiona to go to because their personalities were much more similar.

The opinions of the group members were closely correlated to their leadership style, which seemed to me to be a more significant factor in determining the relationship between the instructor and the student. My issues with Steve were completely nonexistent with John, which I believe, is entirely because of how his instructing style matched with my learning style. Fiona was a necessary and integral part of the instructor team because her consultative style complemented Steve's directive style quite nicely. For people who needed more support and positive reinforcement (myself included), having Fiona there provided a helpful buffer.

Although Steve's style was very different than my own, I can look back on my course and attribute many positive learning experiences to Steve—some of my most valuable lessons, in fact. Despite this, during the backpacking section in the second half of the course, I made a conscious and concerted effort to place myself in Fiona's hiking group every time. I found that I was significantly more comfortable with her not only because I felt as though she understood my leadership style much better than Steve did and would therefore be less critical, but because I genuinely feared Steve's judgment of me. At that point in the course, it was all I could do to make it to the next day. By then, physical, mental and emotional exhaustion were wearing me down. While around Steve, I found myself constantly on my guard. With Fiona, I feared failure less and felt more confident to step up into leadership positions. Conversely, I had to meditate and give myself a pep talk full of positive reinforcement before each of my meetings with Steve. At first, I thought having Steve assigned as my personal advisor was a cruel twist of fate, but ultimately it did bring with it a considerable amount of valuable lessons that led to vast personal growth. However, knowing I could trust in Fiona always being there if I needed her helped me attain that growth rather than just beat myself down.

Another female student in the group would have had a much less valuable or enjoyable experience if it hadn't been for having Fiona as her personal advisor. They came to an agreement that Fiona would never tell her what her grade was after the first report had such a negative impact on her. That student had more trouble reconciling her relationship with Steve into a positive light. His emphasis on criticism affected her greatly in a very negative way. Fiona admitted to that student that her grade reflected Steve's view more than any of the other instructors and was unable to explain to her why she'd earned it. It was after that instance they made the pact to never talk about grades again. Steve, on the other hand, loved to talk about grades. His assertion during our first meeting that I would not make above a C in the course if I did not learn to tie knots was the only thing in that whole trip filled with some of the most challenging experiences of my life that made me very emotional. The issue of grades completely changed the entire course dynamic for all of us. For me, it nearly ruined it, but instead I finished the course with a healthier outlook on grades, pleasing others, and having too much drive for perfection.

Two events on the trip were the most formative for me, and Fiona was present for both. I was unable to please Steve while doing the preliminary practice exercises in the water for learning a kayak roll in a sea kayak. I did not achieve the just-for-pretend 'certificate of achievement' he offered for doing well in the activity. I left the water intensely frustrated. As I have indicated with respect to my high school's soccer teams, my experience with males has taught me that this sort of strategy will usually drive males to prove themselves and can achieve the desired positive results. I, however, felt completely dejected. I came very close to not going back in the water for fear of failure. I was taking the negative feedback and agreeing with it, then putting myself down even further until I almost lost all my confidence.

However, I did go back into the water. Fiona stood next to my kayak to help me flip it over. I told her I'd done it before (I'd never done one in a sea kayak, but I'd been doing rolls in river kayaks for years) but I said I did not expect to be able to do it. She asked me if I wanted to do the preparatory roll, where she would essentially do the paddle part for me, or if I wanted to just go for it. I said I just wanted to go for it. I remember completely clearing my head. My focus was entirely on the task at hand. I knew I had to raise my arm higher than if I was rolling in a river kayak, and that my knee jerk had to be significantly harder to flip the much larger and heavier sea-kayak. I managed to achieve an odd state of mental clarity that allowed me to ignore the frigid iciness of the water as I was plunged into it with the flip of my kayak. I told myself to lift my arms high and then my muscle memory did the rest. All of a sudden, I was seated right side up in my kayak, dripping with freezing water. It shocked everyone. I managed to be the first, and one of only two students, who achieved a kayak roll on the course. I believe it was because Fiona was there, and not Steve, that I was able to do this. If Steve had been there, I would not have been able to get the focus that it took to do it. I would have been so concerned with doing all the things he wanted me to do that I would have most likely been overwhelmed. His comments and lack of surprise at my failure would surely have discouraged me from ever getting the roll on our course. This is especially because physical skills have always taken me longer to learn, so conditions generally have to be ideal for me to achieve significant progress.

At one point in the course we did an activity where individual group members placed the rest of the group members on a leadership spectrum from consultative (input is heavily sought from followers) to directive (authoritarian). We represented the spectrum by standing in a line in the place that corresponded to our leadership style on the spectrum. It was no surprise that Steve was placed on the furthermost "directive" end with Nick, a super-masculine and testosterone-driven young male, right next to him. I was surprised, however, when I was placed on the opposite end on the consultative side, also on the outside. Thanks to being called "bossy" so frequently growing up, I had always seen myself as a directive leader, and was not expecting the group perception of my leadership style to be quite so different from my own perception. The activity was enlightening because, as my father always says, it is perceptions and not intentions that matter for effective use of leadership styles.

I think Steve was miffed to be placed so far on one end of the scale. In our lesson about leadership styles we learned that one style is not inherently better than another but, especially because outdoor leadership is inherently situational, there are times where one style is better used over the other. Directive leadership, for example, is better for emergencies, situations where a decision needs to be made quickly because there is time pressure, where someone's safety is jeopardized, or when the group cannot make a decision. Consultative leadership is better employed when the leader wants the group to feel invested and involved in a decision. Another example is when the leader needs the advice and knowledge of the group members. Overusing one leadership style or the other tends not to have the best effect. One comes off as dictatorial, or perhaps on the other end, maybe too weak. The better leader has a dynamic style that fits each situation as needed. For Steve to be placed so far on one end of the spectrum could be perceived as an indication that he lacked that flexibility. It was easy to conclude in that moment (with both me and the most feminine student on the course on the consultative end, and the very masculine Nick and Steve on the directive end), that perhaps there might be a correlation between gender and leadership style. However, John and Pete, our two other male instructors, were both perfect examples of masculine men who broke the stereotype by having more moderate leadership styles that did not put them firmly in the directive or consultative camp.

My interaction with an instructor whose leadership style differed so dramatically from my own was ultimately worth way more than my temporary discomfort. Being out of my comfort zone was the reason I achieved growth in my leadership abilities. However, I do believe those achievements were only possible because the instructors complemented each other and served different roles when I needed different types of support.

Gender-Related Issues on the Expedition Course

Discussions about feminine hygiene and dealing with menstruation while living in the outdoors ought to be, and generally are led by the female instructor(s). There are concerns and details that only someone with the same body machinery would be able to understand and address. There is also the awkwardness factor of having to go to a male about feminine issues, especially for younger students. Nevertheless, Steve led the talk about menstruating on the course prior to our departure. Fiona was present, but it was Steve who described the procedures and precautions that we needed to take. At the time, as a girl fresh out of high school, I found this discussion quite awkward. There is something to be said, though, for just jumping into the deep end and getting completely comfortable with everyone in the group about all issues. However, if I had ended up having any problems, I would have found it much more difficult to go to Steve than Fiona. It is extremely important to have instructors of all genders, leadership styles, and backgrounds because there will be students of all categories that will need instructors they can connect to on many different levels.

Because different students have different needs, it bears noting that being gender blind in making instructor placement choices could be harmful to the group. My experiences as a female outdoor student with a sister and father who are outdoor instructors have taught me that genders cannot be put into boxes or neat categories, that favored leadership styles vary based more on personality more than gender, and that there is no gender that makes an inherently better outdoor instructor. However, one cannot deny that genders do exist in society, and they also matter and have some differences. Gender equality in leadership is important, but not at the expense of recognizing the different contexts and needs. All genders are equally valuable, but not the same.

Summary

It seems that gender issues cannot be neatly packaged but can have large impacts on leadership, teaching and learning. Using the opposite positive gender traits that exist in us all could be very helpful. Gender issues in outdoor instruction are a fertile area for further study.

References

Clarke, G., & Phipps, M. L. (2010). *An investigation into technical and soft skills instruction using an importance-performance analysis*. Unpublished study. Western Carolina University, Cullowhee, NC.

Mattoon, M., A. (1981). *Jungian psychology in perspective*. New York, NY: Free Press.

Neill, J., T. (1997). *Gender: How does it affect the outdoor experience.* Paper presented at the National Outdoor Education Conference, Sydney, Australia. Retrieved from http://wilderdom.com/abstracts/Neill1997GenderEffectOutdoorEducation.htm

Phipps, M. L., & Claxton, D. B. (1997). An investigation into instructor effectiveness. *The Journal of Experiential Education, 20*(1), 40-46.

Chapter 10

Evaluation and Outcomes Assessment

"Do we really have to do this?"

- Many people

Formative and Summative Assessment

When evaluating students, an instructor usually uses two types of assessment, formative and summative. *Formative assessment* is used during a lesson when you as the instructor may be checking students' performance and giving them feedback on how they are doing and how they can improve while, at the same time, giving support as in Joplin's (1981) five stage model discussed earlier. It may be simple. Gilbertson, Bates, McLaughlin and Ewert (2006) give an example of formative feedback to a student in compass lesson.

> You're doing a good job working with the map to figure out your next bearing. You're lining up your bearing on your compass with great accuracy. Now pay attention to shooting a bearing or looking ahead directly along your bearing to choose a path to walk. (p. 97)

It may be more complex such as using the whole part whole method where you first demonstrate a kayak roll, then break it down into stages as described earlier under *scaffolding. Summative assessment* is done at the end of a lesson or course. One example is the written objective test at the end of a Wilderness First Responder Course. It could be a skills test like setting up a z-drag for a swift water rescue course or performing a skiing ability test as a prospective ski-patroller.

Rubrics

Rubrics, which give clear expectations of what is required, can be used to help students understand how they are being assessed. The Wilderness Education Association (WEA) has very detailed and clear rubrics to aid in student assessments on their certification courses. Students are assessed on a variety of curriculum elements, some of which may seem vague without further detail. The rubrics explain exactly what is being checked. Figure 24 illustrates a rubric for the health and sanitation section of the WEA Certification Curriculum.

Figure 24. WEA Rubric for Health and Sanitation

Rating scale
 NA= Not applicable or not enough information to make a judgment
1= Needs work or inappropriate for situation – is not certifiable at this time
2= Slightly below average for situation – although not certifiable, performance is appropriates for this course
3= Average – certifiable although still needs work
4= Above average - certifiable, demonstrated above average expertise
5= Exemplary – at the level expected for WEA instructors

	Comments
Maintains personal hygiene care practices 1 2 3 4 5	
Bathes and washes regularly 1 2 3 4 5	
Sterilizes eating utensils 1 2 3 4 5	
Uses proper water treatment 1 2 3 4 5	

Reprinted from *The WEA Affiliate Handbook* 7th Ed., (p.53) by D. Berman & C. Teeters, Bloomington IN: The Wilderness Education Association. Copyright, 2006, by The Wilderness Education Association.

Evaluation and Outcomes Assessment

Evaluation can serve a greater purpose than assessing the difficulty of a particular activity or how a project, lesson, or skill may be going. As the instructor, how can you know if the students are learning what you are teaching? How do you know whether your teaching was effective? First, establish the expected outcomes that relate to the goals of the course. These goals can be broken down into more specific program objectives, and even further to performance objectives. To what extent you do this depends on your agency's demands and how fully you are expected to document what you are doing. If you are a volunteer teaching a recreational Boy Scout canoeing session, detailed documentation is probably not expected. If you are working for a public agency or university and you wish to show that you are achieving certain goals, then a complex outcomes assessment program will often be required. Years ago, I worked for an outdoor center where we did fell walking, kayaking, caving, climbing, camping and youth hosteling. It was accepted that these activities were good for youngsters, but it was never clear what we were specifically trying to achieve. We informally talked about it and generally we thought we were about "realization of self and others". Without asking the questions and setting goals and objectives, how could we have known what effects we were having on participants' inner selves or their relationships with others? We knew that we were loosely based on the Outward Bound idea. We saw youngsters cry because they didn't want to leave on the last day, which said a lot about the relationships that they had made. However, we never measured anything, so we couldn't say anything beyond, "They looked like they enjoyed the experience".

Could we have made the experience even better? We didn't know. We didn't evaluate what worked for them and what didn't. What if we had analyzed the specifics of what the center was trying to achieve? It probably was about self-realization and realization of others, so we could have evaluated aspects of self-concept, self-efficacy, self-confidence etc. We could have looked at the group dynamics and how to improve the experience by teaching students about group norms, conflict styles, conflict management, group maintenance, group roles, distributed leadership etc. Once you have decided on specific outcomes, then you have to come up with a way to measure them and of course how to modify the course to make sure that you do actually meet the outcomes. So if you say that you want the students to improve their interpersonal skills, then you would develop effective ways to teach group skills rather than just hope that it happens. Some courses had more specific agendas, such as the British Canoe Union courses or the Mountain Leadership courses that had specific curriculums where you knew that you were supposed to be teaching specific skills like certain strokes and maneuvers in canoeing or navigation techniques for mountaineering.

If you are publicly funded, and especially in hard economic times when funding is very competitive, it would be expected that you could show to what extent you are achieving your stated goals. If you were to apply for a grant to run a program there would be an expectation that you have specific goals, objectives and a way to measure outcomes in some kind of evaluation. If you are expecting students to learn something, then you need to have some way of establishing that they did learn it. This sounds very mechanistic and to be honest it is. Sellick (2006) posted some remarks that could resonate with many of us.

> I recently received advice on some educational material that I had submitted that instructed me to preface each session with statements that defined learning outcomes by using the words: "At the end of the session, you will be able to....". I had at last been confronted by outcomes-based education and I must say it did not warm the cockles of my heart.... If we know what the student is expected to learn then we can assess it.... This seems all very rational except that it subverts the very essence of what education is because it is predicated on the requirements of assessment and not on the enlightening power of the material to be studied. Our focus on education has been taken over by the bean counters who want accountability at all costs and by fixing definite outcomes we think that we can control the educational process, just like we control productive processes in a factory. (p.1)

If we had instigated full blown outcomes assessment at my old center would that have stifled us as instructors? Would my experience as a youngster when being taught by Joe Brown at Whitehall Outdoor Center[8] have been better? At the time I couldn't perceive that the experience could have been better, but then I didn't know what I didn't know. Nicol (2002) quoted Lyn Noble, Whitehall's one-time principal "...at the outset Whitehall was primarily concerned with outdoor pursuits. The belief in their intrinsic value went virtually unquestioned...personal development was bound to happen!" (Hopkins & Putnam, 1993, p.36). I do have a feeling that although I relate somewhat to Sellick's comments, in general -- experiences can be improved with good outcomes assessment.

A good outcomes assessment plan would be one that is planned from the bottom up, one that is worked out with the instructors and not something that is imposed. It would be used for improving programs and teaching, and not as a supervisory technique that could lead people to fear for their jobs. We have to determine to what extent outcomes assessment is necessary. An informal, evening kayak rolling session may need nothing more than participants successfully rolling their kayaks. A university, outdoor kayak course may include more specifics relating to comfort level in the boats and wet exit abilities, as well as rolling. A national body certification, like the American Canoe Association, the Australian Canoe Federation or the British Canoe Union, would have very specific expected outcomes and measures for these outcomes. You may be just taking some youngsters for a hike from Camp Merriewoode to the top of 'Old Bald' next to the camp that doesn't need an outcome assessment, but perhaps feedback from the campers about the whole camp experience would pinpoint something that may need some modification. Camper satisfaction is also measured in terms of returning campers. You know Camp Merriewoode is doing something right when they are full for the following year by the end of September when their last course is in August. You do have to consider being a bean counter though. If the county, federal grant, education authority, board of trustees or whatever supervisory body wants some measurements, then you probably need to go the 'whole hog'. You may need to look at the other side of Sellicks' coin and do it anyway.

---

[8] Whitehall is the Derbyshire Education Outdoor Center in the UK. Joe Brown at the time was regarded as the premier rock climber in the UK.

Another example of blind acceptance was given by Ken Ogilvie, who was the warden of the Ghyll Head Outdoor Education Center in the UK. He talked about planning where, "The assumptions we began with were not articulated at that time" (Ogilvie, 1985, p. 37). However, they used a questionnaire to find out why students were going to Ghyll Head and what they had or had not enjoyed. They found some de-motivating factors among the students but decided rather than "bash on" regardless using "steamroller" tactics, they decided to change radically. The social effects that they thought they were achieving were left too much to chance and were "purely incidental". They questioned whether just doing the activities developed maturity or whether there was any transfer of learning. Having looked at the perceptions of the students, the staff and students consulted to produce a radically changed course that still focused on personal and social development. They changed the format to allow the students choice in activities, decision-making and input into group conflict and problem solving. Checking the assumptions and outcomes at this center totally changed the instruction from being instructor centered, to student and group centered.

Discussing the details of constructing a full-blown outcomes assessment plan is beyond the purview of this book, which is focused at the instructor rather than the administrator level. The administrator establishes the broad, organization and program learning goals. The instructor is then more involved with specific course goals, broken down into course objectives and performance objectives, but always look at the organization's purpose and values and ask yourself why you are really doing a program. Some examples follow for a youth at risk program, a university outings program and a skills course.

Example Goals and Objectives for Different Programs

Program Goals and Objectives
An example for a canoe trip for a youth at risk program could look like this:

The Program Goal
The program will enable the re-habilitation of some youth at risk.

(What you are doing -- in a general statement).

The Program Objective
The program will enable an increase in self-concept and communication skills through a canoe trip on the St. Croix River.

(How you will achieve the goal).

Performance Objectives
1. *The participants* will increase their self-concept by satisfactorily completing a challenging canoe trip of 70 miles on the St Croix River. Measurement will be through a pre and post-test of the *Tennessee Self Concept Scale.*
2. *The participants* will increase their ability to communicate positively by taking part in elements of the Group Dynamics Teaching Model[9] before and throughout the duration of the trip. Measurement will be through completion of the Group Dynamics Questionnaire -- which will be administered twice, once after two days, then again at the end of the trip.

(How you will enable the program objectives and how you will measure them).

An example of a university student activities trip could look like this:

The Program Goal
The Program will provide enjoyment for students at Western Carolina University.
The Program Objective
The Program will provide enjoyment through a friendly hike in Panthertown Valley.

---

[9] See the Group Dynamics Chapter

Performance Objectives
1. *The participants* will complete an ice-breaker at the beginning of the trip and know everyone's names and interests. Measurement will be through observation.
2. *The participants* will enjoy a 4-mile hike via Schoolhouse Falls and Little Green Mountain that will take approximately six hours. Measurement will be through observation and a questionnaire that will be given at the end of the trip.

An example of a skills course could look like this:
The Program Goal
The program will enable safer river kayaking.

The Program Objective
The program will teach river safety and basic river techniques through a two-day workshop on Cedar Cliff Lake and the Tuckaseigee River.

Performance Objectives
1. *The participants* will understand safety about clothing and equipment on this two-day workshop. Measurement will be through observation and a post-test (quiz).
2. *The participants* will understand stretching concepts and perform effective stretching prior to entering the water. Measurement will be through observation.
3. *Participants* will correctly demonstrate basic kayak strokes, including paddling forward, backward, sideways and turns on the first day on the lake followed by a small slalom course to integrate all the strokes. Measurement will be by observation and successful completion of the slalom course.
4. *The participants* will correctly demonstrate wet exits and safe swimming techniques on the lake prior to the river, then again on the river. Measurement will be through observation.
5. *The participants* will correctly demonstrate being pulled in from a swim with a rope on the river. Measurement will be through observation.
6. *The participants* will demonstrate to the best of their ability, the river techniques of ferries, eddy turns and peel-outs, while completing the five-mile stretch of the river. Measurement will be through video and observation.

The number of performance objectives depends on the program. The above examples show how a skills course may have more. The performance objectives, according to Edginton and Hayes (1976), should include a verb about the behavior, the method of performance, factors and conditions, and how it will be measured. A canoe example is shown in Figure 25.

Figure 25. Writing Performance Objectives

Step 1 - State the performance objective using a verb:
　　"The participant *will demonstrate* proficiency in canoeing…"

Step 2 – State the *method* of performance: " by completing a slalom course…"

Step 3 – State *factors* or *conditions*: "of 100 meters and 20 gates…"

Step 4 – Indicate in each performance objective how it will be be *measured:* "covering the course in under 200 seconds."

The participant will demonstrate proficiency in canoeing by completing a slalom course of 100 meters in length, with 20 gates covering the course in under 200 seconds.

The performance objectives should include how they are to be measured. This could be a standardized test that can be obtained from an expert in the field or bought from professional companies.

Some of these tests may require qualifications like a master's degree or doctorate for administering purposes; for example, psychological outcomes for wilderness therapy programs. Questionnaires can be constructed or modified. It is always worth checking if one has already been used before, and often it is possible to get permission to use one without having to pay fees. Poorly constructed questionnaires give poor results that may not be valid or reliable. University professors are a good resource for providing or constructing such questionnaires.

There are other forms of evaluation like a *sociogram* (a technique to look at the social issue of who likes to be with whom) where a question is asked; for example, which students would want to share a tent? Then the data can be shown on a scatter plot - which can reveal information about relationships in the group. Student journals can be used for formative assessment where instructors can be reading them during the course to find out what students are thinking about regarding judgment or decision-making, or they can be used for summative assessment to see if by the end of the course the students thought processes reflect that they have learned how to apply leadership decisions or teaching skills if they are on a teacher education course. Observation can be used, but judgment needs to be made as to whether this should be done in a scientific manner or just 'eyeballed'. This situation, just looking with a generic feeling about a situation is very different to someone with a clipboard looking for specific behaviors.

Collecting quantitative data is useful but limited unless qualitative data in the form of comments are included. You may find out that 60% of participants were dissatisfied but not know why without the comments. Rating scales are useful to better gauge satisfaction levels, along with some yes/no questions. Video can be used for skiing and kayak racing. There is nearly always a way to measure outcomes, but you may need to consult with some experts in the activity, and in measurement and evaluation to ensure that the data you collect is as valid as possible.

Edginton, Compton, and Hanson (1980) maintain that, "An organization can benefit from the use of performance objectives in terms of its accountability" (p. 94). They make the point that formulating them is very time consuming and their precise nature may affect spontaneity, but overall, they do recommend using performance objectives. You will have to make the judgment to what extent you formulate objectives. You may be asked to use them by a program planner trying to inject more into a program than just the activity. For accountability purposes, an agency may need to show that it is achieving specific outcomes and this may affect funding. If a grant proposal is being written for a program, then it is very important that the program is outcomes based with performance objectives linked to a strong evaluation. A benefactor, like a foundation, would want to know how you intend to find out if what you are doing is really working. This means aligning your methods of delivering a program with your goals, and objectives. Hattie (2009) gives an example of this with Outward Bound. "The program provides challenging and specific goals (e.g., successfully negotiating a 60-foot cliff by abseiling or rappelling) and then structures situations (e.g., adequate preparation, social support, etc.) so that participants share a commitment to reaching those goals" (p. 24).

To what degree are you working toward the benefits and outcomes of your program? The following questions developed by Stiehl and Parker (2007, p. 75) can help to determine this:

1. Do you have clearly developed, publicly stated outcomes that underscore the benefits of adventure?
2. Do your outcomes align with the values and beliefs of your sponsors, advocates, and participants?
3. Are your outcomes appropriate for your participants' needs, interests, and abilities; your resources; and your staff knowledge and skills?
4. Do your activities and policies support your stated outcomes?
5. Do you have functional assessments for your stated outcomes?

6.   Is there ongoing evaluation of the extent to which outcomes are being achieved?

Possible Outcomes

There are many different kinds of outcomes to consider as an outdoor instructor. You may be teaching skill-based courses with various skills mastery outcomes. The outcomes for a youth–at–risk program may be for the students to interact with respect for each other and have an increased self-concept. As a WEA or NOLS type instructor you would likely expect an outcome(s) where the students have applied specific leadership techniques. Ewert (1989) in Figure 26 summarized some potential benefits that can be used as targeted outcomes.

Figure 26. Potential Benefits of Outdoor Adventure Pursuits

Psychological	Sociological	Educational	Physical
Self-concept	Compassion	Outdoor Education	Fitness
Confidence	Group cooperation	Nature awareness	Skills
Self-efficacy	Respect for others	Conservation education	Strength
Sensation seeking	Communication	Problem solving	Coordination
Actualization	Behavior feedback	Value clarification	Catharsis
Well-being	Friendship	Outdoor techniques	Exercise
Personal testing	Belonging	Improved academics	Balance

Reprinted from *Outdoor Adventure Pursuits: Foundations, Models, and Theories*, (p.49), by A. Ewert, 1989, Worthington, Ohio: Publishing Horizons. Copyright, 1989, by Publishing Horizons. Reprinted by permission from A Ewert.

Over 25 years later we may add such things as leadership under *education* and toughness (an original aim of Outward Bound aim was to toughen participants) under *physical*. Beames, Higgins, and Nicol's (2012) idea of educating for sustainability is recommended. Working in the outdoors is an ideal environment to teach what is becoming a heavy reality in necessary changes humans need to make. Neill (2006) added Leadership in a list relating to a meta-analysis of outcomes and includes other things like personality traits (femininity/masculinity, achievement motivation, emotional stability, aggression, assertiveness, locus of control, maturity, neurosis reduction, also 'adventuresome' which includes 'challengeness'. Challenge has been the mainstay of Outward Bound along with character building. The concept of character building, however has been challenged by Brookes (2003). He stated that he believes "Outdoor Adventure Education programs do not build character but may provide situations that elicit certain behaviors" (Brookes, 2003, p.49). However, in North Carolina, the term character building is commonly used and accepted. The Student Citizen Act of 2001 is supported by *The Character Education Informational Handbook and Guide* (2002, p. 2), produced by the State Board of Education that defines character education as:

Character Education is a national movement creating schools that foster ethical, responsible, and caring young people by modeling and teaching good character through an emphasis on universal values that we all share. It is the intentional, proactive effort by schools, districts, and states to instill in their students important core ethical values such as respect for self and others, responsibility, integrity, and self-discipline.

The State Board Handbook (2001) lists the following as character traits to be developed.

1. Courage
2. Good judgment
3. Integrity
4. Kindness
5. Perseverance
6. Respect
7. Responsibility
8. Self-discipline (p.15)

There seems to be some differences in regard to character building. No, we can't change someone's total character overnight and we have to realize that change is incremental for all interventions and education is a lifelong pursuit. A positive outdoor experience adds to the picture, the picture here representing the total character. If we look at specific character traits, then we can target them more easily. The eight traits above are targeted by North Carolina Schools with definite teaching and assessment plans. Toughness could be considered another trait and was mentioned above. More and more time is now spent in front of a screen, be it TV, computer, phone, an iPod, an iPad, or whatever comes next. As a result, perhaps disappearing character traits (as we stay cocooned indoors) are both mental toughness (or resilience) and physical toughness. Adventure education can address this need. It is interesting that the highly prestigious Moorhead-McCain Foundation plan for all their academic scholarship recipients to complete an extended expedition style Outward Bound or NOLS course the summer before they start their studies at UNC Chapel Hill. Besides academics, these students are expected to complete service and research overseas, often in tough travel conditions. Being toughened up could be a good thing for many of us, keeping in mind Dewey's miseducation concept – we don't want to put off anyone to any of the activities that we do by them being too challenging. Besides well-established traits, we can brainstorm other outcomes such as interest in lifelong activities, specific skill acquisition whether it is physical like skiing, caving, kayaking climbing etc., social or mental, such as leadership and personal growth. Perhaps we should really examine what our organization is really all about and then decide if we need to change, establish or modify our goals. Then we can plan our programs to fit our students better to enable those outcomes to be realized.

Measuring Outcomes

Neill (2006) noted that the two main objective ways that have been used to research outdoor education outcomes have been post-program surveys and pre-post testing. A post-program questionnaire usually asks questions about the experience. The problem with this type of survey is validity – is it really measuring what you asked with honesty and integrity, and without bias? Answers may be affected by the mood of the group at the end of the course -- which could be a range from euphoric to depressed. Were the respondents given a Mars Bar to enjoy while completing the survey (chocolate can inflate scores), was it done in a rush, in the van, in the rain or in a more controlled environment? According to Neill, in Australia, where there is less rain, end of course surveys are colloquially known as "happy sheets". The same limitations hold true for participants' self-analysis, for their perceptions on personal growth, etc. When looking at post-program survey data, remember that many potential distortions exist. Carefully constructed questionnaires, that are also carefully administered can, however, give useful information.

The second major approach to measure effectiveness of outdoor education outcomes, pre- and post-testing, has been to gather information before and after a program to ascertain how much change has occurred. This has been used with and without comparison or control groups (Neill, 2006). Both of these methods (survey questionnaires and pre-/post-tests) can use statistics to better reveal information. Post-test scores can be analyzed to check whether goals and objectives are being realized, and they can be compared with past program scores. Pre- and post-test scores can be used to check differences before and after a course. Written comments in addition to rating scale information will illicit valuable information, the 'whys' as well as positive or negative perceptions, both quantitatively and qualitatively.

Kleinfield (1983) separated evaluation into what she called "the high road" – formal scientific evaluation with experimental groups, comparison groups, pre-tests, and multiple measures – and "the low road" – questionnaires asking program participants what they liked and didn't like about program activities, staff, special speakers, session lengths, and so forth" (p. 45). Pinch (2009), made the same case -- suggesting that the 'quick and dirty' survey approach and 'the intuitive' approach (seeing cues from participants) are not what is needed for the challenges ahead, which require a systematic approach. Russell (1982) summarized this idea of being systematic:

> Theoretically the purpose of evaluation is to systematically judge, assess and appraise the entire workings of a program to gain information that indicated whether or not the planner is getting results and the program is going where it was intended to go… One of the most fundamental purposes of evaluating the program is to determine whether or not it is doing what it is intended to do. Is the program achieving its objectives? (p. 284-285)

The evaluation in program planning should relate back to the objectives. This is why the performance objectives have to be written to include how they will be measured.

Taking "the high road" with formal scientific evaluation requires research expertise in the organization. However, some outcomes assessment advocates, such as Marchese (1988), suggested that insisting on only perfect data can prevent anything from being attempted. Though better research quality yields more valid information, it is better in most cases to have some information vs. none. Kleinfield (1983) made the additional point that tailoring the questionnaire, especially for the pre-test could add, rather than steal, time from the experience and we should be finding out what students learned as well as what they liked. She suggested linking the process to Joplin's (1981) Experiential Education Model. This could involve pre-test questions 'pointing the way' in the learning. This, however could affect the scientific integrity by introducing what is called a confounding variable (one that impacts the results but is not a variable under study); in this case frontloading. Data collected at the end of the "action" could be subject to a post-experience variable like euphoria. There are many variables that can affect a research study, before, during, and after which have to be taken into account. Ewert and Sibthorpe (2009) contend that researchers and evaluators "…should make informed decisions about which potential confounding variables to address and which ones to ignore, prior to undertaking a study" (p.12). This kind of expertise may well be beyond the abilities of the instructor, but the instructor may be asked to collect data.

Understanding that scientific research needs be done as accurately as possible can help the process. Research in the social sciences that requires input from people will always have some 'ruggedness' but the tighter the research, the better. Warner (1984) noted that sometimes empirical research projects have been done to establish facts "…which can be used in the battle to attract funds and participants. The logic is: we believe our program is effective and we can prove it, then we will have a strong argument in our efforts to get more support" (p.39). This concern is especially relevant for the agency with grant funding or financial concerns. But, we should be doing outcomes assessment to improve the program and the experience for the participant. Hattie et al (2016), emphatically state "What does matter is teachers having a mind frame in which they see it as their role to evaluate their effect on learning." (p. 269).

Once it starts to be used for other purposes, it can lose its appeal for instructors, who will most likely collect the data. Placing emphasis on the results of only one study for agency survival may not be the best idea. If confounding variables affect the results badly, then things may not look good for the agency.

What are program effects that we can consider measuring? Four areas that we can evaluate according to Russell (1982) are:

 1. *Psychomotor*

> a. Development – body image, skill.
> b. Physiological – strength, endurance, fitness, relief from stress.
> c. Rehabilitative – remediation, therapeutic, prescriptive.

 2. *Psychological*

> a. Behavioral aspects – self-concept, attitudes, personality, human need satisfaction.
> b. Self-actualization
> c. Play and play therapy

 3. *Sociological*

> a. Enhancement of group or community
> b. Collective behavior – small and large groups, leisure norms, belongingness, social behavior, integration.
> c. Increased social organization (reduced disorganization such as delinquency)

4. *Education*

> Usually information learned through a particular course.

Research and Evaluation Tools

Much of the discussion above has centered on the questionnaire, but there are other tools with which one can measure program and instructional outcomes. Figure 27 shows a list suggested by Russell (1982).

Figure 27. Research and Evaluation Tools

- Inventories
- Questionnaires
- Interviews
- Anecdotal records
- Observational methods
- Checklists
- Rating scales
- Case studies
- Standardized tests
- Video
- Self-appraisals

- Reaction papers
- Cumulative records
- Delphi
- Sociometric methods
- Journals

These tools, as suggested by Russell, are explained below in relation to outdoor courses.

Inventories

This is basically a detailed list of all resources related to the course, program or organization. This is the place to start.

Questionnaires

These include sets of carefully worded questions. They should be as valid, reliable and objective as possible. Validity refers to whether the questions measure what they are supposed to. Reliability refers to consistency and dependability (which could be over time) – will it measure the same taken two weeks apart assuming there was no interference in between? If several evaluators agree on the questions and scales, it would remove some bias and be more objective. There are coefficients that, through statistical analysis, illustrate to what extent the questionnaire is valid and reliable. Testing instruments is time consuming so using one that is already tested can save that time. Often questionnaires are only checked for 'face' validity (where it is just assessed at face value) and if this method is being considered, then using experts to do the checking would be advisable. Some questionnaires use open-ended questions for comments or qualitative information, which is less easy to measure but does illicit reasons for ratings. They sometimes use yes/no questions, but often use some kind of Likert Scale to evaluate to what extent respondents may be satisfied, perceive things to be true, etc. There are a lot of assumptions with questionnaire. It is assumed that respondents will complete them honestly and seriously, and that they are competent to fill them out. If the respondents do a questionable job filling them out, then the ruggedness of the research goes up. Confounding variables like weather or the group mood (high spirits or low spirits) affect results as well. Questionnaires should be as accurately worded as possible so make sure that care is taken in devising questions and only the questions you really need along with appropriate rating scales, and if at all possible, kept to one page.

Interviews

Interviews can be structured, unstructured, or a mix of both. A questionnaire would be prepared for a structured interview, whereas open-ended questions allow the interviewee to take the discussion where they want. It could be semi-structured in that the interviewer has some specific questions but is prepared to move into other topics. An advantage of an interview is that misconceptions can be eliminated. Exit interviews at the end of a course can be very useful.

Anecdotal records

These are observations you or other staff or instructors make through a course. Usually instructors make mental notes like, next time arrange for a river release so there is more water, or take some spare fleeces on a caving trip, or put a bucket in the back of the Land Rover to supplement the students having their helmets handy on that windy road. There would be many things related specifically to instruction, for example, give river instructions about a hazard sooner, where there is a good eddy, or back off on the amount of feedback for a particular population learning to ski. It is good idea to write down all the observations so that they will be remembered for that particular course next time. It may not be you teaching that course so the information will be useful to other instructors. Anecdotal information, even without scientific rigor, is very useful to enable future improvements and perhaps policy changes, goals and organizational culture. There would be much anecdotal information revealed in interviews.

⚒ Observational methods

Using observation for research purposes requires advanced preparation of what you are looking for, and then preparing a check sheet that a trained, objective observer can fill out. If you were looking for specific behaviors during a ropes course experience, then these would be on the check sheet. The trained observer would be looking for these and checking them off in real time or later from a video. It may be that a new method of teaching skiing is being investigated. In this case the students could be observed prior to a class, then afterwards, where specific aspects like, knees bent or straight, body position, pole planting, etc., would be added to a check sheet for an impartial observer that had the required knowledge of the skill to make checks, pre- and post-course. The observer needs to be as inconspicuous as possible so as not to become a confounding variable. Observational techniques need to be well structured and the observers need to be both conscientious and competent.

⚒ Checklists

Russell (1982) also gives a checklist for what she regarded as minimum competency for a recreation program evaluator:

- ☐ Know the place of evaluation in recreation programs and its relationship to the planning process
- ☐ Understand the subject of the evaluation, or the specific efficiency and effectiveness area that need to be evaluated
- ☐ Select the appropriate evaluation design and put it into effect
- ☐ Identify appropriate evaluation instrumentation for collecting data
- ☐ Analyze and interpret the results
- ☐ Effectively communicate the evaluation results to others and convert them into practice. (p. 301)

All national instruction organizations have checklists for testing the proficiency of students and instructors. Many camps have checklists for awards that students can progress through or to determine if a student is ready to move to a higher level. An example of a checklist for kayakers wishing to progress to class III whitewater could be something like the following:

Perform the following skills on class II water

1. ☐ Ferry gliding
2. ☐ Eddy turns and peel outs
3. ☐ S-turns

4. ☐ Surfing

5. ☐ Rolling

6. ☐ Self-rescue

7. ☐ Swimming in fast currents

Answer questions on:

a. ☐ Safety

b. ☐ The international river grading system

c. ☐ Reading the river

d. ☐ Types of kayaks and equipment

The examiner would check off each item during the examination to determine a pass or fail. Using a checklist formed into a rubric is so examiners have specific things to look for as has more recently been suggested by Cooper (2013).

A Suggested Rubric for American Canoe Association Assessment Courses Paddling Skills (Level 4 Instructor) (Cooper, 2013)

Needs improvement
Is unable to model skills at 1/2 speed. Is unable to perform kayak roll in class II water. Is unable to perform river-running skills in class III whitewater. Is unable to effectively self-rescue in class II whitewater.

Acceptable
Is able to model skills at 1/2 speed when instructing. Is able to perform kayak roll in class II water. Is able to perform river-running skills in class III whitewater. Is able to effectively self-rescue in class III whitewater.

Exemplary
Models 1/2 speed >75% of time on the water. Is able to perform kayak roll on both sides of boat in class II water. Is able to perform advanced maneuvers in class III-IV rapids. Is able to hand roll in whitewater. (Cooper, 2013, p.11)

Checklists may be attached to established standards like safety. Measurements could be made of the number of accidents for different activities, per number of user days compared to national figures. Checklists are used for determining the safety of ropes for rock climbing as it is standard practice to keep a rope log detailing use, falls, and any damage. A check sheet could be used for other equipment such as kayaks, canoes, skis, paddles, poles, etc. For instruction the instructor can use a check sheet to make sure that various aspects of teaching are not missed as in the Instructor Effectiveness Check Sheet (IEC), which will be explained later (under process evaluation). Check sheets are limited in that they only provide basic quantitative measurement. Their efficacy can be improved through comparison with other professionally designated standards such as the National Ski Patrol, British Canoe Union, Australian Canoe Federation, Canoe Kayak Canada, etc.

🛠 Rating Scales

The most widely used rating scale in recreation is the Likert Scale, which has varying scales such as 1-3, 1-5, or 1-7. The qualifiers are many and varied, but could be, for example, from *strongly agree* to *strongly disagree*. They can measure attitudes, perceptions or observations. Statistical analysis is possible as a number can be assigned to each qualifier. Some other examples are:

Completely false
False much of time
Sometimes true and sometimes false
True much of the time
Completely true

Strongly agree
Disagree
Undecided
Agree
Strongly agree

Unacceptable
Poor
Acceptable
Good
Excellent

Poor
Fair
Average
Good
Outstanding

Rating scales are found on questionnaires and check sheets. On the Instructor Effectiveness Questionnaire (IEQ), the completely true to completely false scale is used for students to rate their perceptions of the instruction. Students on a different instrument may be rating their own self-concept, or their attitude to certain things. When developing a questionnaire using a Likert Scale it is important to make sure that the statement or question does match the qualifying descriptor of the scale.

✂ Case Studies

Case studies are intensive study on something like one individual or a group. It could be about instruction in a group, the students, a particular program, policy, or administration. It could include data from anecdotal information, observations, questionnaires, interviews and or testing. A variety of techniques can all add together to produce an overall picture for whatever case is being researched.

✂ Standardized Tests

There are standardized tests for most activities, whether they are educational, psychological, or related to physical skills. Standardized paper and pencil tests have usually been statistically tested for validity (measuring what it purports to measure), reliability (measuring results over time and internal consistency) and objectivity. The statistics give a coefficient to show the extent of the validity or reliability. The evaluator can choose an instrument that has already been tested instead of developing their own to be more confident that the measures will be more accurate –unless there is the time and expertise to develop a new one. National bodies have established physical tests such as the Star tests of the British Canoe Union that measures personal ability through beginner, improver, intermediate and advanced proficiency.

✂ Video

Video can be used to assist with observation techniques as mentioned above. It can also be used for direct comparison of pre-course and post-course skills. Recording a student making turns at the beginning of a skiing course can enable comparison on the slope and/or at the end of the course. A video of a particular skill, say a parallel turn, could be shown at the beginning of a course to show the student what they are trying to achieve by the end of the course. A video can illustrate the techniques required to successfully complete the skills portion of any physical test, whether it is first aid assessment for Ski Patrol, or rope set-ups for climbing certifications.

✂ Self-Appraisals

Instructors are sometimes asked to write a self-appraisal of their current skills or document recent trainings, conferences, and workshops that they have attended. Self-appraisal is also used for programs and can include checklists, interviews, questionnaires, and advisory boards. These are often required as part of accreditation processes.

✂ Reaction Papers

These would be narratives written by participants, instructors or administrators on courses. Some structure explaining what aspects are being considered is helpful – such as, instruction, logistics, equipment, transportation, administration, etc.

✂ Cumulative Records

Two examples of record keeping on accidents in the US are the American Alpine Club and American Whitewater. This data is recorded each year so there is a cumulative record. Individual organizations also keep their own, whether it is for safety where accidents and near misses are recorded, or resumes, qualifications, course evaluations and instructor evaluations. The data can be used for immediate decision-making in safety cases (if there have been near misses, when a change of procedure is called for), and can be used for longitudinal study of what is happening over time.

🛠 Socio-metric Methods

An example of a socio-metric method is a socio-gram, which measures the internal nature of a group by identifying accepted and non-accepted members of a group. It shows the social links of each person. This technique could be used to identify people that can get on well together, and so may be useful for expeditions, or climbing teams within a larger expedition. Organizing climbing teams into compatible units can increase the chances of success for an expedition. To create a socio-gram for a climbing expedition, you would construct a question to ask all members that would relate to the upcoming expedition. The question could be, "Who are three people on the expedition that you would like to have as tent mates?" All responses are then plotted on a graph. Because of the complexity, Russell (1982) suggested a limit of 25 members.

After collecting responses, list the names and write next to each one the number of times they were selected. Draw concentric circles with one more than the greatest number anyone was chosen. Number the rings spaces starting from the outside as 1. Write each person's name inside the ring space according to the number of times he or she was chosen. Draw arrows connecting persons who have selected each other. If the selection is mutual, draw arrowheads on each end of the lines. Inspect the diagram to assess the social links but keep the information confidential and use sensitive communication when forming the actual sub-groups. This technique could prevent some unnecessary conflict and provide for a more enjoyable experience for everyone unless there are some outliers (such as Lee in Figure 28) who no one wants to be with. The question could be asked whether or not a total outlier should be taken on the expedition or should be counseled regarding what may be affecting their unpopularity. Figure 28 shows what this type of diagram would look like.

Figure 28. Example Expedition Socio-Gram

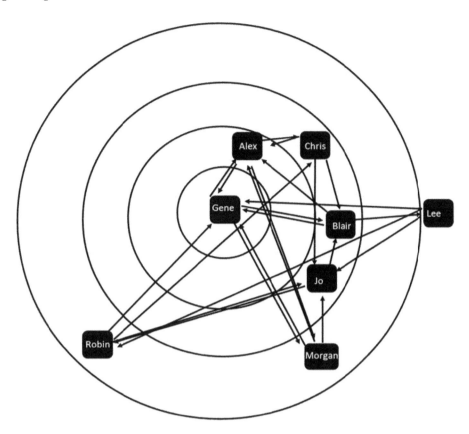

✖ Delphi

The Delphi process would be used more for research. The process consists of sending out questions to experts for usually three rounds. The questions are sent for a written response from each expert, after which, all the responses are again read by all the experts. The questions are then reconsidered in the light of everyone's feedback. The subsequent comments are studied again and a final response from the experts is then summarized.

✖ Journals

Field notes, diaries, personal accounts and journals can be used for evaluation purposes. If they are to be used for evaluation, then to what extent they will be used needs to be stated very clearly. An example was given earlier (in chapter 1) of a structured journal for decision-making assessing student's thoughts on important leader decisions. Sometimes journals or diaries are used for personal or intimate thoughts that are more for the students' personal growth and not for evaluation purpose, so clarification is very important about what kind of content is expected and whether or not the journals will be read by instructors. Trip logs are often used for assessing instructor experience as part of national certifications and for job interviews.

Process Evaluation

Marcia McKenzie (2000) asked the question, "How are adventure education program outcomes achieved?" (p.1). She refers back to Ewert's (1983) suggestion that we have an educational black box in that we know that many outcomes, such as self-concept, work, but we don't know why or how. Some research has related to the 'hows' and 'whys' but most has related to outcomes. McKenzie (2000, pg. 20) suggests that research on the following aspects would maximize program effectiveness:

1. The physical environment
2. Activities
3. Processing
4. The group
5. Instructors
6. The program

The black box refers to how outdoor education works. Neill (2004) explained the problem well in his parody about the elephant in the black box. Different people have different views about what it is that works in outdoor education and he suggested that they could all be true as it is as if they are describing different parts of the elephant. Here is a summary of his parody:

Researchers have studied different parts of the elephant and admit to that but sometimes they pretend they have studied the whole elephant and can describe it as a model. Many elephants were subsequently tested which concerns others who think too much prodding and poking will kill it and that we should just ride it. Some do have a good ride but unfortunately some fall off and get trampled. Some people fight over bits of the elephant and who is qualified to handle them.

So, we have a giant human knot with an innocent elephant in the middle and no light to see what we're doing. By carefully listening to each person describe in turn the part of the elephant which they are holding and asking them questions about how they arrived at their descriptions, it is possible for people to create a more detailed and refined picture of the elephant in the black box. If however we keep shouting back that we've found a python in the black box, we might never realize that we've been fooled by the trunk, and we'll miss the chance to learn about the rest of the magnificent creature that we've called 'outdoor education'.

Published research on effective outdoor instruction has been sparse but some examples follow. Cashel and Gangstead (1986) researched outdoor leadership and teacher effectiveness. Cashel (1994) used kayaking to investigate feedback techniques. Attarian (1996) used an importance-performance analysis to measure instructor effectiveness in rock climbing. Using qualitative research, Kime (2008) investigated Educational Connoisseurship and Criticism to view the conceptual frameworks of intentions, curriculum, pedagogy, outdoor structure and evaluation within each of three cases for teachers in the USA, Canada, and New Zealand.

Phipps and Claxton (1997) researched instructor effectiveness at the Nantahala Outdoor Center (NOC) in North Carolina. Phipps, Hayashi, Lewandoski, and Padgett (2005) studied teaching and evaluating instruction using NOC again and a WEA expedition style course. Richardson, Kalvaitus and Delparte (2013) researched systematic feedback to improve teaching skills in Western Canada. These last three pieces of research used the IEQ and the IEC, suggested by Phipps and Claxton (1997). The two instruments measure aspects of instruction. The questionnaire measures students' perceptions and the check sheet is designed for instructors to check off what they feel they are including in the instruction. The IEQ and IEC (see appendix) measure eleven constructs through 59 questions. The IEQ was tested on Nantahala Outdoor Center Courses in 1997 (Phipps and Claxton 1997). The Alpha reliability of the IEQ was .95 showing consistency between all sections of the instrument. When tested for inter-rater reliability, Spearman's Rho was used to measure a .7 correlation.

The constructs are:

Structure: Logical sequencing, goals, focusing, cooperative, competitive and individual learning;

Communication: Climate, spontaneity, novel information, creativity, demonstrations, and clarity;

Perception: Engagement at correct levels, reflective observation, and judgment;

Motivation: Needs (safety, physiological, group, individual), and enthusiasm;

Arousal Levels: Interest, fear, challenge, confidence, ability and site matching, appropriate timing;

Feedback: Instructor to student: accuracy, timing, praising, amount, positiveness; student to instructor: feedback to instructor;

Group Processing: group norms, group climate, group building, group dynamics, group conflict;

Action/Practice: Amount (physical involvement, experimentation), pace, decision-making, safety;

Leadership: Effectiveness, social skill, competency in complex situations, selflessness, egalitarianism;

People Skills and Safety: Includes selected items from the above concepts.

Using the IEC to check that you are keeping up with all the above aspects of instruction can make sure that you don't forget things. Checking with the students by having them complete the IEQ during the course can illustrate what you need to change or add. Using the IEQ at the end of the course is a way to evaluate students' perceptions of the instruction.

To enable more effective individual lesson planning, a short form of the IEQ can be used. This is shown in Figure 29. The students can use it to evaluate the lesson and the instructor can use it to plan the lesson, by making sure each construct is sufficiently covered.

Figure 29. Instructor Evaluation Questionnaire Short Form

Learning Evaluation
Please check whether you agree or disagree with the following statements and qualify each answer with reasons under comments.

	Agree	Disagree	N/A
1. My *arousal levels* were optimal (I was not over anxious or bored).	☐	☐	☐
Comments			
2. *Communication* was sufficient that I understood the material.	☐	☐	☐
Comments			
3. I was able to clarify my understanding through a *perception check* if needed.	☐	☐	☐
Comments			
4. The amount of novel (new) information was sufficient.	☐	☐	☐
Comments			
5. I was *motivated* to learn during this session.	☐	☐	☐
Comments			
6. I felt that the session was well *focused.*	☐	☐	☐
Comments			
7. I felt that I was given appropriate *feedback and support.*	☐	☐	☐
Comments			
8. I felt that the educational *structure and progression* was appropriate.	☐	☐	☐
Comments			
9. I have *reflected* and am in a position to formulate related abstract concepts.	☐	☐	☐
Comments			
10. I felt *safe* during this session	☐	☐	☐
Comments			
11. *Group work* was well organized for this session.	☐	☐	☐
Comments			
12. I feel that I *learned* a great deal in this session.	☐	☐	☐
Comments			
13. I know here to go to get *further information*	☐	☐	☐
Comments			
14. The instructor was instrumental in *assisting* my learning	☐	☐	☐
Comments			

When investigating teaching looking at hard and soft skills, Clarke & Phipps (2010) used a marketing research technique. The technique is an importance-performance analysis, which uses a pre-test questionnaire that measures what is important to the participant, followed by a matching post-test questionnaire that measures how the participants perceived the performance. Using the information from both tests enables a grid to be constructed that shows where improvements are needed. It is easy to administer and gives a visual representation of important attributes, how important they are, and performance (Guadagnolo, 1985). The grid was developed by Martilla and James (1977) and is illustrated in the Instructor Action Grid below (Figure 30).

Figure 30. Instructor Action Grid

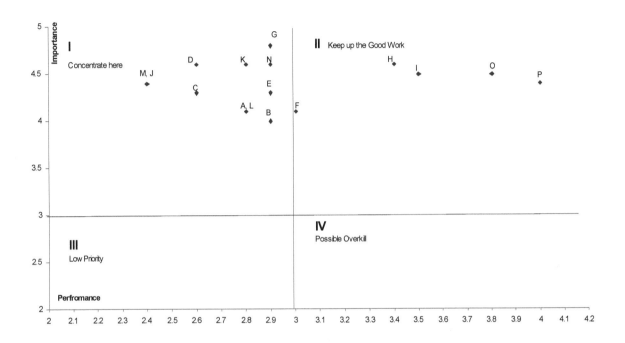

Reprinted from "An Investigation into the Technical and Soft skills of Instruction, using an Importance-Performance Analysis", by G. Clarke and M. Phipps, 2010, p. 15.

The grid illustrates four areas of concern:
I. Concentrate here
II. Keep up the good work
III. Low priority and
IV. Possible overkill

The letters represent the questions on the survey, which are shown in Table 6 below. The data shown in both the table and the grid are the same, but the grid separates the results into the four areas of concern and allows the researcher to see where improvements need to be made.

Table 6. Attribute Results from a Dysfunctional Instructor.

	Importance - Performance Attributes.	Importance Mean	Performance Mean
a	Sensitivity towards students	4.1	2.8
b	Sensitivity towards differences	4.0	2.9
c	Attentive listener	4.3	2.6
d	Dealt with group problems well	4.6	2.6
e	Supportive of students	4.3	2.9
f	Respectful and Polite	4.1	3.0
g	I want to enjoy/enjoyed the experience	4.8	2.9
h	Is skilled/demonstrates skills well	4.6	3.4
i	Handles Logistics well	4.5	3.5
j	Gauges correct level of instruction	4.4	2.4
k	Explains skills effectively	4.6	2.8
l	Variety of teaching strategies	4.1	2.8
m	Diagnoses skill level well	4.4	2.4
n	I want to learn/learned the skill well	4.6	2.9
o	Enthusiasm	4.5	3.8
p	Safety Conscious	4.4	4.0

(N=20)

Note: Likert Scales: Importance, 1= not important to me to 5 = very important to me;
     Performance, 1 = completely false to 5 = completely true

Reprinted from "An Investigation into the Technical and Soft Skills of Instruction, using an Importance-Performance Analysis", by G. Clarke and M. Phipps, 2010, p. 18.

The scores can be assessed by viewing the table or they can be put into the importance-performance grid for better impact as is shown in Figure 30. It can be seen in the above grid that the instructor needs to concentrate on several attributes, including all of the soft and half of the technical skills. The only attributes that merited "keep up the good work" were (h) is skilled, demonstrates well (i) logistics, and (o) enthusiasm. Most of these were related to hard skills. The areas of improvement that is needed can be easily seen on the action grid.

If instructors score highly on all items however, then the grid won't discern where improvements are needed unless the axes are changed, which was suggested by Hollenhurst, Olsen, and Fortney (1992). An alternative to changing the axes can be to compare expectations to performance on bar charts. The grid like the one in Figure 31 can easily be assessed but if the scores are all very high it wouldn't pinpoint anything in the results as shown in the table below (Table 7).

Table 7. Performance Attributes and Performance

Importance- Performance Attributes	Center Performance Mean
a. Sensitivity towards students	4.2
b. Sensitivity towards differences	4.1
c. Attentive listener	4.5
d. Dealt with group problems well	4.5
e. Supportive of students	4.4
f. Respectful and Polite	4.3
g. Enjoyed the experience	4.6
h. Is skilled/demonstrated skills well	4.7
i. Handled logistics well	4.6
j. Gauged correct level of instruction	4.5
k. Explained skills effectively	4.6
l. Used a variety of teaching strategies	4.1
m. Diagnosed skill levels well	4.4
n. Wanted to learn/learned skills well	4.7
o. Enthusiastic	4.7
p. Safety conscious	4.7

(N=20)
Note: Likert Scale, importance, 1= not important to me to 5 = very important to me;
performance, 1 = completely false to 5 = completely true

Reprinted from "An Investigation into the Technical and Soft skills of Instruction, using an Importance-Performance Analysis", by G. Clarke and M. Phipps, 2010, p. 15.

A bar chart can be constructed like the one below in Figure 31 that illustrates expectations *against* performance as mean scores in each of the teaching attributes for all instructors at a Mountain Center.

The difference between the performance and expectations is recorded on each chart where plus figures represent higher than expected performance and minus figures represent lower than expected performance. A check on all individual instructor's data is important besides looking at mean scores as one data set that reveals poor teaching may be hidden by a majority of positive data sets. But as an overall look at how the instruction is going in an agency – this can be useful.

Figure 31. Performance at a Mountain Center

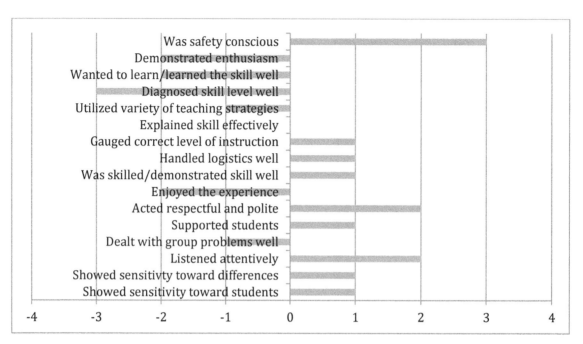

Reprinted from "An Investigation into the Technical and Soft Skills Instruction, using an Importance-Performance Analysis", by G. Clarke and M. Phipps, 2010, p. 16.

The bar chart shows attributes that can be improved as reflected by the minus scores and attributes that exceeded expectations in the positive scores. This technique can tease out small changes that may need to be made. In this case the attributes that need to be considered are: Enthusiasm, learning, teaching strategies, enjoyment, and group issues

Summary

In summary, for outdoor instructors, outcomes assessment may be demanded by program planners as their evaluative research may be based on carefully planned performance objectives. It may be demanded by the administration of an organization to improve instruction levels. Outcomes assessment done by instructors can improve the efficacy of their teaching. If organized by the agency, the following aspects are often considered:

Performance Objectives
Program effectiveness
Agency improvement
Administrative improvements
Instruction

Outcomes assessment can enable better decision-making for an agency. In regard to instructor improvement and student learning, it is best done for exactly that and not for promotion or discipline purposes. Instructor improvement techniques need to be embraced, not feared, by instructors.

This chapter has given some examples of how to proceed but expert advice on setting up outcomes assessment is suggested to enable the most valid and reliable data possible. The instruments designed to measure effective teaching explained in this book, the IEQ, the IEC, and the Technical/Soft Skill Importance/Performance questionnaires can be found in the appendix.

References

Attarian, A. (1996). Importance-performance analysis to evaluate teaching effectiveness. In R. Koesler & R. Watters, (Eds.). *Proceedings of the 1995 International Conference on Outdoor Recreation and Education* (pp.145-150). Pocatello, ID: Idaho State University Press.

Beames, S., Higgins, P., & Nicol, R. (2012). *Learning outside the classroom: Theory and guidelines for practice.* New York, NY: Routledge.

Berman, D., & Teeters, C. (2006). *WEA affiliate handbook* (7th ed). Bloomington, IN: WEA National Office.

Brookes, A. (2003). A critique of neo-Hahnian outdoor education theory. Part one: Challenges to the concept of "character building". *Journal of Adventure Education and Outdoor Learning, 3*(1), 49-62.

Cashel, C. M. (1994). Augmented feedback in outdoor skills instruction. In M. L. Phipps (Ed.), *The 1993 Proceedings of the National Conference for Outdoor Leaders: Wilderness Partnerships* (pp. 29-33). Saranac lake, NY: The Wilderness Education Association.

Cashel, C. M., & Gangstead, S. K. (1986). Outdoor leadership under a microscope: A look at teacher effectiveness. In J. Cederquist, (Ed.), *Proceedings of the 1986 Conference on Outdoor Recreation,* (pp. 57-69). Davis, CA: National Conference on Outdoor Recreation Planning Committee.

Clarke, G., & Phipps, M. L. (2010). *An investigation into the technical and soft skills Instruction using an importance-performance analysis.* Unpublished study. Western Carolina University, Cullowhee, NC.

Cooper, R. (2013). Using academic style rubrics in assessment courses. *Journal of Paddlesport Education.* April.

Edginton, R. C., & Hayes, G. A. (1976). Using performance objectives in the delivery of recreation services. *Journal of Leisurability, 3*(4), p.21.

Edginton, R. C., Compton, D. M., & Hanson, C. J. (1980). *Recreation and leisure programming: A guide for the professional.* Philadelphia, PA: Saunders College/Holt, Rhinehart and Winston.

Ewert, A. W. (1983). *Outdoor adventure and self-concept: A research analysis.* Eugene, OR: University of Oregon, Center of Leisure Studies.

Ewert, A. W. (1989). *Outdoor adventure pursuits: Foundations, models, and theories.* Worthington, OH: Publishing Horizons.

Ewert, A. W., & Sibthorpe, J. (2009). Creating outcomes through experiential education: The challenge of confounding variables. *Journal of Experiential Education, 31*(3), 377-389.

Gilbertson, K., Bates, T., McLaughlin, T., & Ewert A. (2006). *Outdoor education: Methods and strategies.* Champaign, IL: Human Kinetics.

Guadagnolo, F. (1985). The importance-performance analysis: An evaluation and marketing tool. *Journal of Park and Recreation Administration, 3*(2), 13-22.

Hattie, J. A. C. (2009). *Visible Learning: A synthesis of over 800 meta-analyses relating to achievement.* London and New York: Routledge,Taylor & Francis Group.

Hattie, J., Masters, D., & Birch, K. (2016). *Visible learning into action: International case studies of impact.* London and New York: Routledge,Taylor & Francis Group.

Hollenhurst, S., Olsen, D., & Fortney, R. (1992). Use of importance-performance analysis to evaluate state park cabins: The case of the West Virginia State Park system. *Journal of Park and Recreation Administration, 10*(1), 13-22.

Hopkins, D., & Putnam, R. (1993). *Personal growth through adventure.* London, England: E.P. Publishing.

Joplin, L. (1981). On defining experiential education. *The Journal of Experiential Education,* 4(1), 17-20.

Kime, D. B. (2008). *Outdoor adventure education instructor teaching in postsecondary education settings: Educational connoisseurship and criticism case studies in Canada, New Zealand and the United States* (Doctoral Dissertation). University of Denver, Colorado.

Kleinfeld, J. (1983). Practical evaluation for experiential education. *Journal of Experiential Education, 6*(2), 45-47.

Marchese, T. J. (1988). The uses of assessment. *Liberal Education, 74*(3), 23-36.

Martilla, J. A., & James, J. C. (1977). Importance-performance analysis. *Journal of Marketing, 41*(1), 77-79.

McKenzie, M. D. (2000). How are adventure education program outcomes achieved? A review of the literature. *Australian Journal of Outdoor Education, 5*(1), 19-28

Neill, J. (2004). *The elephant in the black box: A parable about outdoor education.* Retrieved from http://www.wilderdom.com/theory/blackbox1.htm).

Neill, J. (2006). *Meta-analytic research on the outcomes of outdoor education.* Retrieved from http://wilderdom.com/research/researchoutcomesmeta-analytic.htm

Nicol, R. (2002). Outdoor education: Research topic or universal value? *Journal of Adventure Education and Outdoor Learning, 2*(1), 29-41.

Ogilvie, K. (1985). Planning an adventure experience in the outdoors. *Adventure Education, The Journal of the National Association for Outdoor Education, 2*(4/5), 37-42.

Phipps, M. L., Hayashi, A., Lewandoski, A., & Padgett, A. (2005). Teaching and evaluating instructor effectiveness using the Instructor Effectiveness Questionnaire and the Instructor Effectiveness Check Sheet combination. *Journal of Adventure Education and Outdoor learning, 5*(1), 69 – 84.

Phipps, M. L., & Claxton, D. B. (1997). An investigation into instructor effectiveness, *The Journal of Experiential Education, 20*(1), 40-46.

Pinch, K. J. (2009). Seer keynote address: The importance of evaluation research. *Journal of Experiential Education, 31*(3), 391-398.

Russell, R. V. (1982). *Planning programs in recreation*. St Louis, MO: C.V. Mosby.

Richardson, R., Kalvaitis, D., & Delparte, D. (2013). Using systematic feedback and reflection to improve adventure education teaching skills. *Journal of Experiential Education, 37*(2) 187-206.

Stiel, J., & Parker, S. (2007). Individual outcomes of participating in adventure. In *Adventure education: Theory and applications* (pp. 63-69). Champaign, IL: Human Kinetics.

Sellick, P. (2006). *The predictable journey of outcomes based education*. Retrieved from http://www.onlineopinion.com.au/view.asp?article=4993

State Board of Education. (2003). *The character education informational handbook and guide public schools of North Carolina*. State Board of Education. Department of Public Instruction, Division of Instructional Services, Character Education. Retrieved from www.ncpublicschools.org

Warner, A. (1984). How to creatively evaluate programs. *Journal of Experiential Education, 7*(2) 38-43.

Appendix

Instructor Effectiveness Questionnaire
Instructor Effectiveness Check Sheet
Importance - Performance Questionnaire (Importance)
Importance – Performance Questionnaire (Performance)
Group Dynamics Questionnaire

Instructor Effectiveness Questionnaire

To be filled out by students/guests/clients

Instructor's Name _____ Group _____ Date _____

Directions: Fill in Column **A** with the points that tell how true each of these statements is, of the instructor and course. Add comments in column **B**.

If the statement is:

    Completely true... 5
    True much of the time.............................. 4
    Sometimes true and sometimes false........ 3
    False much of the time............................. 2
    Completely false... 1

	Column A	Column B
Example: Scheduling was flexible...	5	*Modifications were made to change the teaching sites to suit the group*
Structure		
1. I learned at an appropriate level of difficulty...........................		
2. Goals were clearly defined..		
3. A clear focus on goals was evident....................................		
4. Skills were taught in a logical sequence from easy to more difficult.....		
5. The structure of the course promoted cooperative interactions.............		
6. The structure of the course promoted individual learning......................		
7. The instruction was well focused......................................		
8. The instructor used mental imagery techniques effectively..................		
9. I know where to go for further information.............................		
10. The instructor promoted appropriately competitive interactions.......		
Communication		
11. A positive communication climate encouraged supportive behavior...		
12. Spontaneous communication existed in the group..............................		
13. Appropriate amounts of *new* information was given........................		
14. Information was given in understandable ways..............................		
15. If a block to understanding was encountered, the instructor was creative in trying different ways of teaching.................................		
16. The instructor demonstrated skills well....................................		
17. Verbal instructions were easily heard and understood........................		
Perception		
18. The instructor taught at my level (same wavelength)...........................		
19. I was able to conceptualize different techniques and ideas because of the instructor's teaching.................................		
20. Time was set aside for reflective observations on the reasons why we did things (debriefing).................................		
21. I was able to develop judgment in applying skills in different situations.................................		
22. I learned a great deal during this course.................................		
Motivation		
23. My safety needs were met...		
24. My physiological needs (clothing/food/etc.) were met........................		
25. Group needs were recognized and met...		
26. The instructor made efforts to meet individual needs..........................		
27. The instructor was enthusiastic...		

Completely true... **5**
True much of the time.............................. **4**
Sometimes true and sometimes false........ **3**
False much of the time.............................. **2**
Completely false.. **1**

	Column A	Column B
Arousal Levels		
28. I was interested in the concepts presented...		
29. "Classroom" sessions were interesting...		
30. Practice sessions were interesting...		
31. My fear levels were not high..		
32. The classes provided a correct level of challenge...............................		
33. The instructor helped me increase my confidence level.......................		
34. Sites selected for teaching matched my ability.....................................		
35. Teaching took place at appropriate times of the day............................		
Feedback		
36. The instructor gave *accurate* feedback and corrections.......................		
37. The instructor used *good timing* in giving feedback and corrections..		
38. The instructor used frequent praising for accomplishments.................		
39. There was not too much feedback given..		
40. Feedback was given in a positive manner..		
41. The instructor was open to feedback from individuals and the group..		
Group Processing		
42. Accepted standards of behavior (group norms) were established.........		
43. Group members conformed to group norms...		
44. The instructor set a positive group climate...		
45. The instructor was effective in group building....................................		
46. The overall group dynamics were positive...		
47. Group conflicts were effectively resolved...		
Action/Practice		
48. I was physically involved for an appropriate amount of the time.........		
49. Enough time was available to experiment and practice skills...............		
50. The pace of instruction was just right..		
51. I understand the 'whys' behind the skills that were taught...................		
52. I experienced decision-making that will enable me to make future judgments..		
53. Responsibility for each other's safety was encouraged.......................		
Leadership		
54. The leadership was effective...		
55. The instructor showed good social skills...		
56. The instructor could handle several things at once smoothly..............		
57. The instructor created a relaxed environment.....................................		
58. The instructor focused on the group and individuals rather than self...		
59. The instructor encouraged all participants equally..............................		

Additional Comments

Instructor Effectiveness Check Sheet
Instructor self-report

Instructor's Name _____ **Group** _____ **Date** _____

Directions: Fill in Column **A** with the points that tell how true each of these statements is, of yourself and course. Add comments in column **B** to explain how you accomplished the different aspects.

If the statement is:
- **Completely true**.. 5
- **True much of the time**... 4
- **Sometimes true and sometimes false** 3
- **False much of the time** 2
- **Completely false**.. 1

	Column A	Column B
Example: Scheduling was flexible...	5	*Modifications were made to change the teaching sites to suit the group*
Structure		
1. The students learned at an appropriate level of difficulty....................		
2. Goals were clearly defined...		
3. A clear focus on goals was evident...		
4. Skills were taught in a logical sequence from easy to more difficult....		
5. The structure of the course promoted cooperative interactions.............		
6. The structure of the course promoted individual learning...................		
7. The instruction was well focused..		
8. I used mental imagery techniques effectively...................................		
9. I explained to the students where to go for further information...........		
10. I promoted competitive interactions only when appropriate............		
Communication		
11. A positive communication climate encouraged supportive behavior...		
12. Spontaneous communication existed in the group........................		
13. Appropriate amounts of *new* information was given.....................		
14. Information was given in understandable ways.............................		
15. If a block to understanding was encountered, I was creative in trying different ways of teaching..		
16. I demonstrated skills well...		
17. Verbal instructions were easily heard and understood......................		
Perception		
18. I taught at the students' level (same wavelength)...........................		
19. I enabled the conceptualization of different techniques and ideas through my teaching..		
20. Time was set aside for reflective observations on the reasons why we did things (de-briefing)...		
21. The students were able to develop judgment in applying skills in different situations..		
22. The students learned a great deal during this course......................		
Motivation		
23. The students' safety needs were met..		
24. The students' physiological needs (clothing/food/etc.) were met........		
25. Group needs were recognized and met...		
26. I made efforts to meet individual needs.......................................		
27. I was enthusiastic..		

Completely true.. 5
True much of the time 4
Sometimes true and sometimes false 3
False much of the time...2
Completely false 1

	Column A	Column B
Arousal Levels		
28. The students were interested in the concepts presented....................		
29. "Classroom" sessions were interesting...		
30. Practice sessions were interesting..		
31. Students' fear levels were not too high..		
32. The classes provided a correct level of challenge............................		
33. I helped the students to increase their confidence levels..................		
34. Sites selected for teaching matched the students' abilities...............		
35. Teaching took place at appropriate times of the day......................		
Feedback		
36. I gave *accurate* feedback and corrections....................................		
37. I used *good timing* in giving feedback and corrections...................		
38. I used frequent praising for accomplishments..............................		
39. I gave just the right amount of feedback.....................................		
40. I gave feedback in a positive manner...		
41. I was open to feedback from individuals and the group...................		
Group Processing		
42. Accepted standards of behavior (group norms) were established.........		
43. Group members conformed to group norms................................		
44. I set a positive group climate..		
45. I was effective in group building..		
46. The overall group dynamics were positive...................................		
47. Group conflicts were effectively resolved...................................		
Action/Practice		
48. Students were physically involved for an appropriate amount of the time..		
49. Enough time was available for students to experiment and practice skills..		
50. The pace of instruction was just right......................................		
51. The students understand the 'whys' behind the skills that were taught...		
52. The students experienced decision-making that will enable them to make future judgments..		
53. Responsibility for each other's safety was encouraged...................		
Leadership		
54. My leadership was effective..		
55. I showed good social skills...		
56. I handled several things at once smoothly...................................		
57. I created a relaxed environment...		
58. I focused on the group and individuals rather than self..................		
59. I encouraged all participants equally...		

Additional Comments

Importance-Performance Instruction Questionnaire (Importance)

Instructor's Name _____ Group _____ Date _____

Directions: Different people come on courses for different reasons, so we would like you to give **your** opinion on the relative importance of the following aspects of instruction. *Thank you for completing this questionnaire with care.*

Please rate the **importance** of following aspects **to you** about this particular course that you are about to do, using the following scale.

If the statement is:

Very important to me... 5
Between very important and neutral.............. 4
Neutral.. 3
Between neutral and not important to me 2
Not important to me 1

Example: Scheduling should be flexible	5
1. The instructor should be sensitive towards needs of individual students	
2. The instructor should be sensitive to individual differences	
3. The instructor should be an attentive listener	
4. The instructor should be skilled in dealing with problems that affect the whole group	
5. The instructor should be encouraging of supportive behavior from students	
6. The instructor should be skilled at setting a respectful and polite atmosphere	
7. I want to enjoy the experience	
8. The instructor should demonstrate outdoor skills well	
9. The instructor should handle logistics well e.g., equipment needs, transportation, scheduling, etc.	
10. The instructor should gauge the correct level of challenge	
11. The instructor should explain skills effectively	
12. The instructor should use a variety of teaching strategies	
13. The instructor should be able to diagnose skill levels and assist in enabling improvements	
14. I want to learn the skill well	
15. The instructor should be enthusiastic	
16. The instructor should be very safety conscious	

Importance- Performance Instruction Questionnaire (Performance)

Instructor's Name _____ **Group** _____ **Date** _____

Directions: Different people come on courses for different reasons, so we would like you to give **your** opinion on the relative importance of the following aspects of instruction. *Thank you for completing this questionnaire with care.*

Please rate the **performance** of following aspects **as viewed by you** about this particular course that you just completed, using the following scale.

If the statement is:

Completely true **5**
True much of the time **4**
Sometimes true and sometimes false **3**
False much of the time **2**
Completely false **1**

1. The instructor showed sensitivity towards the needs of individual students	
2. The instructor showed sensitivity to individual differences	
3. The instructor was an attentive listener	
4. The instructor was skilled in dealing with problems that affect the whole group	
5. The instructor was encouraging of supportive behavior from students	
6. The instructor was skilled at setting a respectful and polite atmosphere	
7. I enjoyed the experience	
8. The instructor demonstrated his/her skills well	
9. The instructor handled logistics well e.g., equipment needs, transportation, scheduling, etc.	
10. The instructor gauged the correct level of challenge	
11. The instructor explained skills effectively	
12. The instructor used a variety of teaching strategies	
13. The instructor was able to diagnose outdoor skill levels and assist in enabling improvements	
14. I learned the skill well	
15. The instructor was enthusiastic	
16. The instructor was very safety conscious	

Additional Comments

THE GROUP DYNAMICS QUESTIONNAIRE

Directions: Fill in column A the points which tell how true each of these statements is of the group. Add comments in column C

<u>If the statement is:</u>

                    Points

Completely false.. 1
False much of the time.......................................2
Sometimes true and sometimes false............3
True much of the time.......................................4
Completely true...5

Column	A	B	C
Example: *There are too many group members* **GOALS AND OBJECTIVES**	5		*We have 30 members which decreases the personal interaction*
1. The goals are clearly defined			
2. There is definite recognition of present position in relation to goals			
3. Means and activities are instituted which will lead to goal attainment			
4. Means to goal attainment are cooperatively set			
5. Members are generally assigned to particular tasks			
6. Completing the day's tasks takes precedence over personal struggles			
7. Judgment is the top priority in decision making			
8. Uniform procedures are encouraged			
9. Scheduling is flexible			
10. The goals that were originally set are being met			
Communication, Atmosphere and Climate			
11. There is an air of permissiveness and warmth			
12. People are inhibited			
13. There are unresolved personal tensions			
14. All members communicate equally well with each other			
15. The members talk "Head talk"			
16. Sufficient information is given to complete set tasks			
17. Specific communication skills are dealt with in teaching situations			
18. The communication climate is personal control oriented (unnecessarily manipulative)			
19. Communication is spontaneous			
20. The members feel free to talk "Feeling talk"			

Participation			
21. All members contribute to the group process			
22. All members are assuming responsibility			
23. There is encouragement for all to participate			
24. Certain members consistently "get lost"			
Group interaction and Social Control			
25. Interaction patterns in the group are individual			
26. Interaction patterns in the group are cooperative			
27. Interaction patterns in the group are competitive			
28. There are hidden agendas			
29. Members conform to group norms			
30. Members are given recognition for meeting group norms			
Role Structure			
31. Members understand the nature of productive group member roles			
32. Members are engaged in both group task and group building roles			
Cohesiveness			
33. The group exhibits a definite "we" feeling			
34. Members demonstrate a common concern with regard to other members and the group as a whole			
35. Members understand that groups normally develop through a "conflict of interest" stage			
36. Members show a genuine willingness to work and sacrifice for group consensus and group goals			
37. Members regard the group and its activities as attractive			
Leadership			
38. There is a definite feeling that leadership is present			
39. Clear-cut decisions are made			
40. The members are accepting of the leadership style			
41. Group decisions that are made by the group are generally only changed by the group			
42. The decision making in the group is mainly leader centered			
43. The decision making in the group is mainly group centered			
44. The decision making in the group is determined mainly by the situation			
45. The style of leadership is effective			

Additional Comments

Questionnaire Directions (GDQ)

Filling out column C is extremely important for all group members to enable needed changes to be made. A more detailed explanation of the questions follow:

1. The goals of an organization are extremely important. Is everyone leading in the same direction? Have the goals been discussed?
2. Where is the group in relation to the goals; has this been made clear to the group?
3. Pertinent activities assist in reaching goals.
4. Members of the group participate in setting ways to reach the goals.
5. Members are given specific roles to assist in the task.
6. This could be positive or negative depending on the type of group/life-cycle/environment.
7. Is judgment used to make decisions, or are decisions made without much thought?
8. People are encouraged to follow similar procedures (standard operating procedures).
9. To what extent is the scheduling flexible or fixed?
10. Is the group heading toward the same goal, or has this changed? Has the original goal been forgotten?
11. The group climate is open, warm and supportive.
12. Members are not comfortable in saying what they feel.
13. There are some personal problems within the group interactions.
14. Members for the most part get on with each other in respect to communication.
15. Members talk "thinking" talk (intellectual talk).
16. Tasks seem to be organized clearly.
17. The leader uses definite communication techniques in teaching situations.
18. The leader tends to exert power unnecessarily over followers.
19. People feel free to act and speak when and how they feel without feeling inhibited.
20. Talking about feelings is acceptable in the group.
21. Do all group members contribute or are some members withdrawn?
22. Are some members not taking responsibility for tasks in the group?
23. Encouragement is given for participation to all e.g., compliments, verbal encouragement, group outings, get-togethers, etc., to include everyone.
24. Some members "space out" or withdraw from the group activities inappropriately.
25. People are expected to work on their own.
26. People are expected to work together.
27. There is more than friendly competitiveness between group members.
28. People have ulterior motives in the group.
29. People conform to expected behaviors.
30. Expected behaviors in the group are rewarded with some kind of recognition, e.g., positive comments.
31. There are positive roles in groups such as gatekeepers and group maintenance -- do members understand this kind of thing?
32. Members work towards building relationships as well as completing the tasks in the group.
33. Members of the group feel a sense of togetherness.
34. Everyone is helpful to the needs of others.
35. In all group development, one stage is a conflict stage. Does the group understand this?
36. The use of group consensus is important to develop cohesiveness rather than voting.

The Group Dynamics Questionnaire can be just "eyeballed" for information or if you wish to investigate the group dynamics in real depth to determine the group's perceptions on positive and negative functioning, then you can score it.

Scoring the Group Dynamics Questionnaire

	+2	(5)
	+1	(4)
Transpose the scores from 1-5 to	0	(3)
	-1	(2)
(In column B on the questionnaire)	-2	(1)

Transfer these to Score Sheet I, taking care to **reverse the score** where you see a shaded area (these questions are phrased negatively). For some groups other questions might also need to be reversed, but this depends on the type of climate expected in your group. Check all the questions in relation to whether they should be positive or negative before scoring.

Total the columns on Score Sheet I. This gives the raw score for each column. Divide by the total possible score for that column to give the % score. Do this for each column.

The task and relationship scores should be combined at the bottom left hand corner. Some questions referred to both task and relationship at the same time. To include all task and relationship scores, column A needs to be combined with column C and with column B. This affects statistical information in reference to separating task and relationship scores for the whole instrument because of the interaction of these scores when combined. Divide A + C (raw score) by 48 and A + B (raw scores) by 48 to obtain the % scores.

In the table on the score sheet, place your raw scores, % scores, and the mean % scores of the whole group for each sub-section of the questionnaire. The % scores for the whole group are calculated by adding the % scores for each person in the group on the different components (task, relationship, etc.), then dividing these totals by the number in the group who filled out the questionnaires (see Group Dynamics Score Sheet II). The individual and group % scores allow a comparison to see if a group member is out of sync with the rest of the group; this may mean the individual OR the rest of the group might be out of sync. For example, an individual might rate the communication, atmosphere and climate as -25% while the group rates the same subsection as +40%. This problem can then be addressed by looking at the comments on the questionnaire that qualify the numerical value given in the atmosphere section. It could be that the **individual** needs to change or it could be that **the rest of the group** needs to change.

It is essential that the comments are completed as fully as possible to enable the group to see what actually is causing any negative scores. The group can then do something in regard to the problem which otherwise might have been buried by that person. If many of the scores are negative, then the group dynamics are negative and the comments should be studied to determine which group dynamic needs to be dealt with. Scores will rarely be higher than 60% as it would be unusual to have everyone in the group give full positive scores for everything in the questionnaire. In general, scores 30% and above show a positive functioning group, 0 to 30% is actually positive functioning, but areas should definitely be looked at with a view to possible improvement.

Negative scores mean that something major needs to be done in those areas to improve the group dynamics.

The Group Dynamics Score Sheet's I and II can be found overleaf.

Group Dynamics Questionnaire Score Sheet I

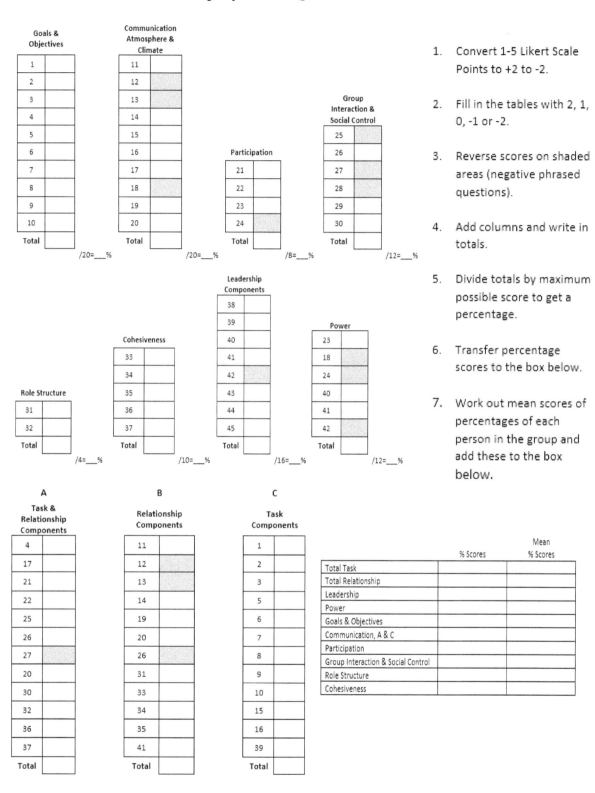

1. Convert 1-5 Likert Scale Points to +2 to -2.

2. Fill in the tables with 2, 1, 0, -1 or -2.

3. Reverse scores on shaded areas (negative phrased questions).

4. Add columns and write in totals.

5. Divide totals by maximum possible score to get a percentage.

6. Transfer percentage scores to the box below.

7. Work out mean scores of percentages of each person in the group and add these to the box below.

TOTAL TASK = A + C _____ / 48 = _____ %

TOTAL RELATIONSHIP = A + B _____ / 48 = _____ %

Score Sheet II for the Group Dynamics Questionnaire

**Calculation of the Mean Scores for
Participant's Perceptions of the Group Dynamics**

	Person #1	Person #2	Person #3	Total	Mean
Total Task					
Total Relationship					
Leadership					
Power					
Goals & Objectives					
Communication, Atmosphere & Climate					
Participation					
Group Interaction & Social Control					
Role Structure					
Cohesiveness					

These mean scores can be transferred onto the table on Score Sheet I.

Additional columns should be added for larger groups.

Index

9 781634 925532